Background in Sunshine

The Hon. Sir Henry H. Juta

BACKGROUND IN SUNSHINE

Memories of South Africa

BY

JAN JUTA

ILLUSTRATIONS BY THE AUTHOR

New York

CHARLES SCRIBNER'S SONS

The poem "The Old Voortrekker" printed on page 26 is from A. G. Visser's *Gedigte* (Pretoria, 1929), and is reprinted by kind permission of the publisher, J. L. van Schaik, Pretoria, South Africa.

Illustrations on the following pages are by Jan Juta: frontispiece, xiv, 1, 7, 137, 162, 171, 182, 194, 220, 229, 237, 238, 275

FOR MY FATHER

The Honorable Sir Henry H. Juta

Contents

LIST OF ILLUSTRATIONS   ix

PREFACE   xi

1. South African Heritage   1

2. Papa   27

3. Mama   102

4. Sisters   136

    I. RÉNÉ   137
    II. HELEN   141
    III. BRENDA   144
    IV. LUIA   150

5. Three Unanswered Questions   162

    I. THE RAIN QUEEN   162
    II. NDEBELE   171
    III. ZIMBABWE   182

6. Domestics   194

7. Flowers in South Africa   220

8. Visitors   238

9. Tot Siens-Au Revoir   275

GLOSSARY   299

BIBLIOGRAPHY   301

"Where there is joy there is fulfillment,
and where there is fulfillment there is joy."

—PAUL TILLICH, *The Meaning of Joy*

List of Illustrations

The Hon. Sir Henry H. Juta   *frontispiece*

A Koodoo   *xiv*

Dutch colonial architecture   *1*

Jan Van Riebeeck arriving at Table Bay   7

Royal Warrant of Knighthood   *27*

The Hon. Sir Henry H. Juta as Speaker of the Cape
House of Assembly   *99*

The Gunning Sisters   *103*

Mama, 1895   *103*

Mama in her presentation gown   *127*

Réné   *137*

Family Group   *147*

Women of the Rain Queen tribe   *162*

The Ndebele   *171*

Zimbabwe   *182*

Domestics   *194*

Flowers   *220, 229*

Sable Antelope   *237*

Flamingos   *238*

BACKGROUND IN SUNSHINE

Crowned Cranes   275

The author working on a mural   277

Preface

FOR a long time, I have been thinking about writing this record
of an era that is past in a part of the world where life has completely changed both in character and pattern. Urged on by
interested friends and admirers of my family, I have at last
attempted to put down some memories of that life as best I can
recall it. If dates are not exact, nor the chronological order of
events precise, it is because time has interfered and memories
have been disturbed by the dramatic experiences of a long life
that has included two world wars. I can but beg the forbearance
of my readers.

From my father's house in what was the Cape Colony at the
tip of the African continent, there flowed such a stream of creative vitality that it has reached me again and again, all through
my life in many parts of the world. It was a house and a family
that, once known, was never forgotten, for the quite unpreten-
tious reason that it was like no other in that land at that time.

Thus it has seemed to me worth recording what I can remember, through the mist of years spent in a number of different countries among people of varied nationality, of the family in our
home. That I was the youngest of five children, the only son surrounded by four sisters, has perhaps enabled me to view the pattern in the round, as it were. I can but hope that my perspective
has not been distorted, nor my opinions biased by the events that
have colored my life.

BACKGROUND IN SUNSHINE

There is not a trace left of the house, which, though built with such loving care, was burned to the ground. Only certain trees and shrubs in the garden, which was my father's pride, still bear silent testimony to his patient care. Two of the family remain, but before it is too late I want to present one brightly colored picture of the past for those who may be interested in what has always been a very potential part of the world.

I have tried to record the atmosphere of the Cape Colony, one of the four states that later became the Union of South Africa, from the death of Queen Victoria in 1901 until the outbreak of the First World War. After that date, everything changed there, as it did the world over.

During those years, I was at a couple of preparatory schools on my way to going to the South African College in Cape Town, and ultimately to Oxford University. But the life of my home was continually colored by the people who came and went through it, drawn as they were from all over the world, it seemed to me, by the interest and charm my parents had infused into our house.

It should be remembered that the colony was then under British rule, with a governor plus high commissioner residing in Government House in Cape Town, with manners and customs imported from England being implanted in a society of very mixed origins.

Painful memories of the Boer War still influenced the thinking of both Dutch and English-speaking Afrikaners. Dutch names were encountered everywhere; my friends at school came from Dutch and Huguenot as well as English families. But by that time a veneer of "Englishness" had been spread over the Cape Province. This was not so true of the Transvaal and the Orange Free State, where reserves of strong Boer resentment against everything English were held in check by people whose national pride has never been extinguished. The Peace of Vereeniging had made deep wounds in the hearts of the Boers.

It was a period of tremendous growth and development of

which I was acutely aware despite my youth, through my father's involvement in many of the events that occurred.

I can remember hearing of the death of ex-President Kruger, that sad, expatriated old man; the coming of Lord Milner, then governor of the Transvaal, to visit our house; the interesting discussions that took place between Papa and his political friends over the idea of a "Union of South Africa," which had just been proposed in the Cape House of Assembly, a new concept, a great plan, many agreed. That was in 1907, and the triumph of that idea came in 1910, when the Constitution of that Union was established.

A great pageant on the history of South Africa was held on the foreshore of Table Bay to celebrate the occasion. It was directed by Mr. E. Lascelles, later knighted for his achievements, who had come from England especially for that purpose. He was a frequent visitor at our house, where many ideas were discussed and resolved, with Mama and our well-informed friends expressing their opinions. The pageant proved tremendously successful, my mother, resplendent in crown and jewels, playing the role of the Queen of Portugal.

Out of the memories of those years loom the great names in South African history: General Botha; General Smuts at the early stages of his tremendous world career; Lord Buxton, the governor general of the new Union; Sir Starr Jameson; and many more. Most of them came at one time or another to our house to add some new excitement, some new interest to our young lives, for I usually had the honor of being presented to them by Mama, a shy, precocious lad who noted every gesture, listened to every word uttered by these leaders of world affairs.

I have attempted to convey the life of that time as seen from a small corner of the world that was changing every day, evolving, growing into political significance; a corner that was full of prejudice, sharp lines of social classification, snobbism—as there was everywhere—but that had a vitality forging its way through the very pressures created by the multiracial inhabitants, who were drawn in all shades of color between white and black.

South Africa has grown from a small colony made up of people with a varied racial background to a flourishing republic dedicated to independence. My father in his time, and I in mine, have watched this change with love and fear in our hearts. What the future of South Africa may be is perhaps written in gold and diamonds.

Background in Sunshine

1. South African Heritage

HERITAGE in the sense under consideration is a subject both complicated and contentious. To evaluate the contributions of the people involved in the establishment of a colony by any one nation on the land of another is a fascinating study, but a most difficult task.

The United States is, of course, the perfect example of the fusion of a multiplicity of characteristics and national traits. But who can say from which quarter of the globe they have come into the welcoming arms of New York harbor, when in so short a time this conglomeration has been boiled down to produce an entity we recognize as "North American" by certain definite traits? This is nothing less than a miracle when one thinks of all that has gone into that boiling pot of nationalities.

Thus, in considering the heritage of South African-born peoples, we must go further than the mere recognition of the Dutch founding fathers, realizing that to the Cape Colony, first peopled by the Dutch in 1652, came other people, other influences during the seventeenth and eighteenth centuries, resulting in a complexity difficult to comprehend. To the new settlement established in Cape Town by the Dutch came other Europeans and Orientals, all of whom both intermingled as well as influenced the South African nation evolving today. More important is it, in view of this evolution, to remember that South Africa lies at the tip of the Dark Continent, mysterious and immense, inhabited by the black man and the brown for centuries before the white man grasped a foothold on her invaluable southern shore.

Though there has been much study and conjecture of the effects of the white man's psychology upon the indigenous natives of various countries, it would seem that we have underestimated, or not taken fully into account, the reverse effect— that of the black man on the white.

The strength of the psychology of the native peoples of a land as old as Africa is something much more powerful than the white man has cared to admit. He has come as a conqueror, with a superior knowledge of a sort that brought him victory, an easy superficial victory; but the dark mysteries that flow through the blood of people native to their own earth are an imponderable that the white man has yet to reckon with. South Africa is obviously no exception; on the contrary, there, in the very land where the blood beat of the Bantu peoples is strongest, great conflicting changes are taking place before our eyes. But what of the past? How do we estimate what the impact was upon the "founding fathers"? How far were they influenced by the very rhythm of an earth alien to their feet, foreign to everything in their own blood, and how deeply this influence has penetrated consciously or unconsciously, into the South African of today is difficult to estimate.

The gradual discovery of the world as we know it seems to

have been achieved as often by accident as by design. Romance and drama connected with any discovery have never ceased to fascinate men through the ages, so that there is no one who at some time has not longed to have been a Robinson Crusoe and seen for the first time the marvels that nature provided for him on his island of adventure. Discoverers are like missionaries, except that their zeal is marked by national pride rather than religious fervor; but the same insatiable desire to implant something new, supposedly better, upon a lately discovered land exists in the hearts of both categories of men.

The fifteenth and sixteenth centuries saw man wandering the uncharted oceans, exploring for unknown lands, urged on by the desire for wealth as by the more precise need of Europe for the spices of the East. India, with the fabulous riches of the Orient had captured the imagination of all, and became the goal of every king and potentate as well as of every sailor on the high seas.

But between Europe and the East stretched the vast continent of Africa, undiscovered, dark, and foreboding. For though Herodotus tells us that in 600 B.C. Necho, king of Egypt, sent his ships down the east coast of that land to return three years later via the Mediterranean, and that for centuries after the Arabs had sailed the coast searching for gold and ivory, Africa was still wrapped in mystery.

Portugal, the very hand of the powerful Roman Catholic Church, was stretching out her fingers of trade through her proud caravels, while her imaginative prince, Henry the Navigator, was sending his fleets to scour the seas for a route to the East. Thus it was that Bartholomeu Diaz in 1488 skirted the apparently endless western shore of the continent and rounded the Cape of Storms, that dangerous, rocky tip of land where the Atlantic and Indian oceans meet with a mighty rush of waters. Diaz, urged on by King John II of Portugal, actually accomplished a revolution in international affairs by his discovery.

When John died and Manuel became king, he inherited this

3

prize of initiative, together with the adventurous spirit of his forebear, Prince Henry. For, under Manuel, the actual discovery of India via the route around the Cape of Good Hope was finally accomplished by Vasco da Gama in 1498. South Africa then assumed a new position of importance in world affairs.

Now the two doors to all the wonders of the continent were open. For centuries the world had known Egypt in the north, though the fabulous empire of Prester John, which rumor had hidden in mystery, had not as yet been reached by anyone from Europe; no contact had been made with that obscure potentate. But now, by opening the most southerly gate, Portugal gave access to all that lay unknown in Africa: the gold of Monomotapa, the riddle of Zimbabwe, and the Bantu peoples that swarmed around the black heart of that continent.

Vasco da Gama's discovery was the reward for long and patient search; the fleets of Henry the Navigator had pushed their way around the coasts of Africa mile after mile with courage and determination. The news of the findings in India sent shivers of excitement from Manuel's court through all the chancelleries of Europe. But neither Table Bay, nor the superb surroundings on the Cape of Good Hope were of any interest to him except as a victualing station for his crews, or as a haven on the road to his much more important goal.

Time watched the rising of the Protestant countries until the fleets of His Most Catholic Majesty of Portugal no longer sailed unchallenged into the harbor under the great flat-topped mountain, though his own commander, Antonio de Saldanha, had climbed the huge rock in 1503 and christened it Table Mountain. So it took an accident, the kind of accident of discovery mentioned, to establish the first white settlement in southern Africa under the powerful Dutch East India Company. In 1648 one of the best ships of the Company's fleet, the *Haarlem*, foundered in Table Bay, when the officers and crew found themselves stranded in an unknown paradise. After rescuing much of the merchandise and the stores from the wreck, they set up a camp beside the flow of sweet water that tumbled down from the sides of the mountain, that very stream from which the barrels of the Portuguese crews had been filled years before. There they planted such seeds as they had with them on board. The almost miraculous advantages of that verdant peninsula were then fully appreciated for the first time. For, as the seeds sprouted quicker than had ever been expected, the native Hottentots became more willing to barter their cattle and wild game, and these Dutchmen began to realize the possibilities, as yet undeveloped or unexploited, that lay around them.

Above them the mountain, flat-topped and tremendous, dominated the wide blue bay like a great acropolis. On its slopes, which undulated to the seashore, they found a variety of animals so far unseen by any simple Hollander: strange antelopes with fantastic horns and golden-striped zebras like heraldic beasts, while the monstrous hippopotamus, a terrifying mammoth, wallowed in the lakes that lay in the shadow of the mountain. But it must have been the flowers that most delighted their Dutch hearts. For they were everywhere—lovely, fragrant, and of unknown forms and colors, illuminating the hillsides with drifts of scarlet, azure, and gold. The trees, too, were of strange foliage and growth, some shining like silver in the sun, through whose branches darted the "honey birds," gleaming iridescent, emerald, and ruby-throated. Everything seemed bathed in an elusive, penetrating light, an atmosphere so clear that even the distant blue ranges of mountains across the bay were sharply defined, cut out jagged from the sky.

One can imagine the pleasure of these mariners at finding themselves in such surroundings. It is no wonder that it was with regret that they sighted the homecoming fleet from the East that was to carry them back to Holland.

The reports of their findings were so enthusiastic that the Council of Seventeen, the supreme directorate of the East India

Company in Amsterdam, was stirred to interest. "The soil is very good in the valley," reads the memorandum presented by the two officers, Leendert Jansz and Nicholas Proot.

> Everything will grow there as well as in any other part of the world, especially pumpkin, watermelon, cabbage, carrot, radish, turnip, onion, garlic, and all kinds of vegetables, as those who were wrecked on the *Haarlem* can testify. It is also beyond doubt that all kinds of fruit trees will thrive there. . . . Please therefore to consider . . . how many sick will be restored to health by God's goodness.

Here was evidence and an appeal that the Seventeen could hardly resist. A halfway house, where the fleets could get water and fresh provisions for the long route to and from the East, was a growing necessity.

On August 20, 1650, it was decided that a "victualing station" as well as a garden should be established at the Cape of Good Hope. Called to their council was Jan van Riebeeck, an officer in the service of the company who, having once spent three weeks at the Cape, gave the plan his full approval, while offering certain suggestions in the light of his own experience.

On December 24, 1651, the expedition, in three ships, set sail under van Riebeeck as commander of the new settlement: with him went his wife and the official gardener, Hendrik Broom, together with a number of artificers, craftsmen, sailors, and soldiers. When he landed on April 7, 1652, from his ship the *Dromidaris,* and the first official garden was dug and planted with seeds specially brought from Holland, the real history of South Africa commenced.

The extraordinary initiative of Governor van Riebeeck resulted in the rapid growth of the settlement, and the story of the building of civilization in that remote wilderness reads like fascinating fiction.

Van Riebeeck built the essential fort, according to instruc-

"The arrival of Jan Van Riebeeck, first Governor of the Dutch settlement at Table Bay, South Africa, 1652." One of a series of historical murals painted by Jan Juta, for South Africa House, Trafalgar Square, London, 1933

tions, as a defense against the Hottentots and Bushmen * on a specially chosen site on the banks of the Fresh River. It is interesting to note that the design closely resembled another fort erected by another group of Hollanders, across the Atlantic in the New Netherlands. When the strong walls and bastions were completed, he christened it with the name of his tiny yacht, the *Goede Hoop* ("good hope").

Then followed the much-needed hospital for the scurvied crew, who were to be restored to health with the products of the company's garden, the only plot of its kind between India and the Netherlands. Then other gardens and farms were planted, bringing to the Cape a variety of trees that flourished as had been predicted.

Van Riebeeck's reports to the Seventeen in Amsterdam made history, as date by date he marked the steps of accomplishment. Reading his records of the first meal of locally produced foods in October 1652; or of the date that butter was first churned; or the harvesting of the first South African wheat, "threshed with enthusiasm in January 1653," one shares the sense of achievement with this extraordinary man, one of the great colonizers of all time.

By 1657 he had established a group of settlers along the banks of the river flowing under the shadow of the mountain, men who asked for their discharge from the company's service in order to take up farming and market gardening for themselves, having realized the possibilities the peninsula offered.

They were the roots that van Riebeeck foresaw would secure the homeland in this new paradise, the roots that would flourish in terms of industry and efficiency, ultimately bearing the fruits of all the culture that Holland had acquired: her taste, her knowledge, and her democratic principles. For eleven eventful years he toiled for his often ungrateful company, wrenching order out of wild nature. But it was not until 1678, with the ar-

* The nomadic, indigenous people they encountered.

rival of another exceptional man as governor, Simon van der Stel, that these national roots began to flower, to express themselves through the media of architecture and a style of living.

Governor van der Stel built his now famous farmhouse, "Constantia," in the verdant valley on the slopes of the mountain. There he implanted a standard of taste on the settlers, who, as trade and imports from Holland increased, built houses for themselves, following the pattern set by the governor. It is partially due to his foresight, as well as that of his equally remarkable son, Adriaan, who followed him as governor, that we owe the particular formula of classicism that we have come to know as the Dutch colonial type of architecture.

The lack of building materials in a land so far away from the progress and advantages of Europe was a serious problem. Transport from the ports of Holland was slow, and it was doubtless due to this very fact that thick plaster covers the walls of locally made bricks, and that thatch of reeds gathered from the nearby lakes replaces the traditional tiles or slate. Most of the wood used had to be imported from Mauritius, for the wooded valleys of the mountains had soon become denuded. However, it is the gables, above all else, that give the Dutch colonial houses their distinction and unusual dignity. For, instead of the rather severe "stepped" design, so often seen in Holland, the Cape settlers indulged their desire for decoration in a variety of the most graceful and ornamental gables.

The interiors of the houses were, of course, decorated in the style of the day, with furnishings mostly imported directly from Holland by the settlers. Dutch china and glass, together with fine pieces brought from the Orient, filled the large, handsome cupboards, copies of which were made of local woods by the craftsmen employed by the company.

These things are all part of the heritage, as characteristic and expressive of the people as the very houses built to contain them. They are strong and useful but of fine taste and workmanship, for above all they were made with a loving integrity for art that is fast disappearing from the world of today. We know nothing of the architects actually responsible for their design, and it is only with the arrival of Francis Michel Thibault toward the end of the eighteenth century, when he became responsible for a number of the more important buildings, that we can refer to historical records.

Born in 1750 near Amiens, and there trained as a military engineer, Thibault had been sent with his regiment in the pay of the Dutch East India Company to garrison the Castle at Cape Town. He assumed certain official appointments, but when the conquest of the Cape by the English deprived him of these he decided to resign, and stay in the country that charmed and interested him. He practiced as an architect, for which his early training had so well befitted him, and befriended a one-time soldier, Anton Anreith, who was a sculptor and wood-carver by profession. These two artists possessed those qualities nurtured in the culture of Europe which were required to bring to the simple architecture of their day the elegance and refinement that marks their work. There is no doubt that they set a standard and a style that was widely copied by their contemporaries.

To appreciate fully the particular beauty of the Dutch houses, they must be seen in their own setting, standing majestically in the pools of blue shadow that the trees around them cast on their white walls. For there is a harmony made of the elements of white plaster, silken, mole-colored thatch, and teakwood that delights the eye, giving them the distinction they all possess.

In the gentle climate of the Cape, much of the leisure of the occupants was spent out of doors. One can conjure up a picture of the homeowner, dressed in somber brown or black, drinking coffee with his family or friends seated on his shaded *stoep*. His lady would be wearing her lace *kappie*, with perhaps a scarf of fine Oriental silk brought from the East by the latest merchantman to anchor in Table Bay. On the tables would be all the fruits of the farm, the wines, both imported and locally made, together with the sweetmeats and Oriental preserves so loved by the Dutch. Scents of jessamine and oleander filled the air, and the cooing of the countless little gray turtledoves added to the contentment of the scene.

In the records of Gui Tachard, a Jesuit priest, a scholar and a member of a scientific expedition sent to the East by Louis XIV, is a description of the company's gardens. He visited the Cape in 1685, and, with the approval of Governor van der Stel, he and his five Jesuit companions set up an observatory in a small pavilion built in the gardens. He writes:

> May 31–June 7, 1685
>
> Great was our surprise to behold in a land so sterile and desolate one of the fairest and most interesting gardens that I have ever seen. . . . Its beauty does not, as in the gardens of France, lie in the design of the flower beds and fountains. . . . But there are walks as far as the eye can see of lemon, pomegranate, and orange trees growing and protected from the wind by thick and high hedges of a sort of laurel that they call "speck" which is always green, and not unlike "filaria."

But whatever else might be considered an expression of a variety of influences, the architecture as designed and built by the first settlers cannot be thought of as anything but purely Dutch heritage, even though it was Holland transplanted onto alien soil, and adapting herself to new conditions. With the architecture came the taste that she had acquired by the seventeenth century, together with an appreciation of the art of fine craftsmanship, which increased by the growth of trade with the East and especially by the importation of porcelains and textiles of oriental execution.

More important still to our evaluation were the traits and characteristics of national character that the Dutch imposed on the growing colony. These might be summed up as a strong Protestant sense of order, a steadfast religious fervor, which filled both burgher and boer farmer alike, and which has persisted in the Dutch people to this day. With it came courage and an unflinching determination, mingled with a sense of personal freedom not untinged by vain self-satisfaction. These traits, even though mixed with other influences we shall further consider, were so powerful that they are found today in almost every South African boasting one drop of Dutch blood.

In 1659, only seven years after his arrival, Governor van Riebeeck recorded in his journal that "wine has been pressed for the first time," though it was reported to have been rather rough and to have found little favor with the passing fleets, who had had some experience of the European wines. But it was the arrival of the Huguenot refugees that brought the real art of viticulture to the Cape. Their love and culture of the vine, which they made to flourish in virgin soil by dint of much hard work, might be considered the main, tangible contribution made by the French settlers to the colony.

Fleeing from persecution after the revocation of the Edict of Nantes, these French people escaped to Holland, where they were welcomed by the Dutch company and sent out to add to the growing settlement under Governor van der Stel. He in turn, anxious to expand his agricultural policy, encouraged them to settle on land granted to them by the company, which became known as Coin Français, and later on as French Hoek ("corner").

The refugees, who had arrived in dozens on the visiting ships of the company, were for the most part farmers, growers of grapes, and makers of wine and brandy. Lonely and sad at the loss of country and possessions, their French hearts must at least have rejoiced at the lovely valleys they were given to live in, valleys where the sun shone on the sloping hills, flooding the ranges of blue mountains that enclosed them from a hostile world. Here they planted their vines for the tremendous benefit of the future, building their houses on the pattern set by their Dutch colleagues, and giving them names nostalgic of their beloved France—names that are kept to this day, such as "La Provence," "Picardie," "Rhône," and "Bien Donné." But being a small minority, in the end they had to yield their language, their graceful manners and customs, together with their "Frenchness" to the more powerful Dutch. Van der Stel had a vision of what he wanted to see accomplished, and as one writer has said, "French regrets could not be allowed to mar the splendid 'vision' of a new Holland rising up in Africa."

François Leguat, a French Protestant who visited the Cape in 1698, during the last year of Simon van der Stel's administration, writes of the settlement with enthusiasm. "All things considered," he says, " 'tis certain the Cape is an extraordinary refuge for the poor French protestants. . . . They live in good correspondence with the Hollanders who, as everyone knows, are of a frank and downright humour."

Later, writing of the wines, which up until that time had been criticized by the fleets and the government of Batavia, he says: "They have plenty of red and white Muscadel wine . . . nearly as possible like our small wines of Champagne."

The impact of the French, not only on the cultivative possibilities of the land but on the people with whom they mixed and later intermarried, was more far-reaching than is perhaps recognized. But though their very names were ultimately pronounced and mostly spelled in the Dutch style, their French customs absorbed or lost, the fusion of the Gallic and Dutch bloods has resulted in a rich contribution to the culture and character of the South African. It would be interesting to discover whether any Dutch South African of distinction since 1886 can be found without a strain of Gallic blood within his veins. For it should be remembered that it was from the Cape Colony, their first settlement, that the Dutch moved northward, stretching further and further into the hinterland. So that, together with their worldly possessions packed into their "trek wagons," they took with them their evolving character, which had by this time absorbed much from contact with the French.

But by establishing themselves in the north, known as the Transvaal, the Dutch became completely cut off from the contacts they had so eagerly desired to leave behind. For about fifty

in history, despite the fact that England had made more than one abortive attempt at colonization there. In 1615, many years before the Dutch had settled their first governor, ten British convicts, sentenced for various crimes, had been banished and landed at Robben Island in Table Bay, some miles from Cape Town. Their story is told by the Reverend C. Terry, chaplain to Sir Thomas Roe, English ambassador to the Great Mogul, in his *Voyage to East India*, published in 1655. The unfortunate men were left helpless on a dry, waterless, rocky island, with only a few provisions to sustain them for a while—in fact, under conditions guaranteed to prove fatal to them. Most of them perished miserably, and those that managed to escape, or were rescued by passing ships, ultimately found their "just reward" by being sentenced to death in England.

Britain did not concern herself with the settlement until the questionable rule of the Dutch East India Company had ceased, and the temporary authority of the Batavian Republic had given way to British government by the capitulation of 1795. The memorandum laid before the Batavian Republic by their commissary, General de Mist, who had been sent to the Cape to report on conditions, is a most serious indictment on the rule of the Dutch East India Company. So it was a colony sadly deteriorated from the standards aimed at by the great Governor van der Stel that was taken over by Great Britain.

Despite the fact that Britain had eyed the Cape of Good Hope since the Dutch East India Company had first established a station there, the strange, unexpected events that make history brought her eventually into control of the colony.

France was at war with Holland, and by 1795 had forced the stadtholder William V to escape to England, subjugating Holland to the position of a dependency of France under the name of the Batavian Republic. Britain now took possession of the Cape Colony to save it from France, holding it in trust for the stadtholder until the Peace of Amiens in 1802 upset all calculations by handing over the colony to the Batavian Republic, still a puppet of France, rather than to the unpopular stadtholder or to the now-bankrupt East India Company.

Once more war, this time with France, forced the British in 1806 to occupy the Cape rather than let it fall to the French. Finally, on Napoleon's defeat, when the Batavian Republic threw off the yoke of France and reasserted herself, William I, the exiled stadtholder's son and king of the Netherlands, ceded the Cape, together with some small South American possessions, to the British, in payment of a sum of money and an exchange of territory in Europe.

The rule of the British governors that followed after this date had a very definite effect upon the colony. The power of Great Britain was mounting gradually to its zenith at the end of the century, and had there been a succession of governors with enough sympathy or understanding of the people under their rule, the change of one control for another in 1795 might not have disturbed the Dutch settlers as much as it did.

But unfortunately the British government, whose ideas of what a colony should be were not only outdated but narrowed by insular pride, chose men totally unsuited to the task given them. Thus, the bitterness bred in the hearts of the Dutch was more against England herself than against her shortsighted, often stupid officials. It is well expressed by Frederick C. Selous, the famous hunter and explorer, in his fascinating book *A Hunter's Wanderings in Africa*, when he writes of the Boers as "hating the British Government with a bitterness that can only be understood by those who know the cruel, mean, unmanly policy pursued by many of our Cape Colonial Governors towards the Boers."

One can easily imagine the effect of this rule upon a young man, for example the son of a Dutch father and a Huguenot mother, one of the future citizens who would later be fighting in the Boer War. The pride of possession through the achievements of his forebears would naturally have centered in his very heart, there to burn slowly until overcome by good common sense, or else sustained by resentment for the newcomer, the English interloper. There were many, as later events proved, who, though forced silently to admire much that Britain brought with her, still kept to the "old ways" and upheld the national bonds that tied them to their pioneering forefathers.

Suffice it to say here that the discontent, resentment, and anger, not always restrained in the hearts of the Dutch, took many years to finally find expression in their decision to emigrate, get away from all they detested, and establish an independent community in the unknown north. The culmination of their restlessness came in what is known as the Great Trek, which was a movement that together with the Boer War was certainly the most far-reaching influential action in the history of South Africa, while the "manifesto" sent by the trekkers to the government of the day is one of the great public statements of all time.

There were certainly other contributing causes for the discontent brought about by British rule, not the least of these being the missionaries sent out by the London Missionary Society, some of whose representatives proved themselves quite unworthy of their calling. For, with the coming of the British to the colony at the Cape, a faint sound like the tolling of a faraway bell might have been heard in the ears of the established Dutch colonists; it might have been tolling the death knell of all Afrikaner dreams, or it might have been a church bell being rung by the active missionaries who had arrived from England together with the emigrants.

These were to become an added burden to the Dutch, what with their mission stations, their "Englishness," and their dangerous gospel of "equality." Understandably, their attitude was to embrace the dark races as souls to save, rather than to consider them as the Dutch did, merely as laborers whose education and social advance did not then interest their Afrikaner masters.

The reports of the missionaries on the situation they found were often critical of the colonists, but their attitude only added to the irritation of the farmers.

Then followed the more unfortunate mistake the British made, which was their attempt to anglicize the Afrikaners with little understanding of the psychology of their opponents. English took the place of Dutch as the official language. Dutch organization was replaced by British custom, with English currency introduced and only English and Latin taught in state-aided schools.

The Dutch farmers watched these changes with growing intolerance, so that, when the slaves of the colony were emancipated in 1834, they foresaw the inevitable future. They made their now famous resolution to leave their farms, their very homes, and go, with all their movable possessions, herds, and servants, north into the unknown. There they were certain that God would reward them with miles of sun-drenched land to cultivate, where they could live according to their own laws, their vigorous faith, undisturbed by outsiders from a world they wished to leave. The Great Trek of 1836 began.

At their departure they sent the government their "manifesto," written by Pieter Retief, one of their foremost leaders. "We quit this Colony," he wrote, "under the full assurance that the English Government has nothing more to require of us, and will allow us to govern ourselves without its interference in future . . ."

They were to learn later how wrong they were.

However, the advances of civilization that Britain represented were bound to fascinate the people of this remote colony, as once again upon the growing inhabitants a new influence was brought to bear. They felt the stirring of great forces in the world: science was developing; man was evolving; advantages they had never dreamed of were being suggested to them for the first time. Though the governorship (1814–1827) and the tactics of such a man as Lord Charles Somerset cannot be justified, he did represent something powerful, a great force emanating from a little island across the seas, something that was only fully understood by the coming of the British settlers.

For the British people only became firmly established in South Africa in 1820, when their contribution to the country as a whole was as important to the resulting heritage under discussion as that brought by the Dutch.

For though pioneers have much in common—the zeal, courage, and determination that carves their names into the very rocks of the lands they founded, and makes their intangible characteristics difficult to distinguish—there are certain national traits still recognizable in each of them. So to the already mixed nationalities growing at the south of the African continent, there were brought standards and points of view that mark the year 1820 as a milestone in the development of the country. The effect of these hundreds of British settlers, transported through an emigration scheme of their government to the promising El Dorado of South Africa, was more widespread than we can easily estimate. They came from the full range of the middle class in Britain, though most of them were farmers, mechanics and technicians; only a few were professional men anxious to escape from the growing struggle for livelihood in Britain that had been caused by the return of the victorious armies from the Napoleonic wars.

The main purpose of this scheme of emigration, which had been initiated by the governor, Lord Charles Somerset, was largely political. Even so, it was also with a certain national ambition and pride in British character that he urged the government in London with all persuasiveness to induce as large a number of emigrants as possible to come to South Africa. To say that he misrepresented the facts, and that he deluded a government that trusted him to do whatever he thought would benefit Britain as a whole, would be putting the matter lightly. The bitter truth was only discovered by the settlers themselves, too late for them to do anything about it.

The story of their journey is a long one: their departure from England in separate parties on different ships; their arrival in Delagoa Bay, dramatic and tragic in various aspects; and their struggle against appalling conditions through the first few years that followed would all take volumes to tell. For our purposes, it will suffice to recognize their contribution to the country in which most of them remained. And for this it must be appreciated that they were also pioneers, like the Dutch before them, with just as many problems to reckon with, many of the same difficulties, all of which called forth in them the British grit and fortitude for which their country had long been famous. The "Britishness" that flows in the blood of every Briton is not easily absorbed, but under the most surprising circumstances retains its national characteristics.

And this leads us to the one vitally important difference between the British settlers and their fellow pioneers, the Dutch. This was the tie, the vital, umbilical bond that bound the British to their motherland, which was never broken. Despite betrayal, despite lack of consideration, despite much that one might have expected would sever them forever from the government that had seduced them falsely, as far as they knew, into leaving their homes and coming to what had been described to them as "a paradise, awaiting development to bear rich fruits of reward," they remained fundamentally loyal to Britain.

How unlike the Dutch, who wished to sever all contacts with the world they had known, who, in fact, seemed to have disliked rather than loved their native land; who sought to escape from all connecting links in order to live as they wished to, and develop their own distinct, egotistical pattern. They held no loyalty to anything except their own self-made state, proudly conscious of having created it with the specific approval of the Almighty. Even today there is still a tone of pride in the voice of the nationalist Dutch South African, when he accuses his fellow South Africans of British descent of "harboring a love for the mother country—this England!"

This is not the place to dwell on the promotion of the emigration scheme, or of the unsatisfactory method of its execution; nor indeed of the political "play-behind-the-scenes" that brought it about. Rather, we should recognize that among the settlers came men of imagination; men with a sense of loyalty, whose standards were the result of centuries of evolving law and order; men, above all, with a sense of justice, who held love of their fellow men as one of their essential principles. They brought with them a vitality and an intelligence that had had to compete with the developed European mind of the day. Perhaps most important of all was their determination to fight for the rights of the individual, such rights as they had been taught to expect. They established the liberty of the press in 1828, erected their own Church with a much more liberal and humane teaching than the Dutch Reformed Church, and introduced English as an official language.

These were all important steps in bringing the settlement into greater contact with the world at large, the powerful English-speaking world, beneficial to the growing country in so many ways. English, Scotch, and Irish names are all over South Africa today, and the descendants of the emigrants have intermarried with the Dutch and French people who had settled there before them; indeed, the fusion of cultures has been going on since the first generation of English-bred South Africans took portions of the African land as their own. Their influence has continued through all the succeeding years, through the tragedy of the Boer War and the many changes of government. It will continue to be felt as long as there remains a man in South Africa who bears an Anglo-Saxon name.

These verses from the poem "The Old Voortrekker," * by A. G. Visser, an Afrikaner poet, give one a picture of the *voortrekker*, whose courage, loyalty, and faith were completely expressed by his Bible and his gun, which formed the mainstay of the whole life of the Boers.

* Translated by T. J. Haarhoff from A. G. Visser's *Gedigte* (Pretoria: 1929).

BACKGROUND IN SUNSHINE

With children ranged around my bed
  I feel my pilgrimage is done;
This is the last outspan.
  Thanks to the Lord, on yonder shore
This trekker worn will find his rest
  From uphill long and steep.

The family Bible that is there
You should regard as more than gold.
  Through hardship it has been
My guide and comfort when in need
Now, in the hour of death it is
  My buttress and support.

There on the wall hangs my old gun;
Just keep it still; how many times
  When dangers lurked around,
Its ready shot, so quick and sure,
Delivered us from certain death
  Through savage man or beast.

My children, never leave the land;
Remember your forebears, be true;
  Yield not to customs strange.
Though thunders roar around your heads,
We still shall be a people free,
  And ever shall be so.

There still remains the Transvaal flag,
Guard it . . . who knows . . . perhaps . . . some day,
  When I shall be no more,
You yet may wave that flag aloft,
And seize the gun, and shoot, and load
  And . . . Lord receive my soul.

2. *Papa*

OURS was essentially a happy house, large, comfortable, considered luxurious for those days, suited by design and good taste to a family of five children. Architecturally it was not a beautiful house, nor was it very old, for it had been built by my father, who had it designed especially to suit my mother's own wishes. Hence she had called it "Mon Desir."

BACKGROUND IN SUNSHINE

It was built near Cape Town, the capital of what was in those days the Cape Colony, the most southerly area of South Africa known as the Cape Peninsula. This peninsula lies at the turned-up tip of the African continent, caught between the ebb and flow of the Indian and Atlantic Oceans. An equable climate bathes it in sunshine for most of the year, which accounts for the wild, gardenlike look of the whole countryside. Everything flourishes: trees, shrubs, and flowers in varied undergrowth cover the landscape with a carpet of greens. Everywhere is shimmering sunlight or shadow, blue mountains or bays of emerald sea. In some ways one is reminded of Europe—a harbor of the Mediterranean, a port in southern Spain—then one is suddenly struck by something alien—an oriental shrub, a brilliant bird, a scent reminiscent of the East—and one might be in Ceylon or a haven in the Malayan islands. Pine and oak trees shelter the town sprawled around the harbor, which curves along the foot of Table Mountain, majestic, dominating the landscape.

All around our house lay the tree-shaded valley of open fields and country gardens over which loomed Table Mountain. The family had lived in it for ten years before I was born, so my memories of it begin at the turn of the twentieth century.

I can remember thinking, as I used to creep out into the early morning light flooding our garden, that it must surely be the most beautiful place on earth. No one was yet awake, and, in the stillness spread over everything except the birds, there was a clarity of every form, a sparkle in the colors and scents of all the varieties of vegetation that seemed to combine to produce a kind of magic. But I think it was the light, the special, extraordinary brilliance of the light that illumines the whole of that tip of the African continent and gives to everything an added beauty.

About sunset time, if I could escape from the family, my nurse, or my homework, I would take my dog and together we would climb the steep lane near our house to the high tip of the hill where there was a wooden stile leading into the adjoining fields, just to watch the glory of the skies in the fading light. On the top step I would sit to gaze at the blue shadow of Table Mountain move like a living, creeping thing over the vast plains stretching to the north. The whole wonderful display of blazing sunlight on the far mountain ranges, with the blue shadow lapping at their feet, would make me hear majestic sounds like music. And, as the glory of light was eaten by the shadow, I would run home in the gathering dusk, my heart thumping from the sheer beauty of it all.

The large rooms of the ground floor of the house, cool, with high ceilings and polished floors smelling of beeswax, had long French windows opening onto a spacious *stoep* or verandah shaded by oak trees. Up the wide stairs curving from the entrance hall were spaced our parents' rooms, with dressing rooms attached; beyond, a room for each of us children. As we were seldom all there together at one time, these were available as guest rooms for the many friends who constantly came to stay with us. There was the nursery with rooms for nurse or governess, while beyond stretched the servants' wing above pantries, kitchen, with outdoor amenities. There were corridors, cupboards, attics, ample space for all necessities, though, as the house was of Victorian design, bathrooms were few and far between, a constant center of competition.

Beyond the paneled entrance hall a long, dark passage led to the library. This was my father's study and workroom. Here he kept his numerous books, his trophies, the lares and penates of his own personal life. The passage to Papa's library was somehow sacrosanct; to us it had special significance, for, when he was there, we were never allowed to disturb him. Only when I knew he was out did I venture there, the better perhaps to know him, to understand, if not to love, him. The books, in languages I didn't then know, bound in fine, shining leather, delighted my eye; his guns stacked in a glass case against the wall, the silver cups he had won during his younger life of sport, all were part of the man I hardly knew. Only the horned trophies mounted and hung high were something I could really appreciate: the buffalo he had shot in the bushveld, the lovely impala buck with lyrate horns and huge, limpid eyes, the eland, the waterbuck, all the lords of the animal world I longed to see alive and galloping across the endless acres of their own domain, the untamed, unconquered kings of Africa. He had shot them in danger and in sport. I used to feel I should apologize to them, for even as a boy I swore I would never kill an animal just for the fun of it.

Throughout the rest of the house my mother ruled undisputed. Only his library and his gardens belonged to Papa. Yet even the garden was made to flourish and produce, for mother's pleasure, the flowers she most loved to pick and arrange to decorate the rooms she presided over. She had a sense of comfort, Papa had better taste. Between them they made a house considered beautiful, at once luxurious, original in its contents, distinctly personal in atmosphere.

On three sides of the house flower gardens, lawns, and terraces stretched out into woods of pine and oak trees; beyond were the stables, flanked by orchards of vines and fruit trees, while further still lay the open country full of wild flowers, birds, and sunshine. Land was cheap then, so many houses were surrounded by huge acreage. We had fields in which the horses and cows grazed, while at the far end of the property was a pond, filled with water lilies, from which the cattle drank. The haunt of wild water birds, which nested in among the masses of arum lilies, it was one of my favorite hideaways. There I was out of call; I could sit undisturbed with my dog, watching the life on the sanctuary of the pond.

Dominating everything was Table Mountain, the great flat rock guarding Table Bay. The mountain was like some powerful living presence. One could see it from everywhere, eloquent against the sky, looming tremendous over us, changing from sun to shadow, from misty blue to angry purple dark. Our lives were affected by the mountain's moods, our pleasures and states of mind influenced by this power presiding over our house. As a child, I used to think that God lived somewhere in its blue ravines, a God who would smile at us for a while, then retire, completely hidden beneath the great rolling white clouds known as the Tablecloth. My nurse, who was a colored woman, * passionately Christian, was shocked by my pagan ideas.

"Dey do say," Nannie confided to me one day, "dat it's de Debbil smoking up dere trying to drive de Dutchmen away wid all his clouds of smoke." But I could never associate the mountain with anything evil, even on the days when the Tablecloth rolled over to hide it entirely and the southeast wind howled through the gorges.

One side of the mountain slopes down to Cape Town on the blue curve of the bay, where the Dutch had anchored their high-prowed ships sailing to and from the Spice Islands of the East. On the other side, among the velvety pines and spreading oaks planted by the same Dutch settlers of the seventeenth century, nestle the suburbs.

When the Dutch pioneers arrived in 1652, it was a paradise, a garden of wild flowers where the animals reigned undisputed;

---

* This adjective, "colored," does not connote a Negro to a South African, but rather an individual with a skin that is not black but rather brown, sometimes more yellow even than brown, but distinctly neither white nor negroid in feature. The colored community, now a large minority in Cape Town—a political thorn in the side of the Nationalist Government of today—is the result of the mixture of the white races, the early settlers on the Cape Peninsula, with either some of the indigenous native people or with the imported Orientals. These latter with their slim features, their elegant manners and customs came, as we have already seen, from the Dutch islands of the East, and have always been known as Malays in Cape Town. The members of this minority, whether Moslem or Christian, who have mingled with the white world as storekeepers, fruit vendors, or as household workers, have been given the very appropriate title of "God's stepchildren" by our famous South African writer Sarah G. Millin, for they do not seem to belong either to the white world or to their darker brethren, the Bantu, but remain as it were *sui generis*, a growing, developing people full of hidden potential.

only the vagrant little bands of Bushmen or Hottentots with their poisoned arrows disturbed their peace. Into this unknown realm of nature stepped the white man, arrogant, greedy, and rapacious, shattering the calm harmony, beginning the turbulent history of South Africa. By my time, however, Cape Town had grown from the simple victualing station, a market garden planted by the Dutch in 1652, into a busy flourishing city, the capital of the Cape Colony.

I cannot disassociate our house from the complicated political atmosphere surrounding it when I was a child. The wide catholic tastes of my parents made the house a center of cultural, political, and intellectual activities. Through the doors flowed people of many nationalities, varied interests, different walks of life: musicians, artists, politicians, missionaries, all the intelligentsia of the colony. My mother loved people and enjoyed entertaining. Anyone of interest, whether a visitor from overseas bearing letters of introduction, or someone from the hinterland with an idea or a mission, was welcomed with all the hospitality that made her house renowned.

The history of the Cape Colony where I was born, though short, had been full of drama. It was one of four states—the others being the Transvaal, the Orange Free State, and Natal —which were later, in 1910, unified to become the Union of South Africa and ultimately, in 1960, the Republic of South Africa. The various nationalities settled at the Cape accounted largely for the confusion of loyalties and division of public opinion. In my childhood it was a British colony, with all that entailed in the Victorian era of vanity, intolerance, and snobbism.

By the time I was at school and beginning to understand such things, the British and Dutch appeared on the surface to have adjusted their differences and to be living peaceably together. There were many, however, who sympathized with the Boers, as well as their descendants still living in the Cape Colony. And while there had been intermarriage between the two peoples with happy results, with families claiming descent from both nationalities, through it all the Dutch Reformed Church, the religious strength behind the pioneers, kept fanning the embers of nationalism which some foretold would one day burst into furious flames. A relative of ours by marriage expressed strong feelings about British injustice to the Dutch settlers, with whom he openly sympathized; he was not invited to our house.

In the way children have of sensing things, we became aware that there were strongly conflicting points of view among our friends and their parents. We also discovered there were many considered disloyal to Her Majesty the Queen and the hierarchy ruling in Westminster. These were mentioned only in hushed whispers by my sister, who was five years older than I and gathered her information from our Nannie.

The focal point of disagreement was the British prime minister of the colony, Cecil John Rhodes—the "arch conspirator," as some said, or "the greatest champion of British ideals," as others maintained. Even our relatives were divided in their opinion of Rhodes. My aunt prepared to defend him with passionate adoration, my uncle was ready to swear that Rhodes "would sell the whole colony down the river" and betray it as he would "betray every man that opposed him." I listened, often confused at the behavior of the grown-ups.

It should be remembered that the great turning point in the dramatic history of South Africa began with the first discovery of diamonds in 1867. The story of their discovery, in the light of what happened later, reads like a fairy tale. Two friends, a hunter and a farmer, noticed some children playing with a large glittering stone among the pebbles on the bank of the Orange River. Because of their interest in it, the mother of the children, Mrs. Jacobz, gave it to them, and they sent it for analysis to an authority in far-off Grahamstown, who pronounced it to be a first-class diamond. Two years later the same farmer bought another stone for as much as five hundred sheep from a native witch doctor. This stone turned out to be the now famous "Star of South Africa," valued at twenty-five thousand pounds sterling.

The diamond rush of the world began, with men from every

quarter of the globe coming to seek their fortunes. It is said that from their river diggings diamonds worth three hundred thousand pounds had been taken by 1871, while the new town, called Kimberley, became the Mecca of every man with initiative, courage, and enough cash to get to such an outlandish place.

Cecil Rhodes, whose name will forever be associated with diamonds, established the De Beers Consolidated Mines with a check for over five million pounds, having lured, cajoled, and won over to his side every rival in the field. Did he not, with uncanny foresight, almost ordain that every man throughout the civilized world should give to his fiancée a ring of the one stone truly representative of all he hoped to find in his ideal partner —shining, alluring purity—the glittering white flash of a brilliant, cut diamond? What genius lay in that idea!

Almost twenty years later, while the world was still recovering from the effects of the diamond rush, gold was discovered in the same desert area of the Witwatersrand, the "ridge of white waters." Ironically, this was the very area where the Dutch settlers had ultimately chosen to settle after their long trek from the south. It almost seems to have been the fate of the Dutch that the "main reef" of the gold should have been found beneath their very feet, for once more the world rushed in to share, this time, the riches of gold. Now tens of thousands made their way to Johannesburg, by wagon or mule cart, by train as far as was then possible, even on foot. Mining this mineral was a very different undertaking from digging for diamonds. Great skill and tremendous labor were required, for the gold lay deep, thousands of feet under the ground, to be extracted only at enormous cost. Fortunately, there was an unlimited supply of labor.*

---

* Was there not the dark man in his millions ready to come and earn what seemed to him valuable wages for his hard labor with pick and shovel? This was a very different sort of life from working somewhat casually on the land for his Boer masters; the work was hard, the conditions appalling, and he had

But in less than ten years, out of the desert veld rose the glittering city of Johannesburg, filled with the cosmopolitan world of money-grubbing, ruthless fortune hunters, a world of strangers to the Boers, who watched with horror this invasion of their long-sought peace. The struggle between the white races for South Africa had begun; the struggle between the white man and the dark was not then even foreseen.

At the end of the nineteenth century, South Africa, shattered by the Jameson Raid and torn by political disagreement, was a divided country. Loyalties were being tested and found wanting. The Dutch, or the Afrikaners as they were called, were nursing their hatred of foreign intrusion, while the British elements were rallying their forces in an effort to impose their will upon a recalcitrant people.

History has recorded over and over again the fiasco of the abortive "raid" led by Dr. L. Starr Jameson, the friend, confidant, and vassal of Cecil Rhodes, who at the time was prime minister of the Cape Colony. Designed supposedly to "rescue" the dissatisfied group of British and foreign *uitlanders*, as they were called, from the grip of the Dutch government of the Transvaal, whose gold mines at Johannesburg were being taken over by the foreigners, the raid failed. The foreigners wanted control, even total possession; the rightfully suspicious Boers prepared to resist and hold onto what they felt was theirs by right. The committee of foreigners set up in Johannesburg failed to cooperate with Jameson; communications were slow or nonexistent. Dr. Jameson, with his ill-organized troop of raiders, was hot-headed, impatient to achieve his goal of British domination. Rhodes, who supposedly had connived at the plot to take Johannesburg, found things had gone awry but was unable to prevent Jameson from advancing, and the raiders were caught by the Dutch president Kruger's defending Boers. Jameson and

---

no conception of the value of the mineral he was digging up for the benefit of his white employers.

his ringleaders were tried, condemned to prison, and fined, while Rhodes, his career ruined by his best friend, was forced to resign and face accusations from Whitehall. Boer and Briton eyed each other with growing suspicion. War seemed inevitable.

Into this complex pattern of racial and political viewpoints my father brought a fine, astute mind, together with a fund of common sense. His foreign blood, his knowledge of languages, his study for the law at the Inner Temple in London, all gave him a cultural advantage over many of his colleagues. He had come back from England accustomed to British ways, a full-fledged barrister, to practice law in Cape Town, there to join his great friends, Will Schreiner and Will Solomon, who had also studied in London. It was said later that from the first he appeared destined for politics, as indeed was "Uncle" Will Schreiner, who helped him along that path. For it was Schreiner who suggested to his friend, Cecil Rhodes, then prime minister of the colony, that Papa be appointed his attorney general.

My father was an extraordinary man. Richly gifted, he had inherited talents of all sorts from a highly intelligent Dutch father and an equally exceptional mother, who had been born in Germany. My grandfather had moved from Zalt Bommel, not far from Dordrecht, Holland, which had been the family center for over a hundred years, and in 1860 had gone to the Cape of Good Hope, taking with him a large library of books in various languages. This first became a "lending library" at the Cape but later developed into the publishing firm that today bears my name. Grandfather had three sons, of whom my father was the second, and two daughters, who both married and went to live in Europe. My two uncles both died quite young, leaving my father the sole male heir to his family's Dutch inheritance.

In the front hall of our house hung two seventeenth-century portraits in large, oval wooden frames. They were commonly known in the family as "the ancestors," although Papa did not know whose portraits they were, nor who had painted them.

But they were obviously a couple, probably man and wife, dressed in the rich clothes of the period, exquisitely painted. Together with some old Dutch silver and a few pieces of Delft porcelain, they were the only remaining items of the many possessions sent by Grandfather from his home in Holland to the Cape of Good Hope.

The story of their arrival at Cape Town was told me by my father, but only years later did I discover in the family archives the authentic record as reported by the captain of the ship that carried the family possessions from Rotterdam. The captain, a cousin of my grandfather, was in command of a cargo ship trading between Holland and Batavia. Following the tradition of the Dutch East India Company's ships, he stopped regularly in Table Bay for fresh supplies. Thus, it was obvious that my grandfather would entrust his most valuable possessions to the care of his cousin, whose reputation as a sailor was of the highest order.

Grandfather had decided to settle on the Cape in which his father had become interested while serving many years before with the Dutch East India Company. But the move from Zalt Bommel entailed a tremendous upheaval for the family, for, though they only brought their most treasured possessions, these proved to be far more bulky and numerous than had been anticipated. The biggest boxes were sent by trading ship, while my grandparents traveled by another boat. The dramatic story of the family tragedy I report in the translation of the original words, as found in the archives.

On the sixteenth day of November, 1779, the Dutch bark *Zalt Bommel*, Captain C. J. Klerck in command, anchored off the promontory in Table Bay. She was a sailing ship of 600 tons and had brought from Rotterdam both cargo and a few passengers and equipment for Batavia. On the morning of November 18, the captain braced the yards to cast off shore and weighed anchor in a northeast breeze, but the anchor came up foul and at the same moment the vessel was taken aback by a northwesterly wind. Although the crew worked feverishly, the captain found that the ship would not answer her helm and he could not get control. She drifted onto the rocks in the strong current, and, although anchors were run out and hove well tight, a running swell caused the ship to ground and she bilged. Passengers and crew were landed as quickly as possible, and with a heavy heart the captain abandoned his ship.

Although he was completely exonerated by the Court of Inquiries, Captain Klerck swore never to go to sea again, and when he swore it was an education even to his *scheeps-jongen* and a challenge to the most hardened hands.

Fortunately, the packing case containing the portraits was rescued before too much damage had been done, and, although several others were ruined, the two portraits survived safely. I inherited them and they are still in my possession. When my father died, I moved my belongings from Cape Town to London, where I was then living with my wife. Came the war in 1939 and the contents of our house were rapidly packed and stored with a company near Putney on the river Thames. Although the building housing our things was badly bombed, our cases were not damaged, and the portraits continue their lives to this day.

We were all taught to regard our father with a reverence that in a way removed him from my sphere. I was afraid of him and often felt embarrassed when with him for long; but I remember just as clearly his gentleness, his amazing patience, his love of children and flowers. All his Dutchness showed itself in his love of nature. I can see him now, working among his plants with his eloquent hands, which he used to such effect when pleading a case in the courts of justice. He would disbud the chrysanthemums with great care while I, aged six, would stand beside him holding my small watering can, watching his every move, fascinated.

"You must nip off the first bud of the zinnias to encourage the plants to branch out," he said. "In that way you get more flowers, and you should also remember to prune off the dead heads of any flower before it turns to seed, for you will then get a second flowering from almost any annual."

We were a happy family, full of good humor, all of us creative. I had four sisters, a fact I was never allowed to forget as I grew older. I was the only son. My youngest sister, Luia, and I grew up together, as the other sisters were a good deal older and left home to study in Europe while I was still a boy.

On Sunday afternoons, Luia and I were regularly taken by Papa for a walk through the countryside. We loved our walks because Papa always told us so many amusing and interesting things. He taught us about the birds, their names and habits, the color of their eggs.

"D'you see the butcher-bird," he said, pointing at the vicious looking shrike, "so smart in his black and white plumage?"

"Why is he called that?" I asked.

"Because he is the killer of all the caged birds he can find."

"But how, if they are caged?"

"That's the evil part of it," Father said. "He lures them to the bars of their cage, then nips off their heads with his long razor beak."

"Does he eat them then?" asked my sister.

"No, just kills them for the joy of killing. Some birds are like some people—they just hate and want to kill those they hate."

Or we would see the lovely gold and black bokmakierie, whose name was onomotapoeic, exactly like his strange, repetitive song. Traveling always with his mate, the pair sing a ringing duet as they flit through the undergrowth.

Often we were told a story attached to some particular bird we saw, like the hoopoe, sacred to the Assyrians, or the bright-eyed honey bird, famous for guiding his human friends, by his insistent calls, to the golden storehouse of the bees, in expectation of a share of the sweet spoil from the hive.

"Is that really true?" I asked incredulously.

39

"Oh, yes," said Papa. "We followed one once in Swaziland and he led us to a dead tree trunk literally dripping with honey."

"I hope you gave him some of the comb," I said.

"He practically snatched it from us, not a bit afraid," answered Papa.

He knew all about the flowers, too, their habits of growth and variety, with perhaps a legend or some story related to their origin in other parts of the world. Once when we found a big anthill in a field, he told us of the huge terra-cotta-colored castles built by the termites in the north.

"They look just like animals rearing out of the tawny grass," said Papa, "sometimes ten feet high—you almost expect them to move," he went on, "and then . . ." He stopped suddenly. "Then one of them does move and you realize you had been looking at a lioness crouching in the grass."

"Heavens," said my sister, "I'd be so scared."

We children had never then been in lion country, but Papa had, and we never tired of hearing of his adventures among the animals. In his individual way, he told us fascinating things about the bees and the mystery of the termitarium, for we had read everything that Fabre and Maeterlinck had written. It was his interest in all natural history, together with his bent for scientific inquiry, which led him to discover the works of the South African naturalist, Eugene N. Marais.* This extraordi-

---

* My father, who read everything written about nature that he could find, whether in Afrikaans or any other language he could read, and had become fascinated by the experiments of Eugene Marais, told me the whole tragic story of Marais, who, born of an old Afrikaner family, became a student of medicine and then of the law. The Boer War caught him still studying for the bar in London.

Papa always said that Marais was half a century ahead of any other scientist in his own field, but because of his violent patriotic fervor for the cause of the Boers, the accounts of his intensive observations could only be published in an Afrikaans newspaper, and his extraordinary work went unrecognized.

nary genius, almost unrecognized by his own countrymen, personally carried on a variety of experiments that resulted in a series of articles published in France and Belgium as well as in the Afrikaans press. In these Marais propounded an entirely original theory based on his experiments with the termite or white ant. My father was one of Marais's great champions, having met him in legal circles while he was practicing as an advocate in Johannesburg; and though he did not agree with him politically, nevertheless he admired the studies and experiments he was making at his home in the Transvaal. Later I was to enjoy and cherish his two best-known books, *The Soul of the White Ant* and *My Friends the Baboons*, as among my most valued possessions.

His articles were not translated into English until 1939, by which time he was dead.

Papa told me that years after Marais's articles on his study of the white ant had appeared in Afrikaans, a Belgian named Maurice Maeterlinck had published a popular scientific book called *La Vie des Termites*, the basic material for which was the report of Marais's experiments on the spot. Marais sued Maeterlinck, but the latter was a scientist of high renown, a Nobel Prize winner, and his works on scientific subjects were generally accepted. Disgusted, Marais retired from the world to live with a troop of baboons in an isolated area of the Transvaal for three whole years. From his observations of these primates he produced articles on his findings, originally published in a newspaper called *Die Vaderland* and later collected and published in book form under the title of *Burgers van die Berge* by J. L. van Schaik, Ltd. of Pretoria, South Africa. These were studies for a much more detailed scientific work to be called "The Soul of the Ape," the ultimate manuscript of which was unfortunately lost.

It was not until after his death, when his articles were translated into English and published under the title of *The Soul of the White Ant*, that the basis of Maeterlinck's book became apparent to the scientific world and Marais was recognized at last for the genius that he was.

Ultimately, he found that morphine and finally suicide replaced justice, though he remained unrecognized throughout his life. It was this that my father found intolerable and unjust; had he been able, he would have fought for Marais with all his strength, to establish him in that place among his peers where he believed the exploited scientist rightly belonged.

No children were ever taught in a more entertaining manner than we were, for my father had a way of telling facts that illumined them with originality. Whether it was to do with termites or bees or even the stones and rocks we found, we always learned something about them from him. Stones might evoke some reference to Mycenae or Crete, which we had read about, and he would launch into the story of Troy or the lovely mythology of Greece, where he had never been but longed to visit. But Greece seemed terribly far away, and we enjoyed the things that were part of our lives.

I remember a story he used to tell about lions that made us laugh.

There were two Dutch farmers traveling together, in an ox wagon drawn by a span of eighteen oxen, across the high veld through lion country. As the sun began to set, one said to the other, "We had better outspan now, Piet, and build a big fire to scare off the lions." They tethered their oxen close to the huge covered wagon, built a fire, and sat down with their loaded guns at their sides to eat their evening piece of biltong (dried venison) and drink a cup of black coffee.

"*Ach*, Piet," said his friend, "I've got a bottle of brandy wine. Let's have a nip to keep us warm."

With one nip followed by another and another, they were soon asleep and snoring heavily. Suddenly, in the late night, one woke with the grunting of lions in his ears.

"D'you hear them, Piet?" he asked in a loud whisper. "It's the lions after our oxen. . . . I will scare them off and we must quickly inspan the wagon and get away from here."

He fired a shot into the first pair of gleaming eyes he could see, and together they rapidly spanned in the oxen. The animals seemed nervous and restless to be gone.

"The lions have frightened them," Piet said as the oxen broke into a gallop, the wagon lurching, rolling, and creaking over the stony veld. How those oxen ran—neither of the farmers had ever seen anything like it.

"*Magtig*," said Piet, "what has happened to the oxen? I have never seen them gallop like this," and he clung to the reins, trying to keep the wagon straight on its wheels. As the dawn began to break over the veld, they saw to their amazement that, in the dark hurry of their departure, they had inspanned a lion instead of their usual trek ox!

I was a delicate child, having at an early age contracted double pneumonia and pleurisy, by which one lung was dangerously affected. For years I was plagued by the fear of tuberculosis and frequently sent away from any risk of cold or recurrent pneumonia, sometimes to the high karroo where the air was cold and clear, sometimes taken abroad to avoid the winter at the Cape. I am afraid that out of her natural anxiety my mother exaggerated the dangers and made me self-conscious of my health. But I know that her care of me through those delicate years gave me the necessary stamina to resist the frequent attacks of pneumonia that laid me low for many years afterwards. Any sign of even a cold in the head sent me straight to bed, where I had to spend a great deal of time, filled with disappointment at missing either a party or a special anniversary, a picnic or a theater, to which I had looked forward for months ahead. Both she and my father guarded me from every possible risk.

But the one compensation for all I suffered by having to stay in bed was the joy of being read to by Papa. I would lie waiting patiently, looking forward to his return from town when, if he was not too tired, he would come and sit at my bedside to read to me. It was a wonderful experience, hearing him read with his gentle voice and beautiful diction, acting the stories, as it were, until they came alive. Nobody could read as he did! No actor could bring more power to his speech.

While a student in London, living in Pump Court near the Inns of Court and eating his "dinners" at the Inner Temple, Papa had become fascinated by the theater and took lessons in acting and elocution. Whenever possible, he went to watch the great performances of Sir Henry Irving, who, together with Ellen Terry, was the reigning star of the London theater. Luckily for him he was introduced one day to Miss Terry who, realizing his talent, allowed him to try one or two small parts in their productions. He might have made acting his career, but his parents heard of the venture, dangerous in their eyes, and he was sternly persuaded to give up the idea altogether in favor of the law. The experience, however, proved invaluable for his later career as Speaker of the House of Assembly, and accounted for the fact that he spoke far better than most of his contemporaries. It was often said in my hearing as I grew older that "Parliament had never had a better Speaker."

Daily my father left home at eight-thirty in the morning in frock coat and shining top hat, carrying his walking stick and satchel, to go to town, where, first as a barrister or member of Parliament, then as Speaker of the House, he was becoming more and more respected and renowned. But to me he seemed severe, intolerant, I used to think, almost merciless in his judgment of people. He could not forgive them for straying from the narrow path; "noblesse," from his point of view, obliged one to keep to the recognized standards at whatever cost to oneself.

He loved his books as much as his flowers, reading everything he could lay his hands on, and, as he possessed the most extraordinary retentive memory, his fund of knowledge was prodigious. But he equally enjoyed his sports, for he was a fine shot as well as an excellent cricketer.

As his son, I was doomed to disappoint him, for neither of these sports interested me. I remember the first time he took me out shooting the small antelope called springbok on the farm of one of his wealthy clients. By then I had been taught to shoot, practicing first with an air gun, then with a rifle at the butts, until finally he had given me my own gun, a .22 rifle, and told me we were going to stay with his friends to get some "real" shooting. I shall never forget sitting crouched behind the blind made of cactus and boughs of wattle, waiting in the pale, clear light of the early dawn for the bucks to pass that way. I had only seen these beautiful little antelopes stuffed and set up in the natural history museum I frequented, admiring their thin, elegant legs and delicate heads, the graceful tan body with its wide dark stripe and white belly. But I was completely unprepared for the first sight of these creatures galloping over the brow of the hill, flying more like birds than animals, leaping, springing, flowing down the hill slope toward me. "Now," said Papa briskly, "Shoot!" He blazed away, while I knelt, hypnotized, made impotent by the sheer beauty of the animals, unable to do anything but gaze in rapture.

For months afterwards I could sense his displeasure, his unexpressed scorn at my excuses, his disappointment that his only son should have no sporting blood. My own misery in failing him was as bad as his sorrow, yet I could find no way, no words to excuse my feeling of love for these wild creatures, whose untamed freedom I vowed to myself I would never destroy for my own pleasure.

For there had been an incident that had stuck in my memory—an early morning in the woods at the bottom of our garden. There, in a large oak, a pair of squirrels had made their nest. I had tamed the female so that she would come to my whistle and take pieces of food I had collected for her the night before—nuts, fruit, and even bread and butter. I went very quietly into the first bright light that morning, into the hush of the woods, for I knew that the squirrel had babies in her nest. There at the bottom of her tree lay her little body—gnawed, torn to shreds, bloody bits of fur scattered about. My stomach heaved with emotion and I vomited. Suddenly I remembered the babies in the nest without milk or warmth, and I swore quietly to myself that I would never kill an animal, except in self-defense, as long as I lived.

I rescued the two babies from the nest and gave one to a school friend. I kept the other, a male, and called him Jimminy. He stayed with us until the lure of all his friends in the fir trees

grew too strong to resist. One morning he left, and my heart
sank, heavy as a stone, though I secretly hoped he would some
day return to where he had found food and comfort.

I knew my father loved me, which made his disappointment
worse, for he loved his whole family with reckless generosity.
He loved my mother above all and spoiled her as only a man
who loves a woman could spoil her. He was proud of her for
every reason, so he forgave her everything. Even as a small
child I was aware of the power she wielded over him.

Despite all his gifts, his exceptional mind, his handsome looks,
for he was six feet one and a half inches tall, he was essentially
humble, with a hard core of pride deep in his heart. He naturally
assumed the superior position, but was saved from pomposity by
his sense of humor, which I learned later never failed him, even
in his public work.

By the time I was old enough to take part in the life of our
house, he had been knighted by Queen Victoria, and was among
the men trying to carve South Africa into a form that suited the
political pattern of their day. First and foremost among these
men was Cecil John Rhodes, the imperial fanatic who possessed
the vision, intelligence, and charm to bring most men to his feet.
When Rhodes became prime minister of the Cape Colony, my
father was made his attorney general for a time, so that Rhodes
inevitably entered our lives. When later Papa voluntarily resigned, much to Rhodes's regret it was said, they continued a
friendship that had far-reaching results.

That he was associated with Rhodes and the distinguished
men who surrounded him made me feel very proud. For though
I was young, Rhodes had assumed a sort of godhead in my im-
pressionable eyes; his power, his reputation, all made him the
greatest man in the country.

I shall never forget my first meeting with him. I had heard so
much about him, so much that was contradictory, that I became
more and more inquisitive to see him for myself. I had often
been to see his house from the wide terraces of his garden, fa-

mous for the masses of blue hydrangeas he had planted in a dell near the house; when in flower, these created a solid lake of blue. But I had never met the owner, though my father was often summoned to private cabinet meetings held there. Rhodes had had the house designed to suit his own taste by Herbert Baker, a young architect who, through the encouragement of his patron, went on to fame both in South Africa and in England. Ultimately, he shared with Sir Edwin Lutyens the honor of designing New Delhi, where his distinctive sense of style is still visible. Rhodes, who had better taste than Baker, wanted him to develop and adapt the early Dutch architecture of the eighteenth century to the more modern requirements of living. His house, called "Groot Schuur" ("great barn"), was built on the site of an old Dutch granary and remains as a monument to their combined efforts, for it was left by the owner as a residence for all succeeding prime ministers of the Republic of South Africa.

One afternoon, Papa told me he had to drive over to "Groot Schuur" for a meeting and that I could go with him. I remember how excited I felt, for it might mean that I should see the great man face to face at last.

"Shall we see Mr. Rhodes?" I asked impatiently as we drove along.

"I think you had better wait outside," said Papa. "I don't expect I shall be very long."

My heart sank at his words, for it had happened before, when I had wandered up over the slopes behind the house to visit the animals that Rhodes had enclosed in various paddocks. He had brought the animals from his beloved north: zebras in their handsome stripes; koodoo with their magnificent curling horns, standing static, gazing across the valley at their own domain; springbok and impala fenced in against their fighting relatives, the wildebeest or gnu, who pranced up and down the length of their paddock, eager to escape. Each time I had hoped to be allowed to go inside the house. Now I felt I should risk a rebuff.

Gathering my courage, I said to Papa, "D'you think Mr. Rhodes would mind if I waited inside? You've always told me about his wonderful things. Couldn't I see them this once?"

"I expect he'd let you look around if I asked him."

We got to the door, which was answered by a footman in livery. "My son will wait for me in here," Papa said. "I'll tell Mr. Rhodes. You go on in there," ushering me into a large, shaded room. "I'll be down there at the end of the passage. Just look around quietly," he added as he left me.

The room had an immediate effect upon me, for it was like a museum, with things of every sort everywhere, on the walls, the tables, the floor. I stood hypnotized, my eyes trying to take it all in at once. On the walls hung the great heads of the big animals, rhino, eland, buffalo, their glass eyes lit by pinpoints of light. Below them were native weapons, assegais, beadwork, musical instruments, all belonging to the Bantu from the great northlands. The tables, too, seemed full: carved wood figures, bits of sculpture standing unexpectedly among photographs in silver frames. And over all was the strange smell of fur, from the fur skins scattered over the polished floor—leopard, lion, jackal, antelope. I had never seen such a room, filled as it was with all such things as interested me, things I wanted to possess, to look at, to touch. As my eyes grew accustomed to the light, I realized that on one wall hung an immense map, an old map covered with lovely designs of the winds and the sun and moon, with a proud galleon riding wavy seas where whales spouted high plumes of foam. What a wonderful map it was, all of Africa, gigantic, magnified, the huge continent stretching up and up from the tiny point of the Cape of Good Hope. I moved closer to see exactly where on the map I was actually standing, then started to trace my way up to the places whose names I knew, Johannesburg, Pretoria, on up to Salisbury and the immense Zambezi, where I knew the Falls were, the Victoria Falls of Livingston, whose name suddenly conjured up all the dark, exciting mystery of Africa. Someday I will see it all, I said to myself, hot with the excitement of imagination.

Then my eye lit on something that held my attention. I wasn't sure what it was, a strange, archaic-looking piece of stone sculpture standing on a pedestal by itself. Something about it so fascinated me that I stood staring, lost in wondering what it was meant to be.

Suddenly, a voice behind me startled me into the realization that someone had come into the room. "So you like my bird, young fellow," and I turned to stare up at Rhodes himself.

"Yes, sir," I said, as nervous and confused as though I had been caught doing something I should not have done. "I was wondering what it was," I said, excusing myself.

"It's a bird," said Rhodes, "and he comes from here," striding over toward the map. "From here," he said, pointing at a spot on the map ringed around with red ink.

"What is it?" I asked.

"That's just what we don't know," said Rhodes, "but it's called Zimbabwe. Isn't that a lovely name? It's a place all in ruins and possibly the answer to the whole secret of Africa."

"Is there a secret?" I asked excitedly.

"Oh, there are lots of secrets in Africa. I'm after a few myself, and Zimbabwe might give us the key. You must get your dad to take you up there one day. I found that bird there and brought him here because I liked him; they say he was one of Astarte's vultures. . . . Anyway, enjoy yourself—we won't be long, and I'll tell your dad you are having a good time." He strode out of the room as silently as he had come in.

He is like a colossus, I thought, or a great tree, like my favorite tree—the big oak at the bottom of our garden. He was an immense man—tall, with broad shoulders surmounted by a powerful head, just as I had imagined him from his photographs—but his voice made a curious impression upon me. It didn't seem to belong properly to anyone that size.

He left me with my mind reeling at the unexpected meeting, at the surprise that what I had longed for would happen so suddenly, at the things he had said, the secret I knew nothing about. I wondered what he had meant and who Astarte was. I went back to the red spot on the map and spelled out the letters: Z-I-M-B-A-B-W-E; what a strange name, the very sound had a kind of magic! It was like the smooth, singing sound of the Kaffir language spoken by the native boys who came to work in our orchard.

The little history I knew, together with all the stories Papa had told me about the east coast of Africa, rushed to my mind. That part of Africa was a world of romance, one of the oldest coasts of the world, it was said, known to Arabia, Sheba, and the trade with the Orient. As my eye moved from the red spot over to the seacoast, there I saw the port of Sofala, where the navy of Tarshish was supposed to have traded ivory and apes and peacocks, collecting great quantities of gold from the mines of the hinterland in return. In my imagination I could see the harbor filled with every sort of vessel, strange, painted junks from China manned by little men, and the thin dhows of the Arabs with huge lateen sails the colors of the sunset. Every year with the monsoon, Papa said, the dhows sailed from Arabia to trade with Africa for ivory, gold, and rhinoceros horn, the most precious cargo of all.

"Why was that so valuable?" I asked.

"Oh, it was used for things you wouldn't understand," answered Papa. I resented suddenly being made conscious of my age and ignorance.

Further up the coast, I found Mombasa, where I remembered Vasco da Gama had dropped anchor before going on to plant the Portuguese flag on Goa. Papa had told me the whole history of the Portuguese adventurers, beginning with Henry the Navigator and his search for the empire of Prester John. There was a name to excite a boy! Mysterious, Christian before most of the known world, richer than anyone could imagine, Prester John had been a legend to the Europe of his day until Portugal discovered him right there in Abyssinia. A legend who had even been called "king of the Indies"—for Papa said no one in Europe even knew where India was—he had ruled over the whole east coast of Africa from the Red Sea right down to the mines of Zimbabwe. Then I suddenly remembered. Of course, "King Solomon's mines"—that was where they were, that was probably the secret that Rhodes was after, more gold, more even than Johannesburg! I could hardly wait to ask my father about the bird, who Astarte was, and Zimbabwe, the secret so casually mentioned.

That chance conversation started me along a path of inquiry that I followed for years afterwards. With enthusiasm, I read everything I could lay hands on relating to the "mystery" that Rhodes had stumbled on moving north, claiming more and more territory for England. The more I read the more I wanted to see it for myself, so that by the time I was finally taken to Rhodesia I knew most of what was then known or thought about the place. Though Zimbabwe was largely in ruins, who had built it, when, and for what purpose were the questions puzzling the archeologists of the world.

After that first meeting with Mr. Rhodes, my sister and I went more often to "Groot Schuur." Now that we knew the owner I felt quite important, and we saw him occasionally when we took a tea basket to the old summerhouse built on the hillside beyond the house. From the roof, one could see an immense stretch of the flats lying between the two oceans bordered by the jagged mountains of the so-called Hottentots' Holland, which guarded the approach to the north. We loved calling on Alice and Jumbo, the two great lions caged near the roadside, together with a vicious leopard and some jackals, or we would watch the ostriches play-fighting in their fenced paddocks.

A favorite path led through the glen to a small house on the estate called "The Woolsack," where our friends, the Rudyard

Kiplings, lived for part of each year. We used to have tea with Elsie and John, the two children, when we would be allowed to play with a small lion kitten Mrs. Kipling was bringing up by hand. He was very unlike his two dangerous-looking relatives in their cage on the hillside, with his large, soft paws and great, limpid eyes. After tea, Mr. Kipling would sometimes tell us stories on the *stoep*, where, sitting at his feet, we would listen wide-eyed as he brought fascinating tales to life, tales of the elephant, the kangaroo, or the Indian animals we didn't know much about. How much we were to be envied we didn't then realize. But Kipling's stories forever after held a special place in our hearts.

One incident connected with the Kiplings I remember vividly, though I was too young to be allowed to actually participate. This was an afternoon performance of an act from *A Midsummer Night's Dream*. Kipling loved the play and directed the whole idea, acting the role of Bottom himself and casting his daughter Elsie as Titania, his son John as Puck, and my sister Luia as Oberon. He and Mrs. Kipling, assisted by our Nannie, arranged the costumes, making the crowns and the splendid ass's head out of painted cardboard. They rehearsed in the "Woolsack" garden for the performance, which was held in the natural setting of the dell near Mr. Rhodes's house one Saturday afternoon, the sun slanting from behind the mountain adding a magic of its own to the fantasy of the play. Luia looked very regal as Oberon, saying her lines with an almost professional gesture, having been carefully coached by Papa.

We were a very small but appreciative audience, with Nannie nervously patting my hands each time I clapped Luia too loudly. Mr. Rhodes, Mrs. Kipling, and Papa sat in comfortable chairs in the front row, but for some reason Mama was not there. The servants from the houses, together with the workers on the estate, stood respectfully in the background.

Rhodes was fascinated by Kipling, who was the very voice of the British Empire Rhodes had set out to serve. Papa used to tell me that Rhodes invariably carried about with him a copy of Kipling's verses, which he even took with him in his bag when he traveled. Kipling's influence was probably more widespread and influential than we can now appreciate. Papa always said that Baden-Powell, who was also a great friend of Kipling's and stayed with us at "Mon Desir" after Mafeking, got his idea for the Boy Scouts from the stories of Mowgli and his friends. It may be true. He certainly encouraged the use of khaki as a color for the uniforms of the British fighting the Boers in the dun-colored, dusty karroo. The very word *khaki* comes from the Urdu word meaning "dust," and the material had been successfully used by the forces in the field of India.

As the consumption that finally killed Rhodes became worse, he was moved to a little thatched cottage by the sea at False Bay, where it was hoped he would get the fresh air needed for his diseased lungs. My parents had a summer house close by, and I used to look at his cottage and wonder what was happening to the great man, lying fighting for breath. It was common talk that he was going to die, that he probably wouldn't even live to get to England, his own homeland. Each time I passed the cottage I had the greatest longing to see him again, and one day, against all instructions, I skirted the low wall around the cottage plot and tiptoed to the front of the house, where I knew his room was. Peering in the window, I could see him lying, immense and still, propped up on his pillows, a large punkah attached to the ceiling over his head waving back and forth. I remember wondering why he had to die, there out of sight of the mountain he so loved, or the wild north that was his own adopted land. He died a few days later in the hot little cottage, and I sat on the rocks at the sea's edge, watching people come and go, as sad as though I had actually lost a friend.

But that was still in the future, as indeed was the Boer War (1899–1902), which, with the tragic prologue of the Jameson Raid, was yet to shatter the earliest vision of my hero. Our house, like many others, was a center of political discussion, for my father, through his own position, was deeply involved in the upheaval caused by the raid, with the consequent indictment of Mr. Rhodes. We were forbidden even to mention the subject. I don't know to this day just where my father stood in his relations with Rhodes at that time, although years later I was told by my mother about the anxious days of the Jameson Raid, when Papa had stood by his oldest, dearest friend, Will Schreiner, then attorney general. For Schreiner was obliged to resign when he heard from his idol's own lips the revelations that showed that Rhodes had betrayed both him and his cabinet. It was then that his heart broke, for Rhodes had seemed to personify everything he most admired. He had counted on him, believed in him, loved him, even writing when he submitted his resignation, "I have had no more bitter sorrow in my life than my loss of you." Only a few friends of the Schreiner family besides my father knew what the poor man suffered by his disillusionment. (We thought Rhodes found it difficult to forgive my father for his unquestioned loyalty to his friend Schreiner.)

Of the Boer War only a few memories remain, but these are very vivid still. One was the discovery that among people we knew, even our friends, there were some who were disloyal to England, actually some who were what we called "pro-Boer." That was a frightful shock to us children. We gradually discovered that there were many families entirely divided, with members of their clan among the so-called rebels. Even our dear Will Schreiner, who was trying to remain loyal to England and her ideals while at the same time do what seemed best for the country as a whole, was among the unhappiest. His wife was related to some of the leaders of the Boer party.

Another memory is of my visits to the military hospital in Wynberg, a suburb not far from our house. Here my mother helped as a nurse's aide, nursing the many wounded Tommies who were sent back in increasing numbers from the front. Tragedy seemed to surround us, as news of reversals with a fearful loss of life on both sides reached us every day. Mother would come home so sad-eyed and miserable from her days at the hospital that we never dared to ask for news. But I remember clearly being driven in the pony cart with Nannie to deliver homemade soups and jellies to the ward where Mama worked. I can still see the rows of beds with the wounded English Tommies, who had been sent to fight in a country no one in England knew anything about. They had been led, my father said, by "one idiotic general after another," with no experience whatsoever of the type of warfare used by the Boers or, more important still, any idea of the nature of the enemy. For this lack of basic understanding Britain had to pay dearly. No British man had ever fought over such terrain: the strange African veld red with dust; the snakes and animals; the lack of water, roads, or communications; the treacherous stony *kopjes*, behind each of which lurked an elusive enemy. No wonder they said it was "no land for any decent Englishman to spill his blood," as Mama reported to us in a hushed whisper.

More and more English troops arrived at Cape Town to be rushed up country to the front. "Simply to be slaughtered," said Mama. "Oh, I'm so sorry for them—thrown away like fodder to the Boers, and such splendid men led by those stupid generals."

We had heard a lot about Sir Redvers Buller, Lord Methuen, and Lord Roberts, who had met Papa with Kitchener of Khartoum. Wonderful names they were, all with titles and supposed to be England's greatest generals, though Papa said none of them had ever fought against white men, "only savages," he added contemptuously. Yet the war went on the Boers remained unbeaten!

When the war ended and the bitter Peace of Vereeniging * was signed, there was to be no peace in South Africa. The terrible harm had been done; the wounds of that war were not to heal during my lifetime. As I grew older, I became more con-

* May 31, 1902.

scious of this truth, a truth I had heard vehemently expressed by Olive Schreiner, the famous author and sister of my father's friend. She lived to champion the rights of the Boers and to become famous throughout the world through her writing. She even foretold the union of the then four separate states, which came into being ten years after the peace. But she also foresaw that the relations between Boer and Briton, as well as the equally important relations between the white man and the dark, had not been resolved in any way. Though men have fought and died in the effort to weld these races through my long life, they still remain opposed. South Africa is now a republic with her people's dream fulfilled, but "the white man's burden" is weighing her down more than ever and the end is not yet in sight.

Although he did not discuss it much in our hearing, I know from all Mama said that my father was deeply troubled by the Boer War. He had been elected Speaker of the House of Assembly a year after he had served as Mr. Rhodes's attorney general, which removed him from partaking in the political policies. During the stormy session that followed the fiasco of the Jameson Raid, when his friendship with Rhodes was shattered by the exposé of that disaster, his position as Speaker was not one to be envied. To his everlasting credit let it be said that he performed his duties "with a tact and impartiality that had never been excelled." * Later, when he returned to the House as a member for the town of Port Elizabeth, his opinions of those concerned with the raid had not altered, and he refused cabinet rank in Dr. Jameson's newly formed ministry, which was not surprising.

Papa had an extraordinary gift for storytelling; first, because he had a ripe sense of humor and found much in life that was very entertaining, then because he was a first-rate mimic who could copy anyone's accent or mannerisms to perfection. His travels as a lawyer on circuit, and later as a judge, invariably

* *South African Law Journal,* 1915.

produced a fund of very funny anecdotes, so he became well known as a raconteur among his friends. As children we would look forward to his return home, knowing we could expect to sit around him in peals of laughter while he recounted his experiences, often made more amusing by his imitations in the Taal, or Afrikaans.

Once when Papa returned from an electioneering trip among his constituents he told us a story about one of his friends, a successful farmer who had come to see him about a personal problem. It seemed that he had an excellent overseer, a man of real value who worked hard and appeared to be the answer to all his worries over the farm. However, to his great anxiety, the farmer found that his wife had become very attached to his overseer and that, whenever he returned to his house, he found them seated together on the sofa in the living room, apparently in delightful conversation. At first he tried to overlook the situation, but his suspicions grew and grew until, having spoken to his wife about the matter, he came to see Papa for some advice on how to control the situation.

"Why, my friend," said Papa, "it's very simple. Surely you should at once dismiss the overseer."

"Oh, no," said the farmer, "I will never find another man as good as he is. I must think of another way."

"Well, why not speak again to your wife? You are very close to her, so tell her you do not like her seeing so much of your man."

"It's not as easy as that," said the farmer. "She will only dismiss the whole matter and think badly of me for being suspicious."

Months later Papa went back to the same area and found his friend the farmer wreathed in smiles, happy as a lark.

"Well," said Papa, "I suppose you took my advice and got rid of the overseer."

"Not at all," said the farmer, "I thought of a much better way. I sold the sofa."

Father used to tell a story about himself that happened while he was a judge on circuit in one of the farming districts. He was very fond of walking, and often sent his wagons and staff on for miles ahead of him while he tramped along alone. In the days when the railway had not yet connected all the circuit towns, it was necessary to travel by road, often through lonely, undeveloped areas. But he enjoyed adventures, and, as he used to tell us, he learned a lot through those experiences.

On this particular occasion he had miscalculated the distance to the next town. The road was hot and dusty, so he had sat down to rest, hoping someone with a cart or wagon would give him a lift. He had on his traveling clothes—old hat and boots suitable for tramping through the open veld—and must have looked more like a tramp than a judge.

Before long a farmer, summoned as a juror for the next day's court, drove up in his open cart. Without saying who he was, Papa asked the farmer in Dutch to drive him to the village and offered to pay for the lift. This had the desired effect and, after some uncomplimentary remark about his appearance, the farmer agreed, taking the money, and Papa climbed in behind. On the way the farmer, inquisitive about such a dusty-looking stranger in his countryside, began asking questions.

"Are you looking for work?" he asked Papa.

"No, I'm not," was the reply.

"Have you got a trade? Can you work on a farm?"

"No," said Papa.

"I thought not," said the farmer. "You sound like one of those English loafers that never do any work." Then, as though struck by inspiration, the farmer said, "Have you run away from a ship? Do you want to be a schoolmaster? Can you read and write?"

"Yes, I can read and write," said father, "but I don't want to be a schoolmaster, thank you."

"Of course not," said the farmer, "no chance of loafing then.

But if you don't work, where did you get that money you gave me?"

"I earned it," said Papa. "I dispense justice."

That completely baffled the farmer, but, as they were approaching the long street of the village, he asked, "Where do you want to go?"

"To Schmidt's Hotel, please."

"Heavens," said the farmer. "I thought as much. The first thing you want to do is to go and drink. I suppose it is drink that has brought you to your miserable condition." Papa remained silent as they drove up to the hotel.

On the steps waiting to meet him, as was customary, were the magistrate, the sheriff, and one or two of the ministers. As he got off the cart, having thanked the farmer, the latter threw over his shoulder his last words of warning: "Now take care, don't drink too much. The judge is going to sit tomorrow."

While he was speaking, the hotel keeper came forward to greet my father and the assembled men all rose with hat in hand. In an agonized tone, the farmer whispered loudly to the hotel keeper, "but who is this man?"

"The judge," was the reply.

"My God," said the farmer, and he whipped his horses into a furious gallop and was gone in a cloud of dust.

Next day, one juror did not answer to his name, and Father, thinking of his adviser of the day before, was obliged to inflict the usual fine. But, after such an amusing adventure, he hated having to do it.

He often said he wished he had had an opportunity to preach, for he held very firm although enlightened views on Christianity, despite a somewhat Calvinistic upbringing. He had one story about an incident that occurred while he was serving on a commission appointed to deal with certain concessions in Swaziland. I tell it in his own words as I remember them.

"Among the many attracted by the concession court was one

Danford, the surveyor. Danford was founder of the Eclectic and Pirates Club in Kimberley that had done so much for the young men of that city. We arrived on a Tuesday, I think it was, and with his cooperation I decided to hold some sort of service in the courthouse on the Sunday following. The front part of the building, along which ran a verandah, consisted of three rooms: the middle and larger one was the bar, the next in size was the courthouse and the smaller one was the judge's mess room.

"On Sunday morning, a hot day, with the whole place to ourselves, Danford and I in our shirt sleeves sat on the verandah outside the mess room with the largest whiskies and sodas we could get, writing out hymns! My prayer book I had; but the camp did not boast of a single hymnbook, so we wrote out sixteen copies of each of three hymns as we could best remember, and where we could not remember the words we supplied our own. There was on the premises a little harmonium about two feet high, belonging to the landlord. On this, Danford and I picked out the tunes and wrote them down. Both of us knew something about music, and we managed the bass accompaniment.

"It so happened that the first hymn was 'Praise the Lord. Ye Heavens Adore Him.' The tune was more or less evolved on the harmonium by Danford as the organist before a very small congregation consisting of the commission and their officials, who had come willy-nilly. (I wonder how long it had been since some of them had come to church.) During the singing of the first verse, somewhat disturbed by the conversation of the concession seekers around the bar, I, who acted as parson, noticed five or six men slinking in, and very soon I heard them singing in German. Then I remembered that the hymn was set to the tune of the Austrian national anthem. Next day, I got a 'round robin' signed by a dozen men to the effect that, if I would always sing this hymn, they would always come to church service.

"The following Sunday saw Danford and myself working at two more hymns and writing out twenty-four copies of each. Some fourteen men came to the service that night. The following day, we telegraphed to Pretoria for fifty hymnbooks to be sent to Barberton, from where a Kaffir runner brought them over the mountains in time for the next Sunday. That same week an official arrived, and among his possessions was a larger organ. The manager of a business establishment nearby returned, and he was a violinist, so the third Sunday service began with Gounod's *Ave Maria*, the manager playing first violin, myself second (for I could still play the fiddle), and Danford at the organ. After that, the courthouse was full every Sunday night, but the inevitable round robin came along asking for six hymns!"

In his diary Papa wrote:

My only regret is that I never took the opportunity of preaching a sermon, the only one I ever had. I read a burial service over the only member of the community who died while we were in Swaziland, which no doubt was a finer sermon than any I could have composed. Still I regret the lost opportunity.*

Even though he never preached, he used all his sense of composition, of structure and dramatic suspense, when as a lawyer he pleaded the causes of his clients before the juries. I used to be allowed to go and hear him in cases considered "suitable" to my years. Somehow I felt that, when he was in his gown, acting his role before judge and jury with such effect he was a different person altogether, a person quite unrelated to me, someone I didn't know. Then I would remember him in his garden or on our Sunday walks and feel proud that he was the same person and still my father.

I remember an incident that never ceased to cause us amusement as we grew older and could tease one another about what

* *South African Law Journal*, 1915.

was sheer stupidity. In those days, when plumbing was very primitive and bathrooms scarce, there stood at the side of every bed in the house a "night table," really a cupboard in which reposed a spacious china chamber for night use. It happened that our parents were away and staying in some rather primitive hotel, so we were not astonished when our governess, then in charge of the household, received a telegram that read: "Require immediately three blankets, one pillow, send chambers. . . . Juta." The telegram obviously indicated urgency, though we puzzled a bit over the wording; however, it was decided to carefully pack two china chambers in the heavy bedding and dispatch them in haste to the country hotel.

One can picture the tableau, Papa having meant us to send the package to what were called his "chambers" or offices in Cape Town, whence he could collect it more easily. The additional burden of the two china utensils did not add to his pleasure when he claimed the package.

When we were very young, he used to tell us fairy stories, which he had originally composed for my elder sisters but which he added to as we grew older. They were witty, imaginative, exciting, just the sort of stories that children love to hear. Always staged in a local setting we seldom failed to recognize, they were full of the color, the people, the happenings of the life around us. Sometimes they included songs, the verses of which he composed with meticulous care.

He wrote with ease, which was very surprising in one whose literary efforts had been confined mostly to serious volumes on Roman Dutch law. His best-known works, however, which remain classic books of reference for the legal profession in South Africa, concern the complicated laws on water rights, which, in a land as dry and sparsely settled as it was, caused more litigation than almost anything else in those days. He found a release in writing, just as he did in music. Although he seldom practiced his violin or piano, I was always amazed that his technique remained through the years, so that he could play a violin obli-

gato to some song sung by one of my sisters to the piano accompaniment of Mama, who also kept up her music until her
death.

He used to urge me to practice the piano, for which I had
some talent, telling me that of all the arts music could bring
most comfort to the spirit. Years later, when my mother lay dangerously ill, I remember Papa playing for his own solace old tunes
he had not played for a long time with the gentle yet passionate
touch that only an artist can bring to the piano. Mama died
some years before he did, but I know that he loved her to the
very end, even though the world must have offered many temptations to a man as masculine and attractive as he was. His principles with all the denial they entailed always came first, and he
scorned the idea of weakness in himself as well as in others.
With one look he could make me realize how far below his
standards I had fallen, bringing a blush to my cheeks together
with a wave of resentment at his intolerance. Yet he never failed
me when I needed him. Only too often, I failed him.

He ruled the household with a firm hand, a hand we were all
afraid of, for he had a very bad temper, which he took great
pains to control. At times, the house would be filled with a sort
of trembling gloom, a darkness in the usually bright rooms that
we would instantly recognize. "Papa is in a rage about something." It didn't last for long. Mama would sweep in with flowers in her hand to brush away the darkness with her gaiety, and
his humor would return like sunshine.

But I resented his strictness. Being the youngest and the only
son, perhaps the most revolutionary of the family, I longed to
break away, see the people I liked but of whom he so often disapproved, go to the places I wanted to go whether he approved
or not. I seldom succeeded. He had an uncanny way of guessing
my thoughts, of invariably forestalling my disobedience. Some
times this drove me to find ways to deceive him. I know now
how much that must have hurt him. Certainly, he understood
some aspects of my nature, but that did not endear him to me,

though it should have, for he never ceased to encourage me to develop such tastes and interests as he thought valuable.

When he noticed my growing concern with the birds and animals around us, he said to me one day, "How would you like to study taxidermy at the museum, if I can arrange it?"

My heart leaped at the thought. The local museum of natural history had become one of my favorite haunts. I much preferred to sneak away from football practice to spend an hour or two among the animals and birds I loved. To study the lifelike way the creatures were set up among the dried plants, stones, or dead branches, as in their native habitat, gave me intense pleasure. I had learned their names, their province and habits. Somehow I found myself more and more involved in their life story. They were the Africa I loved; they, and the strange, mysterious dark peoples whose manners and customs I longed to learn about, were to me the real Africa, the Africa of the shaded forests, the blue fathomless lakes, the wide, high mountain ranges. I felt I wanted to share it all with them, though I knew I had few rights as an alien intruder.

"I'd love that," I answered, thrilled at the idea of spending more time among my friends, as I called the animals.

Soon it was all arranged. I went with Papa to meet the director of the museum and the taxidermist, Charlie Smithers, who became my teacher, friend, and counselor. I learned more from Smithers' wonderful philosophy than I realized at the time. The things he taught me about both animals and human beings have helped me all my life. The weekly Saturday mornings I spent with him became my most longed-for pleasure.

Smithers was a small man, with bushy eyebrows shading a twinkle in his bright Irish eyes.

"And is it birds ye want to stuff, me boy," he asked me, "or the creatures ye meet around the countryside, perhaps even the people?" he added with a loud laugh.

"I love them all," I said enthusiastically.

"Weel, the first thing we have to learn is to look at them, the way they perch or sit or fly or run, ivry one peculiar to his own. Then we'll look at the anatomy to see how they move. We can't have them contrary to their nature."

So we began with quiet walks among the trees to study the birds.

"An', d'you see the doves a-drinking at me bird bath? Watch the greedy beggars, drinking away with never a head raised or so much as a 'thank you' to the Lord, not like other birrds, who are more grateful to their maker and lift their heads in thanks after each sip."

In his big workshop, smelling of tow, wax, and the musty odor of drying furs, were three stuffed owls perched lifelike on a branch projecting from the wall. Smithers invariably greeted them as we went in as though they were guardians of his properties.

"An' is it because ye see in the darrk that we all think ye are so wise?" he would stop and say to the owls. "Ye are mighty lucky, ye know," he added with a wink, "to see everything that goes on in the darkness."

With his neat fingers he showed me how to skin a bird, to wire the wings, to make the dummy stuffing for the one we had chosen and shot in the woods. And, while he worked, his whimsical philosophy on life, nature, or people would rumble on to brighten all my amateur efforts with humor.

The day came when I proudly took home my first stuffed bird. I alone had skinned it, stuffed it, wired the thin, dark legs, setting it at the proper angle, to convey the bird's gesture, on a twig of my own choosing. I was more proud when Papa congratulated me, encouraging me to go on and tackle small animals as well. Smithers helped me by insisting on my study of the creature when alive.

"An' no squirrel would sit with a dropping tail, me boy," he said. "Look, watch him as he sits chatterin' there on the branch, his tail a-jerkin' as he curses."

I progressed from squirrel to rabbit, from rabbit to jackal, bearing my treasures home to fill my room to overflowing with my works of art. I knew the day had soon to come when I must ask for the thing I now longed for—my own museum.

"We'll see," said Papa, "your birthday isn't far off."

I prayed, persistently asking God to give me what I wanted.

I remember the day our museum was finished, with the shelves almost filled with our collection. My sister and I shared the pleasure, for she was interested in many of the things we added to our display: the stones we found together on the flats, the arrowheads the Hottentots had used, the pieces of early Dutch china we collected on our wanderings. My choice pieces were given due prominence, carefully docketed. Friends had contributed other items to help us fill the shelves: a bottled scorpion, a deadly looking puff adder, some lovely hummingbirds in a glass case as a special gift from Charlie Smithers. How exciting it was to show our friends around the small, square room! Our parents were proud of us, too, and my father's pleasure gave me a deep-down satisfaction. This was better than shooting springbok—anyone could do that, but this was an art. I had learned it, thanks to Papa.

My father was at his best on a picnic, for he and my mother enjoyed eating out of doors as much as we did. Whenever he had a chance and could get away for a day, we invariably went picnicking. He was a keen fisherman, so we frequently chose to spend a day at the seaside. The two coasts of the peninsula are indented by lovely bays interspersed with smooth beaches, ideal for bathing. From the big rocks many of the fish abounding in the Cape waters could easily be caught with a rod and line. Our favorite spot, which was several hours drive from home, was called Kommetje ("little saucer"). It was a shallow bay full of smooth, rounded rocks on which grew various beautifully colored seaweeds. These were the haunt of a small fish called "klipfish," literally "stonefish." Of delicious flavor but full of small bones, these fish are the same golden, brown, and green color as the weeds they inhabit and are quite invisible through the clear water. But they were always hungry and easily caught by all of us with a simple line and hook carefully baited with catfish.

We would leave at very early dawn in the wagonette drawn by four horses or mules driven by Papa himself. Our fishing tackle and rugs and cushions for the ladies were packed in with us. We were closely followed by a farm wagon filled with everything required in the way of food and drinks, fresh water, and fire kindling, all manned by the colored men—servants and garden boys who enjoyed our picnics as much as we did. Papa had always thought of everything to make the expedition as comfortable and easy as possible, even to reminding the boys to bring along their mouth organs, on which they played expertly all the tunes then popular. The main course of our meal was naturally to be the klipfish we were to catch in quantity, broiled over an open fire and washed down by some light, local white wine.

We would fish all morning, then, after a meal that often lasted for hours, we would go for a long walk over the sand dunes to a hidden stretch of soft, white beach for a bathe. Usually we invited two or three friends of our own age to picnic with us, and our greatest sport was to climb to the tops of the dunes, smooth and windblown, and, racing each other, roll wildly down the next snowy, billowing valley. Nothing grew on the dunes, which were as bare and deserted as we imagined the great deserts of Africa to be, and seemed to flow on interminably. We often wondered whether we would get lost but knew we could always find our way back by our footprints, for no other soul was ever on the dunes and, without wind, the sand never stirred.

The beach from which we bathed was well known for the variety of lovely shells always to be found along the tide's edge: fan shells of every size and color from palest lavender to salmon pink or purple; strange twisted cockles patterned in gold; and sometimes, if we were especially lucky, we would find a pure, milk-white nautilus shell, delicately fluted as finest cambric, fading to pale blue at its transparent edges. All these would be added to the growing collection of shells in our museum.

The greatest fun of all was the drive home through the brilliant sunset, past the fishermen's little thatched cottages along the coast, deep into the blue shadow of the peaks, across the valleys of orchards that led on to home. We children would be allowed to go back in the farm wagon with the native boys, who would play us all our favorite tunes, to which we sang lustily. We knew the words and choruses of all the popular songs and we filled the night air with song as the wagon bounced and jolted on its way. I remember one that had been taught us by English friends, though I have never heard it since those long-ago days. The rhythm seemed to accompany the rumbling of our wagon, and it went like this:

With sousings, with rousings, with bouncings, with trouncings;
With mumblings, with jumblings, with fumblings, with tumblings;
With ramplings and tramplings, with rappings and trappings;
A-spriting, a-spriting, a-spriting go we;
With this face, and that face, and you, goodman good face,
Sing heigh ho, jolly heigh ho, a-spriting go we.

When Papa was judge president, he had to travel to the centers where the courts were held. Sometimes, if it was during my holidays, he took me with him, and it was on such trips that I felt nearest to him, away from the influence of either Mama or any of my sisters. For we journeyed in his special railway car, which was ugly, commodious, and especially built for the comfort of the judges. Besides Papa's registrar, a young man we all liked, we took with us his cook-valet, a colored man named Joseph, who looked after us with as much care as though we were his own family. Nothing was too much trouble, and he thought of everything for our comfort.

Joseph was of the same category as our John, the butler, but much darker, with the blue-black skin of one of the Bantu tribes. He had been trained to his job from an early age, serving several of Papa's predecessors, who had evidently been very particular about their food. For Joseph saw to everything with professional care, planning his menus with forethought and discretion. He had traveled the country many times and knew exactly what specialties could be purchased at which particular place we stopped: a brace of partridges, or certain fresh vegetables, even oysters when we reached the seashore. I discovered that his mother had been a Malay, which accounted for his refined sense of flavoring, but nothing was ever said about his father, who I suspected had been either a Basutu or even a Zulu, so superior were his manners and innate dignity.

Joseph was a great singer of songs, accompanying himself with talent on his little African piano. One can see this little instrument today being played by the thousands of lonely natives wandering the endless dusty roads of South Africa. The pianos are made of flattened pieces of metal of irregular length studded onto a small square of wood, raised on a little metal bridge, as it were, so that their ends may be picked, each to give forth a different note. They are played to accompany the many nostalgic songs sung by the men who in solitude walk over the brown-green hills of the African horizon.

Joseph knew a number of them, some with endless verses to a repetitive tune, but they were almost all mournful. He even knew one or two in Afrikaans, besides some tunes of oriental harmony that he said his mother had taught him. He used to sing one I particularly liked for its droll lyrics in Afrikaans. As I remember, it went like this:

> *Wat maak jij bij die strand?*
> *Wat maak jij bij die pikkenakepolis zij strand?*
> *Ik zoek ver mij sak.*
> *Wat maak jij mit die geld daarin?*
> *Ik koop ver mij een vrouw.*
> *Wat maak jij mit die vrouw?*

What are you doing by the shore?
What are you doing by the "Pikkenakepolis" shore?
I'm looking for my bag.
What will you do with the money in it?
I shall buy myself a wife.
What will you do with the wife?

and so on for many explanatory verses, most of which I couldn't understand but darkly guessed at, as Joseph became more and more hilarious over the words.

Our journeys would take us to different parts of the country, wherever the courts were held. But it always meant going north from the Cape Peninsula, up over the mountains that stood like a huge, blue barricade between the south and the vast hinterland. Crossing the long Hex River Pass, as it is called, was always an exciting experience. To this day, it stands as a triumph of engineering for a narrow-gauge railway. The huge scale of the mountains, the height to which the curving railroad climbed so that the train seemed to double on its tracks, the changing color of the valleys, all held me fascinated at the big window of our "sitting room" carriage.

Halfway up the pass, the train, puffing and snorting after so long a climb, would stop for water. I remember always getting out there into the sharp, high mountain air, feeling the thrill of being up so high among the very peaks, excited by the vast buttresses of the mountains flowing smoothly into the tremendous amphitheater of the valleys. The Cape Peninsula itself is, as I have told, gentle, green, and luxurious, with every sort of plant and flower, but as one travels north onto the desolate plateaux of the karroo, up through the ever-changing landscape of Africa, the light, the flora and fauna all change. Greens give way to gray, amber, topaz, and gold; the gentle landscape alters to the sharp, rugged contours of mountains stark against limitless skies. How I loved it! How much I wanted to identify myself with the extraordinary land and its overpowering spirit, which almost crushes one with the sense of one's own unimportance.

Papa

When the court sat for a week or more in one town and our carriages were shunted onto a siding at the railway station, sometimes Papa would get a day's shooting on a farm of friends, or we would be fetched for a big lunch by one or other of his erstwhile clients. He always took me with him, for, though I didn't shoot, he continued to hope I might some day become keen enough on the sport to want to join him. But he knew that he could always leave me to my own devices, that I would never be either bored or lonely. It was then that I grew to understand more deeply both the people of the country as well as the land itself. I asked interminable questions, but I listened and I learned to appreciate more than one point of view.

There was always something of interest on all the farms we visited, but I preferred the ostrich country, for I had become fascinated by these strange birds—almost half beast, half bird—with their long reptilian necks and their bodies covered with the short black feathers that are more like fur than feathers. Papa had told me not to go near the birds during the breeding season, when the cock bird is a dangerous enemy, ready to rip one to pieces with his huge, malicious claws. But I never tired of watching them, their playacting or their dancing, when they move with a grace and lightness unexpected in so huge a bird.

In those days, ostrich feathers were enjoying a fashionable vogue and the farmers were prosperous. For, though it is mainly the lovely, curling wing feathers of the cocks that are most valuable, at such times even the tails and the humbler feathers of the hens yielded a profit.

On one of the big farms belonging to an old friend of Papa's, a Mr. Olivier, I was shown for the first time the method then used for the clipping of an ostrich's feathers. This was done when the bird was at his mating prime and his wing feathers hung, in snowy masses, low toward the ground. First, the selected bird was caught and a hood quickly slipped over his head to prevent his kicking or slashing anything within reach of his powerful claws. The bird was then guided by two native boys into a

71

sort of trestle, the side bars of which were just the height of the bird's wings. There it was firmly held, too dazed to struggle, while one wing at a time was stretched over the trestle bar, the long curling feathers spread open, ready for the farmer's sharp clippers. The feathers were cut to about two inches from the wing flesh, this length of quill being left to dry and fall out before the new feather tips began to form and push forth. It was said they felt no pain by this method of clipping and only suffered from the indignity of having their great pride of feathers removed.

Once clipped, the bird was released into a separate camp among his fellow victims. How curious, yet how handsome they were together, like a stand of some strange growth, their heads all turned in the same direction, their phalanx of black bodies in close array against any enemy, their big eyes staring toward the gray hens moving restlessly and self-consciously about under the eyes of their future mates!

Later, when the birds had paired off, would commence the extraordinary ritual of the mating dance when, wing tip to wing tip, the huge birds would waltz, prancing around and around, light as dancers on their rubber-lined feet. Then at last, in a tremendous flurry of dust and feathers, with the hen spread-eagled, prostrate beneath her impassioned mate, the ungainly union would occur.

Even in the smaller towns on the circuit, we adhered very strictly to the ritual that accompanied the sitting of the court. I used to think Papa looked very imposing in his black robes and wig, preceded by the usher and followed by his registrar and clerk into the silent Court. I wondered whether he consciously became another individual as he assumed this role, but he retained his humor and certainly became famous for his sense of justice. Counsel for both the Crown and the accused wore their black gowns, while at their side sat a character known as the *tolk* in Afrikaans—the interpreter, who was usually attached to the local court and therefore changed at each succeeding town.

Since, unlike Papa, many of the judges could not talk the Taal, as Afrikaans was then called, let alone the extraordinary dialects used by many of the witnesses, as well as by the natives, the interpreter was expected to be able to translate any one of the languages into the other. In some cases the interpreters, well accustomed to the ways of the court, took great liberties, not only with their translations back and forth to the witnesses, but even in trying to influence the process of justice, having assured themselves that the presiding judge understood nothing of what was being said in anything but English. This often caused great amusement to the local public listening to the cases being tried, for many of them spoke all three tongues equally well. Papa, who was a great stickler about the procedure of the court, often had to put the interpreter in his place by insisting on precise translations.

After a busy day in court, sometimes Papa told very funny stories, brought vividly to life by his imitations of the characters involved, at whose extraordinary behavior and remarks he himself often found it hard to keep a straight face. I remember he told us of a case the local *tolk* was interpreting in which the prisoner was charged with a violent assault upon his alleged wife. The interpreter began all his sentences with "he says" or "she says" and always ended with "My Lord." The complainant, a handsome colored woman, stepped into the witness box holding a baby in her arms. Papa later said he thought at once that he scented the cause of the assault.

"Ask her," he said to the interpreter, "whose child she has in her arms."

"Whose child is that?" asked the interpreter in the Taal.

"*Ach, wat,*" replied the woman, "you know perfectly well it is yours."

Whereupon the interpreter, without a flick of an eyelid,

turned to Papa and said, "She says you know quite well that it is yours, My Lord." . . . Tableau.

On another occasion, the complainant was a colored "lady" in an alleged rape case. Papa told us she tried to look modest and demure, but that her whole appearance obviously showed to what profession she belonged.

"And what is your occupation, what do you do for a living?" asked the interpreter for the counsel.

With all simplicity, she replied, "I am an impartial girl."

Everyone seemed puzzled by this reply. "Ask her what she means by that," said Papa to the interpreter.

The lady, tilting her much befeathered hat, turned a beaming smile upon Papa and said in broken English, "I loves all die gentlemens die same."

I remember hearing an extraordinary case of a trial by jury with Papa as the presiding judge in the town of Bloemfontein, which at the time was the capital of the Orange Free State, since when, of course, that state has become incorporated into the original Union of South Africa which in turn has grown into the Republic.

It was rather the fashion to criticize a trial by jury, mainly because feeling ran so high with respect to certain offenses that juries were considered to be unable to act impartially. They were doubtless influenced by prejudice at times and often made mistakes, but it is the difficult responsibility of the judge to guide the jury perfectly equably concerning the law. In those days, as we have seen, there was the problem of the interpreter, who, often tired, incompetent, even false to his oath, had to be relied upon to a great extent. Many a jury, Papa said, had been badly misled by the haphazard translations of the interpreter.

The case, as I recall it, had its humorous as well as its serious side. As I looked at the jury, summoned much against their will, I felt I was grateful it was not I who was going to be judged by them. They were a motley crew, a cross section of the residents of the area, consisting mostly of farmers in their corduroys but with a few local businessmen among them. Though I have no doubt they were God-fearing, upright men, kindly enough in their personal lives, yet prejudice and intolerance were written across their faces, which seemed to lack any expression of understanding.

An old farmer and his wife living alone had in their employ a little colored girl, who for some theft had been thoroughly punished by her employer. Considering her age and apparent physical weakness, the old woman could not have given a very severe punishment, but the girl, determined to be revenged, one day put some rat poison into the early morning coffee she served to the old people. With considerable cunning, she made it appear as if she were drinking coffee from the same coffeepot—a point made much of later in her defense. The old couple became violently sick and would have died, but for the fact that a doctor had been called in during the night by a near neighbor.

The girl was charged with the crime of attempt to murder by administering poison. The old couple, happily recovered, gave their testimony in court, the medical report was direct, and the evidence showed that no one else but the girl could have had access to the poison or put it in the coffee. The defense counsel raised the points that the poison might have been put into the coffee by mistake for sugar and that the prisoner would not have run the risk of killing herself by drinking the same coffee.

The case seemed very clear, but it was the duty of the judge to explain to the jury the difference between murder and culpable homicide—such as homicide without direct intention, etc., etc.—which was learnedly presented in rather technical language. The interpreter had had a long day in a stuffy, hot court and had become quite indifferent to the situation. His translation of all this learned talk to the jury made them terribly confused. Eventually, the trial came to an end and the interpreter, who anyone could see was greatly relieved, feeling he knew the verdict in advance, hurried the jury off to consider their verdict.

They took far longer than expected to arrive at a decision but finally returned.

"Are you all agreed on your verdict?" asked the interpreter.

"Yes," said the boldest of the jury, who spoke as their foreman.

"Do you find the prisoner guilty or not guilty?" was the routine question.

"Guilty of murder," said the foreman.

At this, the people in the body of the court, who generally sit through a long day with the greatest decorum, broke into a loud laugh, in which I joined. For Papa with meticulous care had to point out that the farmer and his wife were much alive and actually present in the flesh, and once more repeated his learned charge. Once again, the interpreter apparently did his best to make things clear to the jury, who retired and in a little while returned.

The same question was asked: "Do you find the prisoner guilty or not guilty?"

"Guilty of suicide," was the astonishing verdict.

The townspeople rocked with laughter, while the unfortunate jury looked more puzzled than indignant. I felt sorry for Papa, who must have been embarrassed at having to go over the whole thing again at even greater length. Once more the jury were charged. They sat perfectly still, making no movement to show that they wished to retire. They looked stolidly at each other, nodded, and sat still.

"Don't you want to retire?" asked the interpreter in astonishment.

They looked at each other and said, "No."

"But are you agreed on a verdict?"

The answer was a firm "Yes."

"Do you find the prisoner guilty or not guilty?"

The foreman got up, wiped the sweat from his forehead and seemed about to speak when suddenly, "Not guilty!" was the unanimous cry.

They were determined not to be laughed at a third time.

After experiences such as this, it was impossible to discuss the doings of the day when we returned to our waiting "railway hotel." Papa and I would immerse ourselves in chess, which he had taught me to play but which I seldom won.

As we traveled through the interminable plains of the karroo, covered with nothing but the gray-green scrub of the *rhenoster* bush, Papa would be reminded by something he saw in passing —a *kopje* or the dried-up bed of a river—and talk of his experiences in the past. As a young barrister, he had traveled with the court on circuit through most of the Cape Colony and his memories had remained clear and vivid. His registrar and I never tired of hearing him, for his stories were very funny and almost always informative. Once he told a story of an exciting experience he had had when he was imperial judicial commissioner to Swaziland in 1890.

Word was brought him that the queen of the Swazis would be holding an *indaba* the day after his arrival, which she would expect him to attend. An *indaba* is a gathering of the royal court, with chiefs, medicine men, and officials of the nation in attendance. It was extremely hot, but Papa, representing the British government and Her Majesty Queen Victoria, wore the appropriate dress for such an occasion, a frock coat with pin-striped trousers and a top hat.

The queen was already seated on her throne under a spreading thorn tree when he arrived, and indicated where he was to stand with an interpreter at his side. Years later he told me how much the queen resembled Queen Victoria, being plump, yet very regal in appearance. Proceedings began, and my father was reading a personal message from Queen Victoria when he instinctively felt a shudder go through the crowd of native people surrounding the throne. He glanced up from his parchment, and to his horror saw a black mamba snake—the most deadly snake in all Africa—sliding along a branch just above the queen's head. She never moved, and my father, though terrified, had naturally to stand his ground as the mamba began to sway from the branch between him and the queen.

"Proceed," she said, "this is the spirit of my late husband, who has come to hear if you are speaking the truth, and truly wish my people well. If you are speaking the truth, nothing unpleasant will occur." The crowd held its breath, nervously watching the snake's movements, as Papa continued, with sweat pouring down his spine, to present his queen's good wishes, as well as offers of economic help if required. Then, with intense relief, he saw that the snake had stopped swaying and was recoiling to slide down the tree trunk to the ground. The Queen was delighted, and congratulated Papa on the excellent delivery of his message and his pronunciation of her language, adding a word of praise through the interpreter for his control under the particular circumstances. I think Papa was rather proud of his behavior, and liked to tell that story.

Sometimes he talked of the early days when the Hottentots still infested certain mountainous parts of the then Cape Colony. Bows and arrows had been their only weapons, but the poisons they had discovered from various indigenous plants and used to tip their arrows were instantaneously effective against both man and animal. The roving tribes of Hottentots, together with the Bushmen, were the only human beings discovered at the Cape of Good Hope by the Dutch settlers in 1652. Cunning as monkeys, the Hottentots, though partially brought under control by superior arms and intelligence, continued to harass the Dutch East India Company's settlement at Cape Town. Their raids upon the company's herds, as well as the gardens so carefully cherished, were a constant embarrassment. Though largely decimated or pushed further and further into the hinterland beyond the mountain barriers, their descendants continued to maraud and rob the outlying farms from their mountain fastnesses. Since the turn of the century, they have completely died out. Only here and there can one still see traces of their very distinctive heads and faces among the many mixed "colored" people living in and around Cape Town.

"I remember," said Papa, "There was a diminutive Hottentot called Solomon Colesberg who was a veritable terror in the district. Living in the mountains in almost inaccessible caves, by daring and strength of character he had made himself the leader of a villainous gang of marauding thieves who thought no more of human life than they did of cutting a sheep's throat. Armed with bows and poisoned arrows and a few stolen rifles, he had successfully escaped all attempts at capture. One day, the rumor spread through the district that Solomon, together with some men, women, and children, had been seen making for the mountains. At once various armed bodies of men, rather like the vigilante committees of America, set out to look for him in the neighborhood, which happened to be a farm owned by three farmers named Steyn.

"At the first signs of dawn, the three brothers, carrying their rifles, silently left their homestead, not unseen by some of the colored laborers on the farm. After some hours they returned. Nothing was said. The various armed bodies returned to their respective farms, and no whisper of anything unusual came to the ears of the officials—only Solomon Colesberg and his gang stopped causing any trouble. Some months had passed when a gruesome discovery was made on the farm of the Steyns. Around what had been a resting place for the night were found the corpses of a number of Hottentot men, women, and children killed by bullets, the children with their skulls smashed in. The intense dry cold of the high veld had preserved the bodies, which no one had bothered to bury, and the whole tragedy was as clear as if it had happened the day before.

"Then Solomon Colesberg emerged from his lair and told his story with force in the witness box. He and his companions were still lying asleep when he was awakened by the sound of gunfire. At once, he tried to escape into some nearby bushes, but not before he was shot, though only wounded, so he rolled over, pretending that he was dead. Thus he was able to see what happened afterwards. In the early light, he could dimly see three men, who kept firing into the group of Hottentots until all the men and women lay motionless. Then they came up to see that all the children were also killed. But for some reason no one bothered to walk the short distance to see whether Solomon was alive or dead.

"You'll never believe this," added Papa, "but the Steyn brothers were acquitted because the Crown could not prove that there were not other men who had also gone out to look for Solomon and had been in the vicinity of the murder that very morning. But with the slaughter of Solomon's gang and he himself in jail, the last of the bows and poisoned arrows disappeared—as far as I know."

"The Hottentots were brutally slaughtered by the white man, weren't they?" I asked.

"Not all," said Papa. "Besides, you must remember those were different days, when the white man was fighting for his own life, trying to establish his foothold in a new country. The indigenous people naturally resented him—the land had been theirs to live in as they liked, so they were prepared to steal anything and kill everyone who wanted to control them."

"But wherever the white man went, he always enslaved the indigenous natives, didn't he?"

"Well, he had to," said Papa, "if he was going to be top dog, but it was the way he did it that is going to cause all the trouble in the future."

Little did he know how prophetic were his words.

As my interest in painting developed, Papa tried to find ways both to encourage and train my talent. I studied at the local school of art, whose gifted director wore Harris tweeds and frequently smelled of Scotch whisky, but had little ability to impart his knowledge to others. On Saturday mornings throughout the winter months of one year, I was also taught by a charming old man, whose meticulous brushwork on old-fashioned subjects particularly appealed to Papa, who favored the classical school of painting.

I was more interested in what I felt was typical of my own surroundings—the brilliance of the local color, the vivid light and shade of mountains and skies, the sweeping effects along the beaches edging the two famous seas of the peninsula. Dear old Mr. Moreland—English, gentle, and an ardent worshiper of Constable—did not seem to respond as I did to the vigor of our landscape, but he taught me the technique of painting, besides training my eye to the essentials of good composition.

One day Papa brought to our house a man who was the sort of painter I then longed to become. He was a South African by birth and background but, like many distinguished men of the country, had Huguenot blood, which brought him his name of Hugo Naude. Papa had become interested in his work, bought one of his paintings, and brought him to "Mon Desir" to look at my poor amateur efforts. I liked him immediately, his gentle, almost shy manner and quiet humor. Besides, as he seemed enthusiastic about my few paintings, I was naturally flattered. Papa was delighted.

Hugo lived in the little town of Worcester, in those days twenty-four hours by train north of Cape Town. He had studied in France, having been aided by sponsors and admirers to go there instead of Italy, whose classical masterpieces were the standard for all students at that time. He had come back to the Cape with his eyes opened wide by the cultural influences of France, the thinking, the ideas, the clichés of the ateliers of Paris. All this he applied to his own vision of his beloved South Africa and painted with an imagination that immediately distinguished him from his pedestrian fellow artists.

I was fascinated by him as I was by anyone whose creative abilities seemed to mark them as unusual. I told Papa that I would like to study with him, but my education stood in the way, inasmuch as Hugo lived so far from Cape Town, where I was still in school. Had my future as a painter there and then been decided upon, I would have been prepared to follow him right through Africa in order to learn from him. However, all that could then be arranged was a short visit to Worcester during my school holidays, with a painting trip into the mountains, when he would give me what instruction he could.

I was excited by the prospect of my visit, for I had never stayed with a real painter, having only met a few artists rather formally at exhibitions or through my parents. But in this adventure I would be alone with a new friend in the sort of atmosphere I longed to experience.

At Cape Town Station Papa saw me into the train, giving me money with instructions to obey Mr. Naude and behave as he would expect me to. I used always to leave Papa in those days wondering what he thought would happen to me, whether he had any real idea of the temptations that might assail me or whether he felt I was so grounded in his high standards of behavior that I would never fail him. I blush now to think how often I did fall from his level, but to this day do not know what he knew or suspected.

It was a new experience going off on my own, to a place among people I did not know, my paint box freshly replenished with brushes, and a palette knife Mama had given me as a parting present.

Worcester lies on the south side of the high jagged range called the Hex River mountains. Beyond them lay the land of Rhodes's dreams, filled with gold and diamonds. It was a spring morning when I stepped into the sparkling sharp air of Worcester, to ask my way to the address where I was to stay for the first few days. I was to be a paying guest in the house of a Mrs. de Koch, a great friend of Hugo Naude, who had kindly agreed to accept an unknown boy into her house until Hugo was ready to start on our painting trip. As I walked down the road, fol-

lowing the directions of the stationmaster, I was at once fascinated by the fact that on either side of the road flowed a fast,
clear stream of water. This fresh water supply I later learned
could be diverted by individual house owners along the stream
and canalized into private property for a variety of purposes, as
I was duly to discover. There was an avenue of fresh green oak
trees all down the broad dirt road, in turn lined on either side
by neat gardens full of flowers, either fenced or hedged along
the footpath beneath the trees.

The place seemed peaceful, drowsy with quiet; there were
few people in the street, no motorcars or trucks, no apparent
activity. It was in those days a very small country town with no
pretensions and very little interest. Beyond the town lay the
farms, and between the houses I could catch glimpses across the
bright, open fields of the far, blue ranges of mountains.

I found Number 27 Main Road and was greeted at the door
by Mrs. de Koch herself, who had been expecting me on the
morning train. "*Ach*, come in, come in," she said in broken
English, "you are Hugo's pupil, no? You will have some coffee,
yes? Of course you will, come with me and we will get some."

She was fat, motherly, and smiling, a woman of good family,
the widow of a man who had held political office and twice
been mayor of the town. She asked me questions about my journey, my home, the health of my family, and about Cape Town,
which she had not visited since her husband's death ten years
before.

"*Ach*, so you want to paint like Hugo. Now there is a good
man. I have loved him like my own son all his life. You are a
lucky boy even to know him," she said.

"I know I am," I answered. "I think he's wonderful."

Mrs. de Koch showed me my room, then through the whole
house and garden to the bathroom. This was a small adobe
structure with a corrugated iron roof that housed merely a
large, square hole in the ground about three feet deep and lined

with cement. At that moment it was completely empty. A small canal led into it at one end from a furrow in the garden, and out of it again through the opposite wall.

"You see," said Mrs. de Koch, pointing a fat finger, "the water comes in there when we bring the stream from the street into my property, and it flows out of that sluice if the bath is too full." She spoke without emphasis, as though everyone had two large openings in the walls of their bathroom. "You pull out that plug in the ground when you have had your bath. The water is quite cold but you can wash in it, we all do," she chatted on. "It is not like Cape Town up here. There is no hot water in any bathroom in the whole of Worcester."

I had a sudden vision of my bath being what my nurse called a "quick promise." But the next morning at seven o'clock I went to the bathroom to find the bath already half full and the stream flowing in rapidly from the garden furrow. I felt the clear, limpid water with my fingers, shivering at the thought of getting into it, but, gathering my courage, I stripped off my pajamas and stepped into the bath for the quickest possible wash. Suddenly two large, white ducks, quacking noisily, swept in with the stream to join me in the bath. Outraged, they swam around as I rapidly stepped out onto the floorboard, wondering how I would ever get them out against the stream flow except by catching them bodily. But that was not so easy—they flapped and wriggled out of my reach, squawking loudly enough to waken the whole neighborhood. I was rescued by the colored gardener who, hearing the noise, came to see what had happened. He took one look at me and the ducks and broke into a loud laugh.

"*Magtig*," he said, "wot strange swimming frens you got," and, grabbing the now infuriated ducks, carried them outside. I realized that using the town water supply had certain disadvantages.

Later that morning Hugo came to fetch me, and we walked a few blocks to his studio, passing a grove of tall, strong-smelling eucalyptus trees, their silvery bark fallen in long streamers from their opalescent trunks. Hugo stopped to look at the trees. "Aren't they lovely?" he said. "They have such wonderful color, but it is difficult to paint that iridescence." I looked and began to see just what he meant. It was my first lesson in learning to see.

The studio, on the second floor of a large two-story house, with living quarters on the ground level, was reached by an outside stairway. The moment I entered I knew it was the sort of room I longed to have myself. Smelling of turpentine and linseed oil, cluttered with canvases, easels, and tables, it had an atmosphere that immediately captured the imagination. Here was a room only an artist could create, a place to work in, but one full of color and interesting things to stimulate the eye. The huge windows opened onto the flowing countryside, the shapes and contours of the veld rolling up to the low hills below the mountains.

I thought suddenly of the only studios I had ever seen, so dull, so uninteresting compared to this ideal place.

"Here we shall paint," said Hugo. "You can have that easel and stool over there, so bring your paint box and we shall begin."

"What shall I paint?" I asked, rather afraid of what I might be told to do.

"What would you like to paint?" he asked. "A still life, perhaps? I will set one up for you and we will start right after lunch."

So began my painting lessons with a man who seemed to know exactly how to convey what he wanted me to see, above all what he knew I needed to think.

"If you look carefully," I remember he said, "you will see much more, but, what is really important, you will feel— something—a communication, d'you know what I mean?"

I nodded.

"I can't explain," he went on. "To an artist, beauty is an experience, not just a set of forms or colors that please the eye."

"D'you mean what I have been told is beautiful?"

He laughed. "Look out," he said. "That is the most dangerous of all the traps, the things we are told are beautiful. If you don't feel them, Jannie, it is no good—a perfect copy, lines, forms, colors, all of them, but dead."

I tried to think of the pictures Mama had shown me, the "great" pictures universally admired for their lifelikeness, their composition, or atmosphere; now I was made aware of something I could only guess at. Hugo had talked about the "spirit."

That word had always conjured up in my mind the idea of the Holy Ghost, the Dove, but this was surely something different—but the same in essence, a life force?

"That is what you must try and convey," he said. "I can't do it, but I'm still trying."

He grinned at me, sitting attempting to puzzle it all out.

"There is more to art than just brains, you know," he added, as he fixed my easel and started to collect objects for the still life I was going to paint. "It isn't a science," he added finally.

I tried to separate my responses to what I could see, my reactions to what I called beautiful. Was it always my brain that responded, or was there something else? Hugo said art wasn't always brains. What was it then? Emotion? What I felt about flowers, music, shapes of things, a sudden stirring in the depths of me that could even bring tears to my eyes for no apparent reason, an instant emotion like a fire springing from somewhere?

Each day I had a lesson, and each time I learned something more from my enthusiastic friend: dimensions, color, the principles of good composition, some of the things I would have to face if and when I became a painter. He taught me not only about painting, but about how to see. Most entertaining of all were his stories of the artist's life he had lived abroad, among the models, the students from all over the world. I sat wide-eyed, thinking of the future in terms of Hugo's experiences, of the dedication required if one expected to succeed.

"D'you think I could be any good?" I asked him.

"That all depends on you, my boy. You have lots of talent, lots of imagination. With those gifts you could do anything you want to do. But I warn you, it's so easy to let it all slide—too many girls, too many drinks in cozy bars, not enough guts."

I wondered what God would have me do.

The most exciting part of my visit was to be the painting expedition to a serene and lovely valley tucked away in the mountains. It was arranged that we were to travel to the hideaway in the car of Hugo's great friend, Stephan, who was a teacher in the local school and a passionate lover of art. He was engaged to be married to an attractive girl who was to come with us to manage the commissariat department. We were to stay in an old farmhouse among the mountain foothills, with only a local colored woman to help with the kitchen chores. Much as I loved Worcester and Mrs. de Koch's good food, I grew daily more excited at the prospect of this longed-for experience.

Our journey took us through the foothills I had seen from the studio balcony. Great drifts of bright-colored mesembryanthemums, stretches of heather among groups of yellow ursinia and venidiums, decorated the hillsides. It was the moment when all the wild flowers of that natural garden were in their full beauty. Hugo and his friends, whose real relationships had already begun to puzzle me, enjoyed it as much as I did, though I was impatient to look more closely at the riot of flowers we were passing.

"I'll only be a moment," I said, as I begged Hugo to stop and let me dash over to examine some lovely plant unknown to me in the south—a new form, another smell, but as ever fascinating to my botanical interest.

As we started to climb into the mountains, the air grew cooler, until, beneath the high overhanging *kloofs* already deep in purple shade, it was almost cold.

"We'll soon be there now," Hugo encouraged us as our road emerged into a flowing valley among the mountains, green and well watered by streams from the high, snow-covered peaks.

The farmhouse stood on a slope surrounded by trees and open, uncultivated fields. Indeed, the whole place looked deserted, forgotten. Through the trees, I could see two or three derelict-looking cottages, which I imagined belonged to colored workers on the farm.

"Does anybody live here?" I asked, as we stopped on the graveled area in front of the door.

"The owners have moved to town and the place is for sale," Hugo said. "It hasn't been lived in for some time, but old Saartje, who used to work for them, still lives over there and keeps things in some sort of order."

We unloaded the car of our boxes of provisions, for we had brought everything from Worcester except milk, which could be bought fresh nearby. There was no sign of our colored kitchen help, but Hugo seemed quite resigned to the fact that she might not appear at all. "You know these folk are so unreliable," he said.

There were three bedrooms sparsely furnished but without doors, the hinges rusty from long neglect, a fairly large kitchen with a dining area in front of the windows looking out over the fields. From the rafters there still hung cobs of dried corn and withered bunches of herbs. And since there was a queer musty smell in the house, we flung open the windows at once. There was no bathroom; the very primitive toilet was in a little ramshackle hut some yards away from the kitchen door. All the water, icy and crystal clear, was drawn in buckets from the well.

"Tomorrow we will go out and paint," Hugo announced over our evening meal of cold meat, vegetables, and bread and butter with honey. The honey was dark and thick with the sugar of wild flowers, the tang stronger even than the smell of the bunch on our table that Katrina, the much-loved fiancée, had arranged.

"At what time?" I asked eagerly.

"I like to go out early," said Hugo, "while there are still shadows. The light in the middle of the day is never good, too flat. Shall we say coffee at six o'clock, then we'll take the mountain path to a spot I have wanted to paint for a long time. I know you'll like it."

The two men were to share one room, while down the passage Katrina and I each had a small room adjoining a little hall with a washtable boasting the only jug and basin the house possessed. We went early to bed, tired after a long day's driving. But I was too excited to go to sleep right away. Besides, there was a bright moon whose light streamed in at the curtainless window, something that had always disturbed me from infancy.

I don't know how long I did sleep, but I woke suddenly conscious of voices. I lay dead still, my senses sharply alert, as from what was barely a murmur I gradually began to distinguish the voices of Stephan and Katrina. I wondered, consumed with curiosity, what they could be talking about at that hour.

Tiptoeing very quietly to the door of my room, I could overhear their conversation—and stood transfixed, as for the first time in my life I heard the passionate phrases of love between a man and a woman. I stayed hypnotized by guilt, an accessory to the clandestine act, for Papa had always said eavesdropping was despicable. Yet I was as excited as though I were a partner who could not tear himself away from their secret. For though I knew how people made love, everything I had heard at school, all the hidden, smutty things boys talk about, rushed into my mind. Here it was happening within earshot. Papa had told me very self-consciously that I would meet those he called "bad girls" as I grew older, who would tempt me to do all sorts of things that I would find exciting, pleasurable.

"But don't risk it," he said warningly, "unless you are quite certain about the girl, else you might get a disease, and that would be death."

That warning frightened me for a very long time, though I asked one of my friends who was more worldly wise than I to tell me just what he had meant. But this was something else altogether. This was love, I felt sure, from the words they used, from the fact that I knew the people in the next room. It was as though I was watching those two at their most intimate moment, listening to their very hearts beating in urgency, almost aware of the very gestures of their bodies.

I stood rooted to the spot, at one moment horrified, the next almost choking with emotion at the picture my imagination conjured up. Was this what people did, even before marriage? This was the physical ecstasy of sex, the passion I had heard so much about.

These were people one knew and liked, yet their behavior was contrary to what I thought was permitted—Katrina, pale and desirable, locked in the embrace of Stephan, urgent, insistent. Perhaps they belonged to the set Papa referred to scornfully as "Bohemians," who I gathered led a life of indulgence in every sort of license but were not accepted by the kind of people Mama called "nice people." It was all very puzzling, but I realized that I must bury what I had heard deep in my heart and never, never tell anyone what I knew.

I went back to bed shivering, my imagination reeling, somehow shocked by Stephan's passionate pleadings. Yet how wonderful I thought it would be to be loved like that, to have such tender, gentle words caress one, to hear loving answers to one's questions, and then to find such glorious fulfillment in another person. This was the agony and the ecstasy of love that I had read about, this wonderful surging of the senses, the longing and the need, as Stephan had told Katrina in stifled gasps of passion. I lay wide awake for hours, until the first light crept up the hillside into my open window.

I was thankful that only Hugo was up for coffee. I felt I didn't want to see Stephan lest I should behave self-consciously, or in such a way that he might suspect I knew something I was not supposed to know. Given a little time I thought I would be able to control my feelings about him and Katrina, though strangely enough I didn't attach any blame to her. She seemed to me innocent but injured; it was Stephan I felt was taking an unfair advantage. In those days, I was very ignorant of the ways of the world.

Hugo and I climbed the mountain path carrying our paint boxes and sketching easels. The atmosphere was cool, sparkling in the blue shadows beneath the buttresses of the mountains.

"Here is the place," he said, as we emerged through the trees onto a grassy slope from where the view was superb.

"It's lovely," I said, trying to take in the whole dramatic panorama of the mountains down to the sweeping lowlands lying distant in the haze.

As we set up our easels, Hugo said, "Never try to paint effects in nature, you know, sunsets, or even sunrise on the mountains, unless you want to produce a picture postcard. They are very popular, mind you, but try for simple, straightforward renderings of light and shade—that's the secret, shadow and sunlight—and search for the color, always remembering you are composing natural forms, not just copying what you happen to see."

I never forgot the truths he taught me, nor the way I learned to look at an object in the round.

"Don't you see," he said, "it has thickness as well as contour, and don't forget the space between one form and another, because quite apart from any perspective there is atmosphere around everything, fading away into the distance."

I listened and learned more each day. For a week we painted regularly, sometimes in the mornings or on occasion in the evenings.

"You must get used to the difference in the light," said Hugo, "the late light, the half light, so lovely on the trees and grasses."

Then one evening, as we came home to find our friends still out in the gloaming, I felt shivery and cold, as though I had caught a chill. I told Hugo, who made me a hot cup of lemon

juice with whiskey and sent me to bed. But it was too late to
stop the cold. The next morning I was feverish and told to stay
in bed.

Though I remained in bed taking nothing but liquids, I knew
enough about my own health to realize I had caught a very bad
chill, and I dreaded the thought of the bout of pneumonia that
had followed so often in the past. Hugo had no medicines at all
with him, except castor oil, of which he gave me a big dose only
to add to the complications in a house with no conveniences.

Saartje, who had finally appeared to help Katrina in the
house, was most solicitous, and brought over some dark myr-
tle-looking leaves, which she said should be put into boiling
water for me to inhale. She was full of suggestions for cures,
and, although they were to be made from local herbs, had all to
be put into brandy. I overheard her conversation with Katrina,
half in English, half in Dutch, which I later told Papa, much to
his amusement.

"Dat little flower growing dere, missis," said Saartje, "you
can't tink how good it is for de troat."

"Really," questioned Katrina, "do you make a compress of
it?"

"*Ach nie*, missis, *jij set dit op brandewijn* (you put it in
brandy)."

"An' dat leaf is werry werry fine for de chest," Saartje went
on.

"How do you use it, Saartje, rub it in?"

"*Ach*, no, missis. *Jou set it op brandewijn.*"

Despite the value of apparently all the herbs growing around
us, there was only one certain remedy, to put them in brandy!

Katrina and Stephan were kindness itself, but as the hours
passed I grew worse, and Hugo was becoming more and more
anxious about me. There was talk of taking me back to Worcester, either to Mrs. de Koch, or at the worst to the hospital. I
was miserable, conscious of being a great nuisance as well as an

anxiety. All my pleasure had suddenly been cut off, as it had been so often before, by illness. Besides, I was perfectly aware that Hugo felt me a great responsibility even to begin with, and more so now than ever. How I hated having to decide what to say to him, but I knew it was up to me to suggest I go home and not spoil any more of their short holiday. I gathered my courage and told Hugo I might be in for a long siege, and suggested he telephone from the nearest point a telegram to Papa to arrange for someone to come up and fetch me in Worcester. He very politely agreed it might be best, though I was no trouble, etc., etc.; within a few hours came the reply to await the arrival of Papa himself. I had not dreamed of such a possibility, knowing how busy Papa was at that time, and it only added to my misery to know that I was causing trouble and upsetting all his arrangements.

In two days' time Papa arrived, obviously very worried about me, having had to calm Mama's exaggerated fears. He had hired a Cape cart and horses to drive him up to the farm, a whole day's journey from Worcester. I don't know what Hugo had told him, but by the time he arrived I was already on the mend, as I could tell from the condition of my chest and breathing. Papa had with thoughtfulness brought various cures, but above all our favorite, "Elliman's Embrocation," which had seen me through several bouts of pneumonia and was my permanent standby.

Stephan offered to drive us in his car down to Worcester, leaving the cart to follow in its own time. By this kindness I was made very conscious of my feelings toward him, though I was more than grateful not to have to spend so much time in the open Cape cart on the road back.

I hated to leave; it had been my first experience of the kind and I had been utterly happy, for Hugo, besides teaching me so many things I had longed to learn, had grown close to me as a friend. I was afraid I would never be allowed to go away on my own again, and I could already hear Mama in her concern over me saying, "You are simply not responsible enough to look after yourself," which was an insult I deeply resented.

They all saw us off, even Saartje, who had been kept constantly watching the kettle so that I could inhale, though we had no brandy, much to her disgust!

I saw Hugo many times afterwards, though never again either Katrina or Stephan. For a long time after I returned home, I yearned to talk to my father about what I had heard on those nights in that hidden farmhouse and ask him the sort of questions that the whole situation had stirred up in my mind. He was the only person I knew I could rely on, but it seemed impossible to speak of such intimate matters with him. There was no one else with whom I could discuss what I regarded as a sacred trust, for fear of betraying the people involved. Nowadays at least parents have a more frank, more helpful relationship with their children.

Perhaps I misjudged Papa, and he would have helped me had I broached the subject, for somehow I knew that on that moonlit night I had taken a step further toward manhood.

Hugo had given me something far more valuable than painting lessons. For he was the perfect romantic, forever in love with life, forever seeking for something beyond the obvious satisfaction. I had the same deep stirring in myself. Young as I was, I wanted to follow what I instinctively felt was lasting, eternal, inspiring. Art seemed to me to be like that; perhaps love was also, though I didn't know much about that and had only partly discovered it. Hugo often said that the whole point of loving was lost if one looked to gain anything by it—the reward only came through sacrifice. I suspected that was a philosophy born of failure to find what he wanted in any one person. I don't think he ever discovered what he was truly looking for, although he later married. He talked constantly of being in love, and perhaps his greatest love was life itself.

But Papa never talked about such things to me. Perhaps he

was innately shy, or unable to communicate with me, his only son, about life as it was affecting me then. As I think back, I remember how I longed to be able to talk naturally, feel free to ask him the sort of questions that flooded into my mind at that time. But there was a barrier, which we know has nothing to do either with character or intellect, both of which he had, but rather with the spirit in the people concerned. Perhaps he wanted to talk to me, even sensed my need of him and his advice, but could not find a bridge over the chasm that divided us. So that it was to individuals like Hugo that I turned to learn my way and be taught the truth, the awful, shattering, inspiring truth about many things. This, then, is my long delayed thanks and appreciation to Hugo, who taught me far more than he ever realized, and to whom I am eternally indebted.

The day of my sister Brenda's wedding eventually was a tragedy. For weeks before, our lives had been in a state of constant agitation. The preparations were lavish, for Mama was determined it was to be a wedding everyone would remember. My sister Brenda was to marry an English clergyman, the son of our oldest friends in London. He had followed her out to South Africa from England, where she had been at a finishing school. I was somehow suspicious of his nature, believing him to be hypocritical. However, he was handsome, with a splendid record at Christ Church, Oxford, and seemed destined for a successful career in the Church.

The week of the wedding began with a major crisis for Mama. The days were warm, blue summer weather, but, owing to the vast number of guests invited, we were to have the reception in a large marquee to be erected on the croquet lawn. Suddenly, the company supplying the marquee announced that at some function the week before the tent had been blown down in a thunderstorm and would have to be repaired; they didn't know if it could be ready in time. No other firm within reach had as big a tent available. Mama collapsed and could only be consoled by spirits of ammonia, unable to imagine how her guests could possibly be crowded into anything smaller. The company would have to supply a suitable marquee even if they worked all day and night, she said, or she would sue them, for they were under contract.

The whole house seemed to tremble with agitation. We all passed each other on the stairs without a word, Mama with her smelling salts clutched in one hand and lists of things to be ordered in the other. Papa's face seemed to grow grayer, more tense, more strained, every day. He walked very slowly upstairs. I had an uncomfortable sense of premonition, but was told not to imagine things and behave like a child; nevertheless, the atmosphere of the house grew dark with foreboding.

But the wedding day dawned bright; the marquee had been erected at the last moment late the night before; all was in readiness, and Mama could relax, knowing no detail had been overlooked.

I was to sing in the choir at the service to help with an anthem that had been specially rehearsed for the occasion. The church looked magnificent, having been decorated by my sisters and their friends with nothing but white flowers gathered from many gardens in the district, for in those days such things were often done personally, without the help of hired florists. I can remember the smell of the lilies as I waited nervously in the church, which was packed with inquisitive guests also waiting for the bride's late arrival. But when they did arrive, though my sister, like most brides, looked her loveliest, I was already more concerned about Papa, who appeared quite unlike his buoyant self, looking gray and ill. Something made me sense the coming calamity.

In the midst of the reception, when the speeches were over and the guests were happily garrulous on the best champagne, the blow struck. Papa retired unnoticed to his room, where Mama, anxious at his disappearance, finally found him lying on his bed. The news of his collapse flew round the house. Réné rushed into the bride's room to console her; the servants gathered in knots, speaking in hushed voices; we rallied around Mama, though none of us were allowed to see Papa.

"Your father is very ill," Mama said, her face drawn with anxiety. "I've sent at once for Stevie—I don't know what has happened," she added, stifling her sobs as she rushed downstairs where there were caterers waiting for orders, delivery boys anxious to be tipped, good-byes to be said to departing guests.

My heart sank, supposing my fears were going to be fulfilled. Would Papa die and we be left without a father, without that unwavering force on which we all leaned? Somehow I felt as though the house was beginning to topple, the roof cave in, my future nothing but a mirage.

My godfather, "Stevie," Sir Edmund Stevenson, who had had a French mother named St. Clair, was considered the best doctor in the colony. He was called Stevie by my parents, who were his greatest friends and admirers. It was said that he saved my life when, as a child, I had been near death with double pneumonia and pleurisy combined. With skill he had performed a most unusual and imaginative operation, cutting away my poisoned ribs, fitting me with a tube to drain my damaged lungs, a process scarcely known by the doctors there at that time. "His knife even touched the heart," Nannie would explain dramatically to inquisitive friends.

Stevie duly arrived in his chauffeur-driven car. We all hovered, hoping for news, though he seemed to spend hours in Papa's room. The house held its breath, waiting, as it were, for the climax. At last Mama came out to us, composed, anxious, her handkerchief crushed to her face. "He has had a stroke," she said, "but he is going to be all right, though it may take a very long time. Of course, he can't move, perhaps for months. We must all thank God he is alive."

We remained stunned, unable to speak or console each other; it seemed impossible that this could happen on a wedding day. I felt ill myself, so I went into the garden and was sick in the shrubbery, with my dog Scamp looking on at me in dismay.

For months of anxiety, Papa battled for his life, but did in fact live for many more years. His doctors said his recovery had been largely due to the miraculous bacillus then known as "Metchnikoff's." It had been discovered by a Russian biologist, Elié Metchnikoff, whose revelations on the bacteria infesting the alimentary canal had shaken the medical world of his day and gained him the Nobel Prize. His means of destroying these microbes were known to our friend, Stevie, through his connection with the Pasteur Institute in Paris, where he himself had experimented. I remember the germ had to be cultivated in milk, put into a large gourd, and hung in the sunshine, where it curdled to develop the bacillus. Papa lived on it, drinking a glassful several times a day.

But that was all to happen in the future. All we knew then was that our father's life hung by a very tenuous thread, and our pattern of life might have to change at any moment.

When Peter, the gardener, heard the news of Papa's attack, he spoke to me.

"Dat's terribel," he said, his eyes full of tears. "I've worked for Sir Hennerey all dese years, an' he's powerful, Master Jan, he don' break up none."

In my mind's eye I could see a great edifice crumbling stone by stone. "Perhaps he won't break up," I answered, consolingly.

"No, sir," he said, "we can't let him go. Dere ain't no one dat can take his place."

I knew this deep down in my heart. He was the mainstay of our whole structure; possessor of the imagination, the wit, the knowledge, the humor that made us forget the intolerance, the judgment so often tempered by tenderness.

When all the turmoil of the day was over at last, I remember I stopped at the top of the stairs on my way to bed to look at the full-length portrait of Papa hanging in the stair hall. It was the same portrait of him, done when he was Speaker of the House of Assembly, that now hangs in the House of Parliament

The Hon. Sir Henry H. Juta, K.T. K.C. Speaker of the Cape House of Assembly, Cape Town, South Africa. Painted by Tennyson Cole, 1896

in Cape Town. Painted by Tennyson Cole, a then top-ranking portrait painter, it was the living image of Papa in his flowing wig, black satin knee breeches, and long, gold-ornamented robes.

Conscious of the sick man lying in his bedroom, I felt utterly miserable as I gazed at his handsome face. He would never look the same again, my sister had said, for Mama had confided to her that one side of his face was very crooked and probably paralyzed. I couldn't imagine him so altered. Would he be changed, I wondered, less quick-tempered, less strict, easier to talk to and confide in? Even if he lives, I thought to myself, he won't ever look like that again, tall, upright, his eyes sharp under the dark sweep of his eyebrows. But there was more of him in the face that the painter had captured: the humor that had softened his judgment, helping us through all the pains of childhood; a strength, too, that had calmed our fears, giving us the courage we needed; a tenderness that had dried our tears with understanding.

I wish I could have painted him before this happened, I said to myself, turning out the light that had illumined his perceptive face.

3. Mama

My mother had an equally interesting background. Her father
was a Scotsman whose family had developed an export trade between Scotland and South Africa. But, through her mother, she
was a direct descendant of one of the famous "Gunning sisters,"
who in 1749 came out of Ireland with little but extraordinary
beauty and charm to conquer, not only the king of England,
but his nobility as well.

The story of their dramatic effect upon the English court,
where their beauty became a byword, makes fascinating reading. For Elizabeth Gunning (1734–1790), my ancestor, admit-
tedly the loveliest of the sisters, became not only the duchess of
Hamilton and Brandon and the mother of the seventh duke, but,
after some years of widowhood, also the duchess of Argyll
through her second marriage. Her wit, beauty, and natural talents distinguished her; she was painted by all the court painters
of the day, including Angelica Kauffmann, and praised by poets,
writers, and pamphleteers alike.

The three famous Gunning sisters: *left to right*, Maria, Countess of Coventry; Elizabeth, Duchess of Hamilton and Argyll; Kitty, Mrs. R. Travers

Mama, taken in Paris, 1895

In his *Memoirs* of the day Jesse writes: "The surpassing love-liness of the Gunnings has almost become a matter of history, nor is there any instance of mere beauty having excited so amazing a sensation as that produced by the appearance in the fashionable circles of London of these portionless girls." In 1752, Maria, the eldest, married William, earl of Coventry. And that same year, Elizabeth married the duke of Hamilton, the ceremony taking place at midnight, according to Horace Walpole, "a curtain ring [sic] being used for the occasion."

The sisters had only one brother, John, who went into the army, serving with distinction in America at Bunker Hill. He rose to the rank of major general and died in Naples in 1797.

Thus legitimately my mother inherited from her famous ancestor her charm, talents, and exceptional beauty. For her mother, my grandmother, was directly descended from Elizabeth Gunning through her second marriage to John Campbell, the duke of Argyll, bringing to her doting Scotch husband a wealth of talent and good looks. As a girl, Mama was spoiled by adoring parents, and she continued to be spoiled by my father from the moment he married her. Her striking good looks made her not so much vain as assured of her prerogatives and her effect upon people, for it was not unusual for them to stop just to look at her, making flattering remarks as she passed. She was essentially feminine, knowing how to exert her charm. Both generous and thoughtful of others, a good, if overanxious, mother, she was nevertheless an effective helpmate to my successful father. Their marriage had joined together an unusual number of talents, enough to produce a family who were each as gifted as the other.

Though she has been dead now for many years, as I try to recapture her I see her always good-tempered, never unkind, and sparkling with a gaiety that made her very blue eyes twinkle. Her smile, and the grace of her beautifully poised head, added to a sort of bright halo that her radiance created around her. But she was proud, critical, and used to her own way.

BACKGROUND IN SUNSHINE

"I cannot think what you can see in her," she would say to me as my eyes strayed to some pretty girl of my own age but not of Mama's choosing. "Surely, I have taught you better taste," and I would inwardly rage against her for her lack of appreciation of my favorite girl of the moment. Only later did I begin to understand her jealousy of me, although I never doubted her love. I was after all her lamb and, though she would have ruined me by spoiling me had it not been for Papa, she nevertheless had nursed me with loving care, prayer, and patience through years of critical illness. In that perspective, her possessiveness was understandable, though much to be regretted.

I can remember her now, sitting before her mirror while her maid brushed and combed her beautiful, bright hair, which she fastened with jeweled combs. Usually I was allowed, in fact invited in to see her finish dressing for some public or important dinner party, possibly packed with political dynamite, a party at which she would shine, the loveliest star in an otherwise pedestrian sky. On the dressing table before her I can see the array of silver-topped brushes, bottles, little jars, and elegant puffs and buffers. I can even remember how she turned her head, directing her maid to curve the curls here and there on the bronze aureole of her hair. Then, when it was all finished, she would get up, slim, her straight back flowing up to her lovely shoulders like some flower rising out of flounces of lace and satin, gleaming like a lily in her newest Paris gown.

Then, having looked at herself for the last of many times while the last hook was fastened, she would turn to me, scenting the air around her with a seduction she knew all about, and would bend to kiss me good night—not a very warm kiss, rather a kiss of affection mixed with condescension. I longed to crush her beauty, and kiss her smooth, white skin all over, but I was held at arm's length to admire and applaud. In my heart I knew how my father must have felt waiting impatiently in the hall below, waiting for this radiant vision of someone I am sure

106

now was fundamentally cold, despite all her affectionate expressions.

Yet when she sang at the piano, accompanying herself with musical understanding, she could convey the essence of the song to her listeners with real feeling. She played the piano with a sensitive touch, having studied under excellent teachers, for she belonged to an era when young ladies of good birth and fortune all learned music, painting, and the art of deportment.

Mama enjoyed entertaining, knowing that she excelled at it, making her house, the food she served, and the manner of presenting it matters of great importance. I used to watch her as she surveyed the dining table, all glittering in crystal and silver, before some large dinner party, moving the glasses, rearranging the fruit or flowers of the centerpiece, even on occasion changing the name cards to agree with the seating list she had written and rewritten twenty times on her special pad. Unlike many a housewife in that part of the world, she was meticulous about the appearance of the dining table, the flowers, the various plates and glasses to be used.

She was thought to have exquisite taste in her house as well as in her clothes, which arrived regularly by the long sea journey to the Cape from her dressmaker in Paris, whom she visited about every two years. For travel, or "going abroad," was considered part of our education, and, as both my parents still really belonged to their European background, they enjoyed returning to the countries they had known. There were also the relations to be visited, which Mama considered essential to our future, for neither she nor my father ever felt completely South African—they were too European, which possibly accounted for the fact that neither of them subscribed to what was then a growing "national" viewpoint. In fact, I remember being told years later that my mother's indifference to the Boers or the republican Dutch had not always helped my father's political career. However, he did not apparently suffer from her lack of support but rather, through his own good common sense, gathered his constituents to his banner without fail.

As he progressed in his career and was made Judge President, then Judge of the Appeal Court, my mother concerned herself more and more with public charities and women's organizations. She spoke (or read from pages that Papa had carefully written for her) with a certain facility, easily assuming a leadership through her own initiative.

I can remember the atmosphere of excitement that pervaded our house for several days before she gave a big dinner party, possibly in honor of some visiting dignitary or for my father's associates from the judiciary.

As our colored cook was not considered worthy to prepare so special a menu, my mother employed a certain Mrs. Bowen, famous throughout the countryside for her cooking. Mrs. Bowen, with a cockney accent but a Scotch upbringing, moved into our house with a variety of utensils of her own without which she never functioned, bringing with her a sense of order and arrangement to counteract the natural pandemonium among our native domestic help. My sister and I, though not allowed to "worry in the kitchen," were old, established friends of Mrs. Bowen, who would promise us "a nice bit of orl right" after dinner had been served. Then, with the connivance of our colored butler, we would each be served a plateful of Mrs. Bowen's "specials" smuggled up the back stairs to be eaten with relish on the landing, from where we could watch the fascinating parade of guests moving across from the dining room to the drawing room, two by two, before the gentlemen went to the smoking room. We knew them all, criticized their looks, the ladies' dresses, figures, and behavior. "Look at old Lady X.'s hair—exactly like a bird's nest," my sister would say scornfully.

"And Mrs. Y. has on that same satin dress," I would add, always carefully noting what every woman wore.

"I don't know what you can see in Lady P.; she's so laced in she can hardly breathe."

"But her diamonds all come from Johannesburg, Nannie says."

"They don't make her look anything like Mother," replied my sister, as Mama, the best-dressed, the loveliest, would wave a fond good night, knowing that we were well provided for in our balcony seats.

Her taste, though far from perfect, influenced us all. For her enthusiasms, whether for a Beethoven symphony or for gardenias (her favorite flower) or her own beautiful new dress, were all infectious. She always picked flowers as though she had to possess them, often leaving them to die from neglect. On the other hand, she never forgot a sick friend in need, or the birthday of some relative she did not care much about but on whose behalf she would go to endless trouble. Her heart and her vanity often became confused, in that she would go to great lengths to assist and patronize a new or unknown talent in which she genuinely believed, for she loved to play the Lady Bountiful. But there were many who would never have progressed had it not been for her thoughtfulness, her boundless encouragement, her real appreciation of accomplishment. To further this, she would sacrifice herself, her time, and her pleasures. She was loved by the most surprising people, and disliked by some she wished had loved her.

Mother's adherence to what was right in her eyes, as well as expected of us as her children, never wavered, though I always suspected that she was doing what her upbringing had taught her to do. Her correction of our behavior was invariably oblique. I never remember her saying, "I forbid you to do this or that," but rather, "I don't think that would be very suitable for you to do," or "You wouldn't be very proud of yourselves for doing that, now would you?"

She suffered a lot from rheumatism and sciatica, to alleviate which she tried many cures in France and Germany. I was usually lucky enough to go with her as long as the trips did not interfere with my education.

There were known to be healing springs in the colony itself which were highly recommended by the doctors. One year, it was decided that for financial reasons we would not go abroad but try a local cure instead, where it would also be possible for my father to be with us at the time of his leave of absence. There was a small village called Caledon, not far from Cape Town, which was already famous even in those days for its springs of healing waters that bubbled hot from the mineral earth. They were credited with miraculous cures of various maladies, though the village had remained undeveloped and the medical value of the springs quite unexploited. This was largely due to the fact that it was difficult to reach, lying as it does over the range of mountains that border the Cape Peninsula. At that time, the railway, which was a most difficult feat of engineering, had not been completed, and the line only ran as far as a junction known as Sir Lowry's Pass, which lay at the base of the mountains. From there the stony, perilous road started to climb through the gorges to the hinterland—and this was the only way to get to the springs from Capetown.

In the early days of the Dutch settlement at the Cape, the Hottentots had christened the valleys beneath the range their "Holland," having heard the settlers so name their motherland. To this day, the district is still called the Hottentots' Holland. These natives had long known of the springs, for the pass over the mountains had originally been made by the herds of eland, the large fawn-colored antelope that they loved to kill and eat. Regularly in seasonal migration the herds crossed the mountains to feed in the higher valleys, making a rough path between the rocks that was used first by the natives and later by the Boer settlers.

A Dutch ensign, who was one of many of the early pioneers to set out from the fort at Table Bay to try and discover the fabulous empire of Monomotapa, about which wonderful reports had reached the ears of the adventurous Dutch, discovered instead the hot, healing springs. For years afterwards, the Dutch officials, and even visiting dignitaries, traveled over the mountains to benefit from the waters, bubbling at 120 degrees Fahrenheit in the valley beyond the pass. Records of the seventeenth century tell us that the pass was so steep and perilous that the wagons had to be unloaded at the base of the range and the contents carried over by pack oxen and slaves. Later, in 1830, after the village had been renamed in honor of the governor of the time, the earl of Caledon, a better road was constructed.

We had heard that the inn at the springs was still quite primitive, so it was necessary to take with us extra furniture and the needs for more comfortable living. I listened with impatience to plans as my father prepared for every contingency and the comfort of my suffering mother. We were to go by train to the base of the mountain, where our belongings would be transferred to a wagon, rented from a local farmer, which would haul us over the pass and deposit us at the springs.

Our party was to include my mother's maid, who was Scotch, and very intolerant of everything "backward and savage" that she found at the Cape of Good Hope. When she heard that we were to travel in an ox wagon, she did not hesitate to express her disapproval of such a form of travel as not fit for "civilized people." Also included was the Basuto groom in my father's employ, who would drive a cart and help with the luggage. Kosi, as he was named, was a great ally of mine, having taught me to ride. I was allowed to take my dog Scamp, on condition that I looked after him myself and kept him out of mischief. He was my constant, closest companion and shared with me many of my most exciting experiences. He was a half-breed spaniel, possessed of an excellent nose, no mean sporting instinct, and tremendous courage, on which I had had to rely on various occasions.

We must have appeared a strange cavalcade to the Dutch innkeeper at Sir Lowry's Pass when we arrived to spend the night before setting off at early dawn the following day. My father had thought of everything; the innkeeper's wife could not believe that anyone could possess as many cushions as we had brought with us to make my mother as comfortable as possible in the wagon.

Late into the night, the men were busy loading it. From my window I could see the yard, or *uitspan*, floodlit by the moon; the twelve oxen tethered, standing in patient groups; the open stalls with the horses in dark silhouettes; the "Cape cart," as it was called, with collapsible hood and high, strong wheels.

Scamp and I were out long before dawn. It was early summer; the sky, like a smooth, celadon bowl, seemed to reach down on all sides. I looked up at the still-dark peaks of the mountains, sloping steeply behind the inn, wondering how the stony, rough road ever found its way between the crags. Nothing stirred in the yard except a few chickens pecking in the straw; only the stamping of the horses broke the silence. I was inquisitive about the wagon that was to carry us and inspected all its details.

Looking at it brought all the dramatic history of the pioneer Boers vividly to mind. I remembered my school history of the Great Trek, in fact of all the treks made by the Dutch. Then there were no roads, and the sturdy wagons drawn by willing oxen were the only form of conveyance strong enough to travel the miles across the arid veld, or climb the rocky passes of the mountains. The Boer families had lived for months at a time in their wagons, facing an unknown world of natural dangers, marauding natives and ferocious animals. Camping out at night under the dome of the star-scattered sky, they had only their courage, their faith in God, and their guns as a defense.

To cross the ranges the wagons often had to be taken apart. Fording the swollen rivers meant the same laborious undertaking, with the oxen driven into the raging current and allowed to find their own way to the opposite shore. But to the pioneers, their reward was to be independent and, they thought, at peace. At least it meant they could live according to their own lights, removed from the restrictions of imposed laws. The land they occupied would be theirs and theirs alone, once they had driven out the natives. They were certain God would reward their determination with the glowing sunshine of productive peace.

There was something magnificent about pioneering, I thought, something that demanded qualities all men admired. To my mind, the wagons somehow partook of all such drama and assumed an equal importance, whether they were mounting the high, blue ranges of South Africa or their counterparts were crossing the vast plains of the United States in the great surge to the West. They were an essential part of these courageous adventures, as personal to the people traveling in them as human character or clothing.

The Boer wagons had only a short shaft, known as the *disselboom*. The front wheels were small in comparison to the two huge back wheels and pivoted free of the shaft to which the oxen, yoked in pairs, were attached along the length of the drag of hide or chain. The driver sat on a box seat, or kist, in front, in which clothes and special possessions of the owners were kept, while inside the canvas hood were flat shelves for the bedding. Our wagon had been differently arranged, for a large wicker armchair for my mother had been placed in the middle. I wondered if she would be able to balance in it, though it had been made secure on the roughly boarded floor, which was raised well above the axle.

I noticed a handle projecting at the back, which I later discovered served both to apply the brake to the wheels, as well as a step to climb on and off the wagon, while beneath the axle hung a bucket and a canvas container of water.

The local farmer who had rented us his team and wagon found me examining the interior. He was dressed in the habitual corduroys, a brown slouch hat shading his eyes. His face was bearded, rugged, the eyes kindly but sharp, typical of his people. I worried him with questions.

"How long will it take to get to Caledon?" I asked.

"The whole day. In fact, unless you travel steadily, until well into the night," he answered in a mixture of English and Afrikaans, most of which I understood.

"And are your oxen strong enough to pull all of us right over those mountains?"

"*Allemachtig*," he said. "My oxen have crossed the pass and back many times. There are no better, stronger-footed beasts in the whole valley." He patted the stupid face of the bony, long-horned ox standing nearest him, passive, chewing the cud.

"But the road is full of stones and rocks," I said. "It's not properly made."

"It's a good enough road for the wagons," he said, bridling. "Good enough even for the horses. We've used it for years. We don't need the *verdomdte* [damn] train to take us over the mountains!" he finished boastfully.

There was the flash of courage, the old, indomitable independence of the Boer that had urged the *voortrekkers* to struggle over the barriers and across the plains to find the peace they sought in the unknown.

As I grew older, I began to understand and appreciate this fire in the character that had helped to forge a nation. But now I couldn't resist a parting shot.

"The train will take you there much quicker, and much more safely," I added as I turned to go.

He appeared to take no notice, busying himself with the ropes on the wagon, but I overheard his mumbling as I left him.

"Thinks he's smart, the boy! Who wants to go quickly? Slow but sure is best!"

I went indoors to help hasten our departure.

The sun was just rising, flooding the valleys below us, as we stopped at a level stretch of road to rest the animals. Scamp and I were allowed to get down and walk beside the wagon for the last slow pull to the summit of the pass. We could still see the blue-green curve of False Bay, edged by a rim of white sand, fading into the distance.

Along the roadside, quantities of wild flowers filled the moun-

tain air with a honey-sweet scent. Groups of sparkling pink im-
mortelles, or everlastings, and white velvet harveyas flourished
among the rocks. Every here and there, shrubs of proteas
pointed their stiff, pink chalices to the sun. The mountain slopes
were famous for the heaths that grew there in great variety, as
sticky, green globular bells and feathery ruby fronds, or colored
pale pink, or a variegated type of orange and green. They had
little perfume but charmed one by their coloring and form. I
picked a bunch of at least twenty different kinds of flowers for
Mama.

She had been seated in her wicker chair, like a queen en-
throned, wedged in with cushions to prevent the jolts and se-
cured against toppling over by holdalls of rugs and counter-
panes. Our valises and portmanteaus were stacked between her
and the sides of the wagon. A long bench seat, fixed at both
ends, supported her chair at the back. On this sat her complain-
ing maid, while Scamp and I perched on the holdalls or on cushions at her feet. From his seat next to the farmer in front, Papa
told us incidents about the countryside to cheer up Mama, who
found the jolting over the stones a painful process.

The road was entirely deserted, the wide, flowing slopes of
the mountain without sign of life. Only from the crags above us
could we hear the bark of the baboons as their sentinel, perched
on some high lookout, issued his warning to the feeding troupe.

The sharp crack of our farmer's gigantic whip snapped along
the whole length of the straining team, echoed and reechoed
among the peaks like a pistol shot. The wagon lurched, groaned
and creaked as, running alongside, with shouts and calls he
urged the dragging beasts to greater effort up the steep slope.

"*Kom*, Wittebooi, Zwaartkop—*Trek!*" he shouted at each
of his animals, as the long, rawhide thong of the whip hissed
through the air to crack again over the pointed horns of the
oxen.

The *towleier* (tow leader), a young Kaffir boy, barefooted
and bareheaded, tugged at the rawhide thong he held that, tied
to the horns of the two front oxen, served as a lead rein. He it

was who guided the team, avoiding the biggest rocks and deepest ruts, picking his way with a precision born of long experience.

By noon we had crossed the pass, leaving the opalescent panorama stretched out behind us, and had arrived at the midway outspan, known as Houw Hoek. Two huge eucalyptus trees guarded the old house, set back from the road. Here we lunched, watered the oxen and the horses before a well-earned rest, for though we were high above sea level on a different plateau, the sun burned hot and the shade of the trees surrounding the inn brought welcome relief.

Here, too, we changed conveyances, traveling the rest of the way by cart drawn by four strong horses, leaving the wagon to follow more leisurely at the oxen's pace. Now the landscape altered in character, opening out on either side of the road, rolling hills and fertile valleys sloping away to more blue and purple ranges of mountains on the horizon known as Zonder End, (literally, "without end").

I remembered that my mother had read to me about this very same journey from a journal written in the eighteenth century by Lady Anne Barnard, the wife of a British attaché to the governor of the Cape Colony at the time. She, too, had crossed the pass over the mountains with her cavalcade, surviving accidents and endless difficulties on the then much more primitive roadway. But there were still the same high peaks, the hazardous boggy streams to be forded and the same superb panorama stretching on all sides below the road as we wound up the hill from the tiny village of Caledon to where the famous "baths" had been built around the springs.

But none of the difficulties daunted the gay, enthusiastic spirit of Lady Anne, who wrote in her witty, informative style of her dramatic experiences on Wednesday, May 19, 1798:

> We arrived about six at Mr. Wolfram's (who rents the Government baths where people go for a variety of complaints).

. . . The House consists of three or four rooms, which could
be divided so as to contain a dozen or two of invalids. . . .
The water is introduced in its own stream into a small house
where there is a bathing place. I put my hand in it and could
just hold it there.

The baths were still primitive, and only provided a modicum
of comfort by the standards of the day. The bathrooms, attached to the small hotel built by an enterprising company,
were merely a series of deep, square holes cut into the ink-black
mineral earth, partitioned and crudely roofed. The hot, steaming water, flowing directly from the springs, was diverted as required into little runnels leading into each room.

There were native attendants, who provided towels and supposedly kept the baths clean, though their main function was to
help the many crippled, sometimes helpless, invalids, who,
wrapped in long, winding sheets, were carefully let down into
the steaming water and there left to soak.

A grove of tall eucalyptus trees stood sentinel before the inn,
providing welcome shade in the yard where the wagons or carts
were outspanned. The air had a strange, hot scent of the mineral
earth as the steam from the nearby springs mingled with the
spicy smell of eucalyptus and flowering undergrowth.

Scamp and I were out early the morning after our arrival to
survey the land. We traced the streams through the bracken and
low ferns to their hot, bubbling source in the rocky hill behind
the inn. I remembered Lady Anne's description as I plunged my
hands into the clear water to test its temperature and found it
too hot to bear!

The hills around the baths were a veritable flower garden, for
the Caledon district was even then famous for the countless varieties that flourished in its temperate climate. Walks with
Scamp yielded more and more of interest in the new plants, the
shrubs that differed from those at the Cape, the birds and insect
life. Scamp learned to play "hide and seek" with *koggelman-
netjies*, the Dutch name for the little lizards with bright blue

heads that peered at us, bobbing up and down from behind the rocks before scuttling out of sight. Their name literally means "little men who mimic," and I don't know of any English equivalent. They are named and noted for their peculiar habit of moving their heads up and down as they watch one through heavy-lidded eyes, supposedly mimicking, or standing static, head on one side, as they listen. Their ear holes are easily seen, and they provide a good example of the difference between lizards and snakes, for the latter have no ear cavities and, as we all know, glistening, lidless eyes. The somewhat menacing action of these lizards, together with their startling colored heads, has given rise to the idea that they are poisonous, but they are, in fact, quite harmless, playful, and inquisitive.

We climbed the rocky slopes to find the lovely lavender-blue "Caledon bells," the name given to another member of the vast gladiolus family, *Gladiolii spathaceus*. Unlike any other of the group, this exquisite flower grows singly on a thin, reedlike stem from which it hangs its large, velvety cup, the color of the periwinkle. The ixias, deep emerald green with a black center sharply accenting each flower, were also a find worth walking for many miles.

On one of our walks across the valley, we came upon the village of Genadenal, which I remembered was supposedly the oldest mission station in South Africa. Neat, quiet, and orderly, the little thatched houses comprising the village seemed to have remained unchanged by time; one could sense the peaceful atmosphere hanging like an aura around them. Originally, it had merely been a camping site of the Hottentots who, driven from their hunting grounds around Table Bay by the Dutch settlers, had receded up over the famous pass and settled in these higher valleys in the hope of remaining undisturbed by the white man.

But, in 1737, a missionary arrived from Germany to work among the natives established in the district. Though they were dirty, barbaric, and unreliable, he set to work to teach them the Christian way of life. For some reason, he was recalled to Holland and never allowed to return to his flock, many of whom he had successfully converted after they had patiently listened to his sermons. Each Sunday, they would gather to hear their pastor, seated under the large spreading tree that served him as a pulpit. Sixty years later, when other missionaries followed, they found two old Hottentots, the first disciples of their predecessor, sitting under the same tree, carrying on the good work and preaching the faith of their teacher.

One of the two, whose name was Solomon, had achieved a great reputation both for his sermons and his extemporaneous prayers. His words went straight to the heart of his listeners. One of his most eloquent appeals was overheard by a visiting listener, who used to tell it translated from the Hottentot-Afrikaans in which it was delivered.

Solomon, with hands folded and eyes closed, was praying fervently: "Dear Lordie, we are very grateful for all you have done for us during the past week. You sent the fine rains and, behold, the veld is green again, the sheep and goats are as fat as can be. But, dear Lordie, you haven't treated our old sexton, Jeremiah, very well. See, his thirst is no longer so great and he puts a penny for you in the plate every Sunday. But what do you do, dear Lordie? You send your old thunder and lightning into the valley and kill all his sheep and goats. How would you like it, dear Lordie, if Jeremiah were to kill all your sheep and goats? No, dear Lordie, if you will think it over, you will see that you have not treated old Jeremiah very fairly."

An earlier missionary, Father Tachard, who was a French Jesuit priest, wrote a vivid picture of these natives as he found them, which Mama gave me to read. His journal, published in 1686, describes them with minute detail, distinguishing between the Hottentots and the Bushmen. The journal says:

> These people, convinced that there is no other sort of life worth living, only do what is necessary to secure an existence for themselves. . . . According to them, they are the owners

of the country and the happiest of men. In spite of the good opinion they have of themselves, they lead a miserable existence. . . . . They take pleasure in making themselves hideous; when they want to adorn themselves, they rub their heads, faces and hands with soot from their cauldrons. . . . . Their hair, which as a matter of fact is naturally almost as woolly as that of negroes, is thus reduced to little tufts to which they attach pieces of copper or glass. Their finery consists of strings of different coloured bones which they put around their necks and waists; . . . but they are faithful to their masters and the Dutch give them free access to their houses. They are charitable and obliging, although they possess scarcely anything. But their great misfortune, one indeed which cannot be sufficiently deplored, is that they have no knowledge of God.

Whatever the truth about these natives may have been, and there are many references to them in the records kept by the Dutch settlers that do not bear out the opinion of the kindly father, the mission station in the hills became a religious center around which there gathered a number of Boer farmers. In time, the village of mud and thatched houses became noted for its tidy, holy, and industrious inhabitants. Today, it stands as a monument to the worthy and virtuous missionaries.

As wagons and carts of all descriptions bearing the sick arrived almost daily at the baths, I became more and more interested in the occupants. The patients apparently came from all over the country, many of them traveling several days from their homes in desperate search of a cure in the healing waters.

Most of the families lived entirely in their wagons outspanned on the open veld, the oxen, knee-haltered, being allowed to wander and feed themselves under the watchful eye of the young tow leaders. At night the fires on which they cooked beside their wagons, in true trek fashion, illumined the hillside, adding something romantic to what was often a pathetic personal or family tragedy.

Sometimes there was music as someone played a mouth organ

or a concertina; occasionally there was hymn singing, the voices floating up into the silent, starlit night as they chanted the hymns of their forefathers, the pioneering Boers. Wandering down among the wagons in the dusk, I could hear families at prayer, saying long loquacious prayers in Dutch, interrupted by sudden bursts of weeping or the muffled sounds of comforting words. Sickness and health, life and death, the living and the dead living, all were brought close to me by the dramas of these lives. I would meet the families going to the springs for water, or the very maimed being carried to the baths. Talking to the native attendants, who were always ready with a bit of news for an inquisitive lad, involved me more with the lives of the patients than they ever imagined. I watched, and I saw patience and resignation, cruelty and pathos, intolerance and love, all intermingled in that strange camp of diverse people. They were mostly drawn from one class of society with which I had had little contact, the farmers and tradesmen from the far-flung area of the Little Karroo.

One morning I noticed a full team of burned brown oxen hauling a wagon into the camping yard. At its side walked a young Boer and two children, a boy and a girl, both about my own age. There was something about them that attracted me, the tall, swinging grace of the man, the thin, upright bearing of the children. Whatever it was, I found myself watching as the man and the boy prepared a roughly made stretcher on the ground. Then, the man, climbing into the wagon, carried out a woman in his arms, laying her gently on the stretcher. Something about the tenderness of the gesture, the infinite care with which he lowered the body, supine but for the bent-up knees, made me more conscious of them as the man and the boy lifted their burden and slowly carried her toward the bathhouse. Later in the day, the man found me at the springs.

"*Dag*," (good day) he said, nodding to me. "Is the water very hot?" He spoke in broken English.

"Not too hot to bathe in," I answered.

"It works miracles, this water, so they say."

"Yes," I said, "lots of people come to be cured by it."

"It isn't only the water," he went on, "it's God. Only if it is God's will are people made well."

Here was the same unquestioning faith that had upheld the Boers through all their struggle to achieve independence. I had been told how the Bible had been their daily guide, their faith in the Holy Word never wavering even when fate itself seemed against them and they were violently murdered by the opposing natives. Faced by this religious fervor in a complete stranger, I was disturbed, uncomfortable.

"My wife is very sick," he went on. "For five years now— it's a long time—each year a little worse, more pain and less able to move about. The doctor says the waters here will help her, but the water cannot cure unless the Lord wills it," he repeated, as though to remind himself of his own belief.

"I'm sure she will get better," I said encouragingly.

"You are English, eh?"

"No," I said, "I was born in Cape Town."

"But you talk like the English. You should learn the Taal. That's what I always tell my children, they should learn the other language. They talk some English, not much, but they understand."

"Have you come a long way?" I ventured.

"From the karroo," he said. "We had to leave the farm, but that's nothing, if the waters help my wife." He looked away across the rolling, sunlit hills, away to somewhere in his mind where there was peace and no more suffering.

"Have you someone ill in your family?" he asked me, suddenly.

"My mother," I said, "but she is getting better. I'm sure your wife will, too."

"Thanks," he said. "We will pray for your mother. We pray every day for my wife and some time," he paused for a moment, "God may answer."

I was silenced by his look, by the twisting of his two browned hands, tearing the strands of the grass he was holding.

As he moved away, he said, "Come and see my children —they are lonely here."

"I'll come," I answered him, moved by a strange feeling of compassion I did not understand.

I told my parents about the incident and my mother went to see if there was anything we could do for the sick woman.

A few days later, I went to their wagon just as they were preparing to carry the woman to the baths. There was something tragic about the little procession: the girl in her cotton *kappie*, walking at her mother's side; the woman, damp and twisted in the agony of her pain, white-faced against the canvas stretcher; the slow, measured tread of the man and his son.

"I hope she is better," I said, as the Boer passed me.

"The water soothes her," was all he answered.

A week later, she died. The innkeeper came to tell us they had found her when they woke in the morning, cold but peaceful, her tortured knees straight and relaxed for the first time in five years. They were to wait until a coffin could be procured in the village, then they would take her back to be buried on the farm.

Late that evening, after sunset, I went out, half hoping to see the children to say how sorry I was, but secretly praying that there would be no one about. Everything was silent; there was no sound from any of the other wagons. Only as I stepped nearer could I hear the man's voice reading slowly, slowly in Dutch, some of the eternal words to bring him the comfort he longed for.

For many years, we went either to Marienbad or Karlsbad in Germany, where Mama used to take the baths for her rheumatism. Considered as part of my education, these trips were usually very exciting experiences for me, for I was just as anxious to see, as Mama was to show me, all the places of interest in that part of Europe.

My formal education did not suffer either, for as a rule we traveled with a governess, though as I got older a local tutor was hired to teach me while Mama was busy with her cure.

But there was another reason that I was allowed to go. Either before or after her cure, I was always taken to see one or other of the best-known lung specialists for an examination. The German doctors were then much in fashion, and, though my health was obviously improving all the time, Mother's constant fear of threatened tuberculosis made her doubly careful. I have memories of exhaustive examinations, being tapped both on my chest and back while saying "ninety-nine" between deep breaths, answering in my youthful German various questions put me by learned-looking professors.

On one occasion, we stopped on our journey across Germany at Cologne. I think it must have been Easter, for Mama took me to hear a High Mass at midnight as a special treat. How well I remember the extraordinary impression the scene made on me: the thousands of glittering candles, the dimly lit arches curving into the dark heights above, the heavenward-soaring voices of the great choir, all enveloped in a scented cloud of incense. Mother pointed out the stained-glass windows, the bishop's miters, the rich copes among the processional crosses, murmuring to me that we were hearing a famous Palestrina *Mass*.

In the art galleries, which seemed very wearying to me in those days, she would take me by the hand and stand me before the famous pictures she was determined I should see. There were others that caught my unsophisticated eye that I would rather have lingered over, but Mama usually described these as "not so important."

All the well-known "cures" in those days provided music and theater, as well as excellent food, though most people taking the waters were on a strict regime. We invariably found friends among the visitors, so I was never at a loss while Mama lay supine in the famous mud baths. I used to be taken to visit her on occasion, lying in the black mud with only her head and ten fingers protruding, her beautifully kept fingernails never being allowed to touch the mud.

These visits gave us the excuse of going to various cities, which delighted me, for from my earliest youth I loved seeing new places, different people, manners and languages unlike our own. Before I was twelve I had visited most of the important towns in Germany and northern France, besides having learned to speak both French and German fluently. All these advantages, which so affected my later life, I owe to my mother, who managed to extract the necessary funds from my ever-generous father, left working at home while we were traveling.

Though I never knew my father's parents, I can clearly remember my maternal grandparents. My grandfather was a Scot with sparkling blue eyes, blond-gray side-whiskers, a cheerful disposition, and a gentle manner with us children. He had made a success of his import-export business in Cape Town, housing his large family in a big house in a flourishing suburb called Rondebosch, not far from Cape Town. He had given his tall, well-born wife thirteen children, a truly unlucky number, as it transpired, for many of them died either in childbirth or very soon after. Thus it was that they lavished extra parental care on the remaining seven, spoiling the four girls with every material advantage.

I can see him now, looking rather like Father Christmas, presiding over the long, enormous table in his dining room, to which we were invited on special occasions. Carving a huge roast, he would lavishly load our plates with delicious food, adding a gay jest to suit either the particular child or the festival. We were waited on by a number of colored servants who adored Grandpapa with awed admiration, for he was a gentle man, though we always thought they were afraid of Grandmama, who watched them with a sharp, critical eye. I got to know her better after Grandpapa died, when she lived in a small house with my uncle. For she would entertain me for lunch on occasional Saturdays, when we would have her "special" dishes, which always required that she take a pinch of bicarbonate of soda after eating them.

My mother was her father's eldest and favorite child. She seemed to have been the answer to many longings in his own nature, for both his Scotch and English blood found full expression in Mama, with her talents, her beauty, and her sympathy for him. He was much less interested in his other daughters or his sons, strange to say, though his youngest boy, Robert, was as musically gifted as his sisters, and had aspirations of becoming a professional singer, for he had a fine baritone voice. I remember him singing our favorite songs accompanied by Mama, who now and then would join him in some well-known duet with a violin obligato played by Papa. What lovely evenings of music we had! And how much they added to our musical knowledge and taste!

After Grandpapa's death, my Uncle Robert had only one dream, which was to escape from the limitations of his mother's strict regime and study in Paris to become an opera singer. After many attempts, he finally managed to get away and lived there his *vie de Bohème*, studying with de Reszke and other French teachers until his debut at Covent Garden in London.

Secretly I envied my uncle, admiring him for his courage and initiative, for I knew what he had gone through in order to break away from the family traditions. I could foresee what I might have to expect from my parents if I attempted to escape a conventional education, for Paris and my own dreams of becoming a painter one day were already synonymous. But though it took me years to accomplish, after study in Rome and then Madrid I finally got a studio in Paris. That was many years after my uncle had blazed the trail.

When we visited him while he was still studying in Paris, I remember how he would entertain me with exciting stories of the famous people in the singing world he had got to know, the lovely women, the interesting men, the composers and renowned conductors of the day. How he used to rave about

Mama, in her presentation gown, Buckingham Palace, London, 1898

Mary Garden's Mélisande at the Opéra-Comique, which Debussy himself had said was the perfect interpretation of the role; Maggie Teyte, who became his great friend while she was studying Garden's roles, which she sang more beautifully than Mary herself, for she had a much lovelier voice; Vanni Marcoux, who knew all the pitfalls and who befriended my uncle, later joining Garden's company in her famous venture in Chicago, where her productions of French opera were far better performed than at the Metropolitan in New York. In those days, these people were just names for me to juggle with, but little did my uncle know how they would become reality in my later life in America. To the end, I cherished the warm, generous friendship of Mary Garden, whom I admired as passionately as did my uncle in the Parisian days. Poor "Uncle Bob," as we called him, only lasted one season at Covent Garden, despite his beautiful voice. We always suspected he was another victim of "overtraining" by too many teachers, for he never sang in public again but retired, a sadly disappointed man, to teach hopeful young singers in London, where he died.

Mama's sisters, rather like their ancestors, the Gunnings, all shared her good looks with some of her talents. They were all musical; the youngest, Evie, who had married a wine farmer and lived in the vine-growing valley not far from our house, had a superb soprano voice. When she was invited to sing to a select group of ladies on Mama's "at home" day, I would sneak into the adjoining hall to hear her sing my favorite Grieg songs, or an aria from some popular Puccini opera. In those days I was anxious to become a composer myself, and was already studying counterpoint and composition with an English music professor in Cape Town. He gave me a thorough understanding of the art, and, though I did not pursue it, it has served me greatly in my ability to hear and understand music.

Finally, one day I had the tremendous satisfaction of hearing Aunt Evie sing one of my own songs to a captive audience. Though I knew the music was a bit derivative, the words were wonderful, and I sat, hot with excitement at hearing that glorious voice singing my song.

Each of my aunts had several children and, as in most large families where there are many children, there was far too much gossip, even slander, in our house. Our various cousins were frequently the butt of our criticism or derision, though never in front of our parents. Papa would not allow that, but vented his intolerance on bad manners and loose moral ethics, castigating the latter mercilessly.

Mama, infinitely more forgiving, nevertheless suffered from a form of snobbishness born of an inherent pride in Papa's achievements. In a society such as ours, sharp lines in class distinction were drawn. Mama supported these, only daring to break them in cases of artists or musicians, who in any event were considered very queer individuals until they had proved themselves successful from a worldly point of view.

There were never any gentlemen on our own "at home" days, but on Sunday afternoons, when sherry would be added to the usual tea, husbands came with their wives to call, followed by a game of croquet. It was the only game allowed on Sunday (though I never could think why), which was otherwise a day of ritual that began with church attended by us all in our appropriate dress. In those days, this meant a frock coat and top hat for my father, with Mama in her latest gown and hat, smelling of the lavender she sprinkled on her handkerchief. It used to scent our whole pew, and I always hoped it would outscent the eau de cologne used by a tiresome old spinster who sat in front of us and flourished her scent as she sat down, giving us all a cold bow. My sister and I didn't like her because she always brushed us aside to accost Papa.

As is usually the case, the house was Mother's domain. She directed it, managed it, and filled it with her own ideas. I think she was strict with the colored domestics, intolerant of their stupidity, but generous when it came to helping them or using her influence on their behalf. She insisted on a standard, however, which gave her the reputation of being an excellent hostess. As was then the custom when dealing with servants, it was always assumed, rightly or wrongly, that they were never to be trusted when it came to taking groceries, eatables, or drinks of any sort. Everything was kept under lock and key, to be doled out daily to the cook in the quantities required.

Mama had a pantry in which all the staples were kept, as well as the stores of choice bottled or canned goods. This was known as "Mother's pantry." But the key to this sacred domain, together with the keys of the wine cupboard and her own private jewel closet as well, were forever being mislaid or lost. The very house seemed to go into paroxysms of anxiety as all of us, family and servants alike, were asked to search for Mother's keys. These would invariably be found in some most unexpected place: on a mantel shelf, hidden behind a picture, almost anywhere, including the garden. But looking for Mama's keys practically became a punishment we dreaded, for we often had to search for hours. I used to suspect our colored cook, Amalie (who thought Mama was stingy with the supplies), hid the keys herself in order to get into the sacred cupboard at her own convenience and take what she most enjoyed. But we never caught her at this, though she never hesitated to impersonate Mama when giving orders to the tradesmen.

There was a famous occasion when one of us overheard her talking in a loud voice over the telephone: "Dis is Lady Juta speakin'. I'se werry cross wid your shop. Why de bloody hell don't you deliver de tings I ordered dis mornin'. Now, hurry up an' no damned excuses." We thought it particularly hard on Mother, who had never been heard to utter one profane word in her whole life.

Mother paid rigorous lip service to the English Church, although I don't think she ever really knew just what she believed. It was what she had been taught, and I am sure she never bothered to question whether it made sense to her or not. So she insisted that we be instructed as she had been.

Indeed, it was Mother who saw to it that we were properly taught the ritual of the Protestant Church. Neither she nor Papa ever allowed us to forget that Sunday meant either communion at 8:00 A.M. without any breakfast whatsoever, or matins at 11:00 A.M., as well as Sunday School in the afternoon. She urged me to sing in the choir of our church and, as I grew older, to study the Bible with two of my friends under the direction of a maiden lady, who served us weak tea with stale cookies after a good hour of Saint Paul or one of the Gospels.

Her attitude to the Dutch Reformed Church, the church of the Boers, was one of condescending disdain, while she viewed the Roman Catholics as distinctly pagan and therefore hardly Christian at all. But she was the first to patronize the Dutch church bazaars, even though she had little time for the congregation, always looking upon the Dutch as uneducated or backward. Her standards were English, with all that that entailed of intolerance of others who fell short of those standards. It is no wonder the Dutch hated the British with all their arrogance and superiority. Even though we were still children, we could sense this critical feeling among our English friends, who never hesitated to express their opinions of the Dutch in our hearing. Mother learned to curb her expressions of criticism as my father moved more and more into the political limelight.

But there were other aspects of my mother, tender, motherly aspects that will never be forgotten. I think of her sitting beside my bed when I was ill, which was so often in the early days, and singing to me in her pretty, gentle voice. Sometimes it was an Irish folk song or an old French melody—she knew so many fascinating songs—but at nighttime it would be one of my favorite hymns: "Now the day is over, Night is drawing nigh, Shadows of the evening Steal across the sky"; then in her anxiety she would put her cool hand on my forehead to feel if my temperature had gone down.

Her continual care for my health used to irritate me, and I am sure it was exaggerated, but I know now that she helped me to get over the barriers that my delicate lungs and chest had imposed upon me.

Then, on Sunday evenings we would all gather around her at the piano to sing a hymn for one or other of the family crossing the ocean to or from England. There seemed always to be one sister or another coming or going on the Union Castle Line, so we regularly said a prayer, which Papa would lead, and sang: "Eternal Father, strong to save, whose arm hath bound the restless wave." When mother finished with crescendo chords for the last line, "Glad hymns of praise from land and sea," she would take her handkerchief to wipe her eyes, thinking of the daughter or a dear friend tossing through the Bay of Biscay.

With her children around her, in her prettiest dress and scented with her favorite scent, and Papa guarding us but joining in the hymns, Mama was at her best; she would kiss me good night with her lovely blue eyes full of tears.

She had been a beautiful dancer in her day, had played tennis rather badly, but rode well to hounds. By the time I remember her clearly she had stopped all sports, having fallen on the tennis court and damaged her back, from which she suffered for the rest of her life. She often went to concerts or the theater with Papa, but in those days entertainment consisted of private parties, dinners, or teas in the houses of friends. She most enjoyed being driven out in her luxurious victoria behind our liveried coachman, who prided himself on the fine pair of bay carriage horses Papa had purchased for her. In her new dress, latest fashionable hat, and feather boa, I remember her looking regally lovely as she drove off to someone's "at home" day party.

As I have grown to know and understand other couples, I think of my parents as a more unusual one. They made our house a happy home, creating an exceptional family unity; they managed to keep their misunderstandings mostly to themselves, though we realized more than they ever knew; their mutual admiration created an atmosphere of harmony; and friction was usually saved by their sense of humor and of fun.

More than anything else, perhaps, I am grateful to them for their varied interests and enthusiasms, which they conveyed to us children, giving us a much wider field of appreciation in our own lives than is given to most.

My mother's complexities were so essentially female that they were easily understood, though not necessarily forgiven, by anyone as intelligent as Papa; her weaknesses, so glaring, her techniques, so naïve. All became unimportant in the warmth of her great heart.

She was awarded the Order of the British Empire for her public services, having in fact done far more than most of the women of her time and place, for she served as president of at least twenty-four charitable organizations. Beginning during the Boer War, when every loyal person rallied to the cause of the Empire, she organized a group formed to help the sick and wounded of Dutch and English alike; it was known as the Cape of Good Hope Society.

I think she was at her best when Papa's illness struck our household. Then she showed her true spirit, her faith and utter devotion. My admiration for her grew as I watched her handling matters she knew little about—things he had always dealt with but now could no longer manage. By his disability she was forced to adjust her thinking, even her way of life, to an entirely different level. Only someone as thoroughbred as she could have done it with such grace, such dignity.

Later in their life together, it came his turn to watch over her with the same tender care she had shown him. For her sake, he had ultimately sold our home. All of us children were either in England or abroad; the big house at the Cape, even though full of their happiest memories, was too large, too lonely. Besides, in England there were the grandchildren as well to brighten life with new interest. Papa retired at the appropriate age and sold the house. I think the loss of his garden broke his heart, but they settled in London, where, although their life was restricted, it was much more interesting.

There Father had to watch Mama die after a serious operation that ended months of failing health. I can hear her now, calling for the one ever-faithful, loving companion, who watched her day and night, knowing the end was near. He would read to her to calm her, just as he had done so often to me, thanking the Lord, as he used to tell me, that she was not being left behind by him to deal with life without him.

Each of us was with them from time to time, but we never discussed "Mon Desir" or the happy life of the past. It was as though leaving the house had ended their lives; they were only sustained through the latter years of waiting for the end by their wonderful memories flooded by sunshine.

The words chosen by my father to be carved on her tombstone perhaps show most clearly what he would never forget about her and wanted everyone to remember: "She never said an unkind word about anyone."

At her death, we received wonderful tributes to her friendship from people scattered from all over the world: the people she had helped or entertained, the artists she had encouraged, the poor she had aided. From among them, I quote a portion of a column written by a great admirer, the wife of the dean of Cape Town Cathedral at the time of her death:

> To her, more than to most women, was given the gift of friendship, for she had the power not only of readily making friends but of keeping them. Those who were in trouble or anxiety knew that her sympathy would never fail them, while her power of rejoicing with those who rejoiced was equally real. It is not unusual to meet with kindness and hospitality among women, but it is given to few to possess that spontaneous generosity of thought and word which characterised all that Lady Juta said and did. How brave she was, and how patient, how childlike her faith through those last days of her illness.

4. Sisters

MY four sisters were very individual, very talented, and, from my point of view, quite unlike each other. Had I been able to view them objectively at the time, I would have found them fascinating, original, and unlike any of their contemporaries. But I was involved emotionally, possessive of each in turn as they came and went from our house to study abroad.

Two of them were more intelligent than Mama, though none of them excelled her in looks or charm. The two elder girls were dark-eyed like Papa, the younger blue-eyed, as was Mama. I don't think all four were ever at home all together during my growing years, which was perhaps just as well for me, the only blue-eyed boy.

I. RÉNÉ

They were all musical, and each of them had a lovely singing voice, my youngest sister, Luia, finally developing a voice of such quality and volume as to make an operatic career her goal. Each inherited very obvious traits from my parents, my eldest sister, Réné, having a mind so like Papa's that they sparred with each other through their mutual admiration. She resented his dictatorial attitude and argued with him. "Just as a man would," I can hear Papa saying under his breath.

Slim, graceful, full of creative imagination and talent, Réné went to school in England and thence to Paris to study painting, though her obvious gifts ultimately found expression in writing. When she returned home from France with several student's canvases to her credit, our house began to assume a different character. She had better taste than Mama, less conventional, always original. Furniture was moved, brighter-colored materials used for curtains and chairs. She arranged the flowers for the house in her own specific manner, using her sense of color and design to make the vases she composed quite different from most others; the mixture of varieties she gathered with her use of foliage or grasses resulting in striking decorations.

Mama looked on, admiring but somewhat disturbed by these changes, indulging her daughter's ideas. Finally, when Réné asked to be allowed to have her bedroom papered in a rich, chocolate brown, Mama could not contain her feelings.

"It's so gloomy," she said, "like a waiting room, and not at all feminine. Wouldn't you rather have rosebuds or some pretty ribboned design?"

The room became brown.

Réné rode well, her delicate hands always sensitive to her horse's mouth. Though she never hunted as Mama had done, she covered the countryside on horseback with some escort or other, gathering into her fertile brain the color, the shape, the history of each landmark. Out of this harvest she started to write, bringing to life the past story of the land and its people. When I became old enough to ride with her, we galloped over the peninsula and produced her first book, appropriately called *The Cape Peninsula*, which she filled with the results of her historical research. Published by A. & C. Black and then again by John Lane, with illustrations by me, it preceded many others by later writers.

She followed this book with articles for local magazines, and ultimately with other travel books illustrated by me, *Cannes and the Hills*, and *Concerning Corsica*, as well as several novels, one of which brought her distinguished recognition.

I remember that she chose her friends with a somewhat reserved discrimination, yet, when we played charades or organized a party, it was her wit and humor that swept us all along. Her beaux, several of whom I got to know quite well as frequent visitors to our home, were always interesting, either talented or gifted in some way. All were intellectual, for apart from riding she was not interested in games.

Naturally, she knew Cecil Rhodes and his "circle" better than any of us, and in the drawing room of "Groot Schuur," where she sang often after dinner parties, she met the great and the then famous. Many remained her friends when later she married and lived in London but, as I look back, I think that men, by and large, were somewhat afraid of her mind, even though charmed by her grace and ready wit. In our drawing room at home, I used to see one or other of her suitors bewitched, fascinated by her looks, her large, lustrous eyes, the movements of her delicate hands, but they hesitated to propose to this somewhat enigmatic female despite her quick understanding of their masculine needs. She suspected them as alien enemies, though in the end she did marry and have one charming, sweet child, "an immaculate conception," she would tell me on the side.

Like Papa, she taught me unconsciously, so I benefited greatly from knowing her complexities and her strange mind. When I grew older, the days of our companionship while doing our book on Corsica were richly rewarding, gay with laughter over her penetrating criticisms, her sense of imagery, and her extraordinary adaptability.

Once, in a remote Corsican village she said to me one morning, clutching a hot water bottle to her breast, as she was always cold, "Madame told me the lavatory was outside, but I had no idea how far it was or that the door doesn't shut. A goat pushed its way in before I could stop it."

"It is pretty primitive here," I agreed, thinking of my own uncomfortable bed.

"Well," she went on, "but it wouldn't go out, so tactless I thought it was, and started eating the straw on the floor. I was terrified."

I laughed at the whole picture.

"It used to be just like that in South Africa, do you remember? Only there, one would meet a large snake in the straw instead of a goat." She shuddered at the memory. "And when I told Madame about the door, to pacify me she suggested I might prefer to sit on straw instead of that cold seat! Imagine the risk if one was joined by a goat!"

But her sense of humor never failed, and we laughed our way all over the island, inconveniences and embarrassments notwithstanding.

As I have said, she had a variety of suitors, but to my knowledge only once met her fate, in a man distinguished in high office, who was unhappily married but unable to divorce. He became ill from some obscure malady and, when he was supposedly dying, she herself lay ill, out of sheer sympathy, I thought afterwards.

"Will you do something for me, Jannie?" she asked me one morning. "Take this letter over for me to Sir H.'s—he is terribly ill, you know—and give it to his valet and ask him please to see that Harry gets it. I can't trust the post, I'm so afraid he'll die before it reaches him." There was a sudden sob in her voice, and I caught my breath in embarrassment.

I rode over on my pony, not telling Mama, who was hovering about René in anxiety, and cantered over the hillside pathways all the way, my mind full of foreboding.

"The doctor is here," said the butler, who answered the front door.

"Could I speak to Sir H.'s valet, please?" I asked. "I have something to give him."

"We want Sir H. to have this letter, please," I said to the valet, who knew me well.

"I have one for you to take back," he answered.

I took the letter and saw that it was addressed "For You." I thanked him and asked, "How is Sir H.?"

"He can't make it," he said. "It's just a matter of time now."

I hurried away. "She won't see him again," I murmured to myself as I rode home.

"He sent you this," I said, as I gave Réné the letter where she lay very still and pale in her bed.

She smiled at me as she took it and turned her face to the wall. I tiptoed out of her room, leaving her to cry out her sorrow, wishing I could have said something to ease her pain.

Sir Harry died the following day and the house seemed very silent for, despite Mama's efforts, "everyone" knew the situation.

Later, after Réné's ultimate marriage ended, she lived with her daughter in the south of France, where she grew jessamine and tuberoses for the scent factories at Grasse. Came the Second World War, together with the hysteria that affected all of France, with rumors of a total invasion by the Germans, forcing foreign residents to seek any means of escape to their own countries. Réné was still a British subject, though she had lived so long in France, and was warned by the British consul to leave as quickly as possible.

But she failed to get away, and died in her lonely farmhouse, deserted by her terrified French workers, with only her daughter and the local priest to comfort her.

II. HELEN

My second sister, Helen, was as rebellious as my first but less intelligent, and made in an entirely different mold, both physically as well as mentally. Luia and I used to tease her, telling her she looked like the portrait of our masculine ancestor that hung in the hall, dark, handsome, and very robust!

She was a fine pianist and a good violinist, studying both instruments for three years in Berlin under the best teachers available. She wanted to become a professional and Mama rallied to her support. How many dreams were dreamed among us all of careers in either music or the arts? How gifted we all were, and yet how unprepared for the life of the artist in those days by our upbringing and our background! For, strange to say, Helen's destiny was to become a singer with a contralto voice of fine timbre but limited range. This never daunted her, however, and she worked hard but achieved only moderate success.

While studying in London, she started to compose and did, in fact, publish two or three ballads, of the type popular with concert singers of the day. Mama was very critical of these to us children.

"I don't think they are very original," she said, "and who would want to sing them?"

Our pride in Helen's achievement was crushed, even though the printed songs were shown off to visitors.

She was fortunate enough to be engaged by the Quinlan Opera Company, with whom she toured a large part of the world, singing contralto roles in both Wagner and Verdi operas. The company came to Cape Town on its world tour, and I was very proud of having sister Helen in the cast of several of their productions. But I remember my great disappointment at the performance of Wagner's *Rhinegold* in which Helen sang the role of Erda. Her scene took place in almost total darkness, with an eerie green light, half illuminating her looming figure, coming from behind a large rock. Her voice was not big enough for the role, and there is no action in the dire warning of the Earth Goddess to reduce the gloom.

I came away from my first Wagnerian opera rather depressed, exhausted by the power of the orchestra and disillusioned by my sister's performance. I knew then that, despite my loyalty, Helen did not have either the volume or the quality of voice needed for grand opera. Had she been a good actress, that might have compensated somewhat, but unlike either Réné or Luia she had no sense of the theater, which both Luia and I inherited directly from Papa, who was a consummate actor.

Mama, who had heard superb opera in Germany, Paris, and London, where she had developed her friendship for Albani, the great Canadian soprano, was critical of the whole company, several of whom were brought to our house by sister Helen.

"They seem so uneducated," said Mama tactlessly.

"I like *real* people," Helen said in defense of her guests, giving a polite dig at Mama's society friends.

Unfortunately, she was involved in a love affair with the chief conductor, an Italian who proposed to her, having developed ideas of future support from my father. However, he soon found that Papa was not interested, and I am afraid that Helen did not receive as much of his attention as before and had to nurse her disillusionment in private.

At home, she showed her qualities as a housewife and became an excellent cook. She played good tennis and rode her horse with a sure rein. To me she was a great friend, a solid, loyal rock on which I knew I could always rely. With my parents she was calm, unruffled by any situation, for she lacked Réné's sharp vision and hypersensitivity; yet her character brought her great affection, her large, kind heart winning her friends in all walks of life.

I saw her through several emotional upheavals, though she seemed fated to choose the wrong man, keeping Mama busy fending off struggling musicians or impecunious suitors who she feared were counting on Papa for a more secure future. I think her heart broke when Frank Webb, about whom I have written in another chapter, left the Cape, never to return. But later in London she married an older English musician, a fine composer, well known in musical circles. Together they had many happy years of married life both in London and abroad, but Helen, who by her nature should have had a large family, died childless, to her great sorrow.

III. BRENDA

I find my third sister Brenda the least easy to recapture now that I want to talk about her, not only because she was so different from the others, but because her very difference is difficult to define.

Blue-eyed, fair, and slim, I did not get to know her well in the days I am writing about; only much later as our paths crossed, either in England or Spain, where I stayed a while with her, did I begin to see her true self and recognize how good, gentle, and patient she was. Her evident simplicity of nature put her in a separate category, quite apart from her dark, more vital sisters. To me, she seemed exquisite, someone to be guarded, protected from onslaughts I knew nothing about but suspected.

She returned from the three years of study in Germany and England an accomplished cellist, not creative as the others were, but a good musician in her own field. She had no wish to become a professional, though she was as much involved with music as were the others. Her religious faith and her cello seemed to be the real sustenance of her life.

Mama was delighted with her. There were no problems to be dealt with in Brenda, no rebellious spirit, no difficult nature, just a lovely, simple, very marriageable daughter. Indeed, she was the first to be married, despite all Mama's efforts with the elder girls. But Mama had very definite ideas about the future for her daughters, no doubt with the memory of the Gunning sisters in her mind. Poor Mama! She was destined to have one disappointment after another, for marriageable men were very scarce, and penniless lieutenants from the flagships of His Majesty's Navy stationed in the bay did not quite come up to her standards, even though some of them were the second sons of the best families in England. Only the best was worthy of these three exceptional girls.

Our house now assumed a new role in the pattern of Cape society. It had always been the center of hospitality, but now Mama's parties were designed with a different object in mind. There were tennis parties with strawberries and cream on the lawns, dances with lavish suppers and the best orchestras, "paper chases" for those who had horses, followed by delicious picnics at some favorite spot. I can still see my three sisters, beautifully habited by the best English tailor, being courted by perspiring captains of the resident British regiments. Everything was focused on the three daughters, and they became known as "the three Graces." This flattered Mama, but within the family we had christened them with far more prosaic names: "The Whim," "The Wog," and "The Worm." I don't know who thought up these names, for they seemed very applicable to each girl, but I suspect it was Papa, who knew his daughters better than they thought he did.

I formed my own ideas about the men who visited us often and seemed to be paying marked attention to one or another of my sisters. I was very critical of most of them and was, in fact, violently jealous of each of the three, and became increasingly possessive the moment I suspected any of them was becoming interested in a particular man.

A few of the suitors remain vividly in my memory for various reasons, mainly because of the manner in which they treated me. There was Lord B., whose father owned a crumbling castle in Ireland but had no cash to give his son, who seemed to spend his life in riding boots and thought of nothing except one form of sport or other in a "fraitfully" English way. With reddish hair and a gay, swaggering manner, he seemed always to get his own way by sheer charm. He was very cheery and chatty with me, and I liked his easy manners, but I soon found out that he was not at all well off, so I knew there was little risk of his walking away with my sister Brenda, with whom he said he was madly in love. I used to think that had she married him she would soon have been forgotten in favor of the foxes or the deer or "the bloody fine grouse" soon after marriage.

Then there was Mr. J., a more serious, dangerous prospect, for he was rich, intelligent, and ambitious. He courted my sister by every known means, and, though I didn't like his condescending manner to me, I very much feared he might succeed in winning her. They rode together regularly, and I used to pull off his riding boots with a view to finding out how "things" were going.

"She's much too good for me, Jannie," he would say with a sigh. I began to suspect he was beginning to discover that she really loved his best friend, and that it might be very awkward; they danced until dawn, but she wouldn't marry him.

There were weekends when my room had to be given over to some ardent visitor and I, cursing his presence under my breath, was relegated to the back porch; when riding boots littered the passages, suppers were prepared for days before a dance, and Peter the gardener worked to exhaustion carrying out Mama's elaborately planned decorations.

It was no wonder that our parties became famous throughout the countryside, and that the three Miss Jutas were the center of every kind of gossip, both friendly and critical, some of which I picked up from my school friends and repeated to Mama.

Sad to say, these efforts proved fruitless. None of my sisters became engaged to be married for quite some time. There were passionate passages, tears over love letters, even talks to Papa in his library at the end of the passage, but no wedding bells. Mama was beginning to be disheartened when along from England came the one suitor that no one really expected, for I doubt that even Brenda, who was the purpose of his visit, really believed that he would come all the way to South Africa. But he did.

He came into our circle heralded by affection and friendship between his parents and ours. He was handsome, a splendid athlete, with various distinctions won at Christ Church, Oxford,

Family group: *left to right*, Brenda, Jan, Mama, Papa, Helen, Réné (Luia was in Paris)

and he was his mother's favorite son. Had Brenda married his elder brother, a warm, charming human being and a captain in the Grenadier Guards, her whole life pattern would have been quite different. He had wooed and won her heart while she was in England, but a cruel fate killed him, leaving Brenda to be courted by his younger brother, a priest in the Anglican Church!

How capable she was to become the wife of an English clergyman and live in cold, drafty vicarages on a financial scale to which she was quite unaccustomed was shown by her difficulty in adapting herself to what was expected of a clergyman's wife in those days. She was no doubt extravagant, but he was certainly parsimonious, and this meant that their married life required careful adjustment. I stayed with them in one cold vicarage after another later in my life, my heart full of sorrow at what I could see was a spiritual hurdle for her to overcome, the natural inclinations she had been used to in the warm, loving comfort of my father's house.

To her everlasting credit, may it be said that wherever they were sent, even into foreign countries, she was beloved by all, and by the generous outgiving of her nature carried the gospel her husband was trying to preach right into the hearts of the people they were working among.

She taught me about God, so that as a boy I was able to understand something of His mystery in a way no one else had ever been able to explain to me. I began to recognize Him in everything I found beautiful: the garden, my home, the people I loved, even the radiant landscape that surrounded us. Suddenly He seemed to be everywhere: she brought to one small pilgrim an understanding only love could have conveyed. For this alone I am eternally indebted to her; the unquestioning faith radiating out of her blue eyes touched me, who was then hardly aware of the path ahead.

IV. LUIA

My youngest sister, Luia, shared with me our "growing-up" years, for, although she was five years older than I was, we were at home together, as our three elder sisters were much older and were already on their way with schooling and study in Europe.

We shared governesses, we shared friends and parties, but above all we shared the excitement of the adventures and discoveries we made together. Of these there was no lack, for we both had imagination, initiative, and a peculiar inquisitiveness guaranteed to lead us into all sorts of problems. Luia, being female, was vain and self-confident, never hesitating to face situations that my rather shy nature would have made me avoid.

"Don't worry," she would say, with a grande-dame gesture, about whatever obstacle to our wishes faced us. "They are bound to agree with us in the end." What often troubled me was that she did so often get her way, but it was her initiative that sparked to life most of our shared experiences.

Our picnics or "escapes," as we called them, away from home, Mama, or a troublesome governess, were always adventures. We both loved the countryside, we reveled in the wonderful variety of wild flowers that grew around us, about which we had gathered some botanical knowledge from Papa, and we had begun to be interested in the history of the peninsula. Perhaps it was because of Papa's association with Cecil Rhodes, or our friendship with the Rudyard Kiplings, or our own eldest sister who had stimulated our reading, but history began to come to life as we connected it with places we went to, old houses we learned to appreciate, or the people whose contribution to the growth of the then Cape Colony we had read about.

I have told elsewhere of our heroine, Lady Anne Barnard, whose letters written to England from the Cape in 1797–1801 while her husband was attached to the staff of the British governor, Lord Macartney, we had absorbed page by page. They described so wittily the life of eighteenth-century Cape Town, no detail of which escaped her sharp eyes, that we laughed through the chapters of the book that had been made of them, together with extracts of her daily journal, called *South Africa a Century Ago*.

In one of them, she described a house that the governor had offered to the Barnards as a country hideaway out of the heat of Cape Town. It was called "Paradise," and was situated not far from our home. It had been so buried by time and changing nature as to become completely hidden, almost like a dream, overgrown by wild shrubs and trees. Lady Anne describes it thus:

> Before the house, charming in no point of architecture . . . there was a row of orange trees loaded with fruit which shadowed the windows. A garden well stocked was behind the house, through which a hasty stream of water descended from the mountain which raised itself three thousand feet perpendicular above.
>
> "Anne, what do you say to this?" said Barnard in a tone of admiration. "Say," I replied, "that I am vexed to own that I like it of all things."
>
> "And if you do, why should we not have it?"
>
> "Because," said I, "the world's end is not so distant as this spot from the busy haunts of men."
>
> "It is very charming, however," said he with a sigh.

They had taken it, put the house into habitable repair, building a road that wound up the hillside, living there happily undisturbed except by the monkeys, who raided their garden from the neighboring woods.

We knew just where the house had stood and, though reputedly in decay, we had a longing to find it for ourselves. So we set out early one morning when the sun was just filtering through the leaves of the old oaks that overspread the Liesbeek River, which flows from the wooded gorges of the mountain. On toward Newlands, a suburb near our home, we trudged, and there, pushing our way through a tangled undergrowth of twisted trees barring our way, we found it . . . "Paradise."

We stood breathless with excitement, gazing at the ruins. There were still traces of the foundations, a tumbled wall, the remains of steps.

"D'you think Anne's room was here?" I questioned, as I uncovered a bit of cemented wall.

"I'm sure her room would have faced the view and the sunset," Luia said. "Don't you remember how she described the hill and the silver trees?"

So we adopted Paradise and the ruined hideout as our very own, and, though the proverbial path was steep and difficult, we would escape there whenever we could get away and eat our luncheon sandwiches in silence among the ghosts of the lovely Lady Anne and her rather more solid, official husband.

We were adventurous enough to climb up what was called the Skeleton Gorge of Table Mountain to try to find the brilliant scarlet and pink orchid, the *Disa grandiflora*. Only once were we lucky; then it was suddenly to see several of these exquisite flowers, perched like some scarlet velvet butterfly on their delicate stems, growing together in the spongy turf of the ravine.

"Just look at these," I called to Luia. "Come quickly! Was anything ever as beautiful? And such a color . . ."

"We can't take more than one," she said firmly, though I longed to fill my hands with the magnificent, exotic blooms.

Or we would walk onto the "flats" to look for birds' nests, even for rare stones or Bushmen's arrowheads, anything to add to our museum. On our way, we would call on the German farmer who battled against winds and drifting sand to produce cabbages as well as other green vegetables for the local market. We knew him well, for he raised beautiful bantam chickens that I envied and longed to possess. His smiling wife would always offer us big glasses of milk fresh from the cow; we thought of them as special friends.

Those were days full of sunshine and excitement, such days as we have all known in our youth, when one could be exalted and wounded in a moment, or when for no reason some secret experience would elate one and joy would flood the whole universe with a beautiful, warm light.

But soon it was time for Luia to leave for school in England, leaving me, the last of the family, alone until my older sisters began to return home, and upon whose arrival life assumed a different tempo.

Even though both my sister Luia and I were at our respective schools, we nevertheless had a succession of resident governesses in our house. They were partly responsible for helping Mama to manage the household (especially if she wished to go away with Papa), as well as for giving us lessons in languages, music, and something called "deportment" for my sister alone.

We disliked most of them, first because they had no idea of how to deal with children (at any rate, that is what we thought), but also because they seemed to lack any sense of adaptability to what were to them entirely unusual surroundings. They were generally either Scotch or English, but, in spite of Mama's meticulous care in choosing someone with only the best of references, we children did not usually think much of her choice.

One of our governesses whom we really loved was named Wilhelmina Winzer. She had come to South Africa from her native Bavaria, where she had had an excellent education, learning to speak several languages as fluently as her own. We had tolerated two of her predecessors with some patience, but they soon proved themselves to be quite unsuitable for the job. Miss Watkins had come from Scotland with a permanent cold in her head, which seemed to add to her strict Presbyterian intolerance of everything we thought of as fun. Poor Miss Amy Lane, who made pathetic efforts to sing in a tremulous soprano, suffered from digestive trouble and lived on laxatives. We teased her mercilessly when we discovered she was full of middle-class prejudices about things "colonial," as she called them, and was quite intolerant of the "natives," the word she always used for our colored domestics. My sister and I soon decided that we would make the situation sufficiently unpleasant, so she would leave us after a short time.

Thus, it was with intense joy and relief that we greeted Miss Winzer, with her wit, her understanding, and her good humor. We quickly found out that there was practically nothing she could not do, from preparing our picnics to suit our tastes, to writing amusing rhymes, as well as thinking of original ways of teaching us French and German. She soon endeared herself to us all except Peter, the gardener, who resented her.

Miss Winzer taught us old French and German songs, which we loved to sing to the excellent accompaniments she played as well as she did Mozart or Chopin, and I shall be grateful forever to her for her patience over my fumbling scales and hesitant sight reading. We soon discovered she was as proud of us, our house, and our various talents as though we belonged to her, entering into our individual lives in a way that left an indelible mark upon us all. Even Mama, usually so critical of anyone who looked after us, was won over by her charm and personality. She kept us well in hand, though even when driven to distraction by our disobedience, her strongest corrective only amounted to *"Ach, aber Luia, das ist nicht schön."* But that was enough to rouse our conscience, so we were invariably really sorry for having failed her.

As a family, we all loved acting, encouraged by Papa's ardent interest in the theater, so it was an added delight to discover that Miss Winzer was just as fond of theatricals as we were. Two of my sisters from their youngest years had proved themselves to be excellent actresses, and at least twice a year for some celebration or other we organized a show consisting of

musical items, songs, and sketches, which we now composed
with the aid of Miss Winzer.

Everyone was drawn into the undertaking. Peter, the gardener, helped by the yard boys, would erect a sizeable stage at
the end of the drawing room with special lighting and curtains
easily worked by hand. For weeks before, after lessons were
over, we would write, adapt, and rehearse under the enthusiastic
eye of Miss Winzer. Sometimes one or other of us would go to
Papa for special coaching, or advice on our acting of some skit
Miss Winzer had thought up, for she had a genius for satire and
some of our sketches were in fact very funny. Only relatives
and close friends were invited as an audience, but how we all
laughed, for we often included some little joke about one or another of them.

I remember my sister Luia, who was even then rather fat for
her age, used to sing a duet with me called "When We Are
Married," which we had taken from some well-known musical
comedy of the time. The lyrics provided us with the opportunity for many rather exaggerated love gestures. I was dressed up
as a dandy of the Victorian era, while my sister, who was twice
my size, wore one of Mama's dresses, complete with cartwheel
hat and ostrich feather boa, and looked exactly like the great
Wagnerian diva she always longed to become. There was not
much room for us both on the love seat, especially chosen for its
size, so what with the excitement, the loving gestures, and dramatic emotion we expressed, we succeeded in both toppling off
the seat in an unexpected climax to the roars of amusement from
our audience. We were terribly embarrassed, but found we
were the hit of the show!

To celebrate an anniversary of our parents' marriage, my sister
Réné wrote a "masque," which was a much more elaborate affair than we had been used to. As usual, we performed it in the
drawing room at home, but it was considered so good that we
were asked to produce it again for some charity in the local
town hall, with added scenes and actors. The parents were de-

lighted, and we were allowed to do it in our holidays. Our play was acclaimed by the public and critics alike, besides which we had the extra satisfaction of making a considerable sum of money for the charity. Papa decided the play should be printed, so it remains the one printed record of our happy days of play-acting, and was the first of several works written by my sister Réné.

It was soon discovered, from a report to my parents by her teacher in England, that my sister Luia had an unusually lovely singing voice. Her future as an operatic singer began to be discussed, while I listened with increasing excitement to the idea that Luia might after all become the "diva" she had always hoped she could be. Finally it was decided that she should be sent to be trained by Madame Albani, a friend of Mama's who was then at the height of her fame singing at Covent Garden. Mama had met her through Canadian friends in London, for Albani had been born a Canadian and only adopted her stage name at the advice of her famous Italian teacher, Lamperti. Mama felt sure that she could persuade the great diva to train Luia, who was another "daughter of the Empire," as it were.

That meant a journey to London, where she was successful, and Luia began studying seriously for an operatic career. We watched her progress with anxiety, though no one doubted she would become a great prima donna, for she had seemed to be destined for that from the very beginning. She was a gifted actress and had a sense of the theater; the only question was whether she had the volume of voice grand opera required, as well as the stamina for the hard training and sustained work. From London she was sent to study with Jean de Reszke in Paris, where her introduction to the fascinating world of opera began. Mama rushed over again to settle her in, more worried over her moral welfare than her success!

The following year, my governess and I went to France with Mama, who was going for her annual cure to Germany. It was arranged that we should stop in Paris en route, see Luia, and hear reports of her progress. I had been there before when I was much younger, but by this time I spoke French fairly fluently and understood what was said to me. It was really the first time I could appreciate Paris, French manners, and French customs, besides that particular quality which makes everything about the French essentially French.

Paris had always been talked about in our house; Mama had lived there with her parents, had studied there, and had always had a Parisian dressmaker, which called for frequent visits to the gay city. She had many French friends whom she had got to know while my sister Réné was studying painting in Julien's atelier. It was fun being with her there, for she knew her way about the city and the many places of interest, which I had grown to recognize from gazing at the countless photographs we had of them in pictorial albums at home.

How beautiful I thought it was, all illumined in a sort of silvery light, almost opalescent; the pulse of the city quick, exciting. No wonder Paris called herself *la ville lumière*. Mama used to talk of it, her eyes sparkling.

"Paris," she would say, "has always prided herself on being the center of all that is most brilliant, artistic, intellectual, in the whole world, because she isn't like any other city. . . . But of course, Paris isn't France. The provinces are very different— you will see for yourself one day."

Years later it all came about, as I am sure Mama knew it would. I studied in Paris, where I had a studio for some years, and traveled the lovely countryside from north to south, learning as I went along, through the beauty of French Gothic art and architecture, much that the French have contributed to our civilization. But that was all to happen in the future. Now I was enraptured by everything I saw as we drove up the Avenue Champs-Élysées, with the Arc de Triomphe eloquent against the sky, feeling a kind of grandeur, a sort of majesty I had never felt before in any city—not even London, where I had spent so much of my childhood, and stood misty-eyed watching the

king and queen as they drove in state between the cheering
crowds to Westminster. Nothing in London was quite compa-
rable; indeed, it seemed to have nothing in common with Paris,
where there was a tingle in the air, almost a lilting tune that I
imagined I could hear.

In London we had lived in a rather rigid fashion, staying with
friends in a large, cold house or hotels, as we came and went.
But the life, so often colored by rain, contrasted vividly with
the easy freedom of the sunshine of the Cape Peninsula. In Paris
we stayed at the Hôtel Vuillemont, then a popular family hos-
telry, where Luia met us, exuberant over her lessons with the
maître. She was living in a pension, well chaperoned by a distant relative of Papa's known as Aunt Kate, a rather dreary lady
from my point of view, who accompanied Luia daily to her lessons at the Rue de la Faisanderie, ever watchful of any masculine approach.

"I have arranged for you to come and hear my lesson
tomorrow," Luia told Mama excitedly, "and perhaps if you
come a little early you will meet Melba, who came in only yes-
terday to work with Jean on her role in *Otello*, which she is
singing here next week. We had a wonderful lunch afterwards,
for she loves Jean's cooking. . . . But what a voice," she added.
"Even if she can't act, one can just listen."

Luia took us to tea with a fascinating woman I shall always
remember, a charming person named Mlle Berthe Merol, who
was teaching her stage deportment. An actress belonging to the
company of the Comédie Française, Miss Merol lived in Whis-
tler's one-time studio in the Rue du Bac, where she taught only
selected pupils. I can see her still, not very tall but exquisitely
graceful in flowing gray chiffon, presiding over her tea tray of
lovely china, chatting to Mama while I looked at bibelots and
varied mementos of the theater. Luia had been sent to her by de
Reszke, for she had trained many of the "great" in opera to act
in her special method, the technique required for all performers
at the Comédie Française.

After the interview with de Reszke, Mama was very encouraged about Luia's future. He had arranged for her to make her debut in Italy singing Santuzza in *Cavalleria Rusticana,* "to gain experience," then, after the debut, study in Milan in preparation for singing *Aïda* in Cairo the following season, with *Tosca* also in her repertoire. This was all to happen in the fateful year that the First World War burst upon humanity. Though she gathered praises for her Santuzza, appearing just before the war broke out, Cairo, together with her future plans, was canceled, so she had to return from Milan with grand opera a dream for the future.

England was in a turmoil, with every thought concentrated on the war effort, and, though she sang for charities and the Red Cross, her career was at a standstill. What would have happened had Luia not married a young Foreign Office official, who was a secretary of Sir Edward Grey as well, is a matter of conjecture. The war was certainly the deciding factor in her decision to marry, the future being darkened by the power of Germany. As the wife of a diplomat, she was not allowed to sing professionally, so that her performances at both the Albert and Queen's Halls were only given by special permission of Her Majesty, Queen Mary, who was her husband's godmother.

Gradually, Sir Courtney Forbes, who had married Luia at the start of his career, climbed the long ladder of the Foreign Office to become minister to Mexico, then Spain, and ultimately ambassador to Peru. Much of his success was due to the sheer force of my sister's personality, her charm, but above all her understanding of the people of the countries where she and her husband served Great Britain—an invaluable gift in diplomatic circles. "We will never forget her," said many to me in my later life.

She was fortunate in inheriting our mother's talent for entertaining, for she made the various embassies she occupied into centers of interest as well as of successful public relations. And when her husband died she used her special training in acting to make a new career for herself as a teacher and lecturer. Wherever she has been, in countries as widely different as India, Latin America, Holland, or the United States, she has earned her own distinction, winning recognition from various heads of states for her efforts. Thus she has continued to earn her own living through these last years.

If my estimation of my youngest sister seems exaggerated, I would say that she is an exaggerated subject. I am, and always have been, perfectly aware of her failings, her feminine sense of the dramatic, but her gallantry and above all her generosity have won the respect of all. That she was born gifted gave her peculiar advantages, but that she used her gifts for the benefit of many is to the credit of her great heart. Throughout my life I have learned to respect the spirit that dwells in some people who, even despite lack of opportunity, money, or other advantages, still carry a sacred spark that lights up their surroundings, and illuminates the paths of others. It has to do with an enthusiasm for life, a joy in God's world of nature that encompasses color and sound. These fortunate ones never seem to grow old, but die singing a canticle of praise. Luia has such a spirit. I remember her scrambling up a stony hillside at the Cape, undeterred by her weight or the difficulties of finding a path, to seize a certain flower we had seen from our passing car. Back she came, radiant, clutching her prize, which shaped like a chalice of pink petals, held within it a thousand glittering stamens.

"Have you ever seen anything as beautiful?" she exclaimed, breathless from her climb. "It is like some fairy creature that lighted on a stem to turn into a lily, and with what a scent!"

One was immediately persuaded by her infectious pleasure.

If I could have viewed my sisters without bias, they would not appear as a "bevy of proper Edwardian young ladies," as one of my critics has said of my picture of them. But I was biased: I did think of them as virtuous, gifted, and superior; I didn't see their failings, though of course they had them.

I knew that Réné's affectations were just that; and Helen's eye drops, which she used constantly, were not only because she had "conjunctivitis," as she would often explain, but because they made her large, luminous eyes that much brighter; or that Luia's exaggerations, which I suspected were never harmful, only added more dramatic content, more excitement to the event or person she was describing.

I sometimes wonder what Siegfried might have thought of his marvelous aunts, the invincible Walküre, though I feel sure that to him they were wonderful, that he thought of them with the same awe that I did my sisters.

As I have said, I never remember having all four at home with me at once, and the three elder girls seemed to enjoy being together without any friction. Papa kept a watchful eye on all of us, and, had there been open rebellion on any of their parts (I was still too afraid of him to have dared), he would have suppressed it rapidly. In the privacy of their bedrooms there may have been arguments and jealousies, but these never reached me. Though their natures were very different their sense of humor smoothed out any discord. They were spoiled, loved, indulged, but it was a happy household, which each of us valued.

5. Three Unanswered Questions

I. THE RAIN QUEEN

As a teen-age boy I think it was the anxiety of my mother over the ever-present threat to me of tuberculosis that necessitated my being sent away from home each winter to avoid the change of climate.

The climate of the Cape is mild and equable for most of the year, but, even though we lived under the protection of Table Mountain, as each winter drew near there arose the question of where I should be sent and how much this break in my education would defer my progress. But it was due to this necessity that I was given the opportunities to see various areas of the country and learn as I did about places and people that might not normally ever have come my way. Sometimes I went to stay on farms on the karroo owned by clients of Papa's, or I was accepted into the family circle of friends of my parents—a judge associate of my father's, or a high commissioner in some area well away from damp or rain. It is to these friends that I owe a debt of gratitude for the varied, often exciting experiences among the animals or natives that made such an impression on my mind as a boy.

It was while I was visiting the high commissioner of an area in the northeastern Transvaal that I heard of a native tribe called the Lovedu living within the jurisdiction of my host. They are said to be an offshoot of the great migration of the Bantu race that swept south from Central Africa like an immense black stream. In what is now South Africa, they settled to form the various peoples known to us as the Zulu, Xhosa, Basutu, and others. But, despite the coming of the white man and the influence of education, even of the missionaries, the Lovedu had retained the customs, beliefs, and old tribal laws of their ancestors. The reason for their resistance, my host told me, was their belief in the magical power of their ancient ruler, the mysterious "rain queen," whose secret knowledge supposedly traverses the centuries to the very heart of Africa.

Her *kraal*, or capital, is in an area where the hills crowd one upon another, and where the people, dependent upon the rainfall, cultivate the hillsides with the necessary crops to sustain the tribe. The "queens," with the extraordinary powers granted to them by their ancestors, have been one of the great mysteries of Africa ever since the coming of the white man, feared but revered through generations. Anthropologists have studied this strange belief in one old dark woman. They tell us that "she is chosen for her role by the ghost of her predecessor, and her destined end is death by her own hands in order that she may rule by divine right." She is believed to be not merely the "transformer of the clouds" but the guardian of the changing seasons as well. This is her sole purpose, her continual care.

"Have you ever met the queen?" I asked my host, inquisitive about this strange ruler.

"Only once," he said. "She received me when I was appointed to this area, but in all matters that concern her tribe I communicate through her councillors."

"Couldn't we visit her?" I asked hopefully.

"I'm afraid not," he replied. "She is sacred, you know, and closely guarded, but you must come with me and we'll visit one of her chiefs, Lobezu. He is quite a pal of mine, full of his own importance, what with twenty-eight wives and a large herd of cattle."

"Does he really believe in the queen's power?" I asked incredulously.

"Rather. Though he is supposedly Christian, I can't help feeling that his faith is somewhat confused."

"I should think so," I said, "and what about the other converts—are there many in the tribe?"

"Plenty, but even they fear the power of the queen, and somehow rationalize their belief in her with the God they now supposedly serve."

It seemed incredible to me, young though I was, that so pagan a practice could still flourish in the midst of the white man's matter-of-fact world, where law and the Christian faith were established. Yet there, hidden in her royal *kraal*, lived this sacred, magical personage still in contact with the gods who could bring life to the lands of the tribe. Mujaji was her name, and she was probably the last of the direct line of queens, for her people are spreading and the influences of a world that knows her not are beyond her control. They are encroaching on her domain, her people, and her powers with all the factual ugliness of mechanics. She cannot escape into the shadowed quiet where she can tend the "rain pots" she has to brew and distill according to the ancient knowledge that she alone possesses.

The method of her magic has never been disclosed as far as I know, but the ingredients of her "rain pots" are said to be both strange and numerous. Such oddities as human skin, specially prepared; parts of the great koodoo bull, one of the larger antelopes; a quantity of seawater carried during the night by her runners from the ocean, many miles away. The hide of the scaly anteater is an important adjunct to the mixture, for it is a royal animal, which, if caught alive, must be brought to the queen. One other item essential to the brew is the termite, the flying ants that appear after the first rain. These must be gathered by the virgins of the tribe, who collect as well the first green sprouts of the crops. All must be fed into the "rain pots," each with its own peculiar significance, though how the pots are used in the working of the magic only the queen knows. The tribe has also to accept the wisdom of the "rain doctor," who works closely with the queen, divining by hidden means the causes of drought, or of forces due to hatred or disobedience that may be at work to hinder the queen from carrying out her mission.

This "rain doctor" is none other than the counterpart of the witch doctor attached to every tribe throughout Africa. Such an individual has been part of the court of every ruler since time immemorial, whether in Egypt, Ethiopia, Babylon, or elsewhere; whether known as a "wise man," "soothsayer," or "prophet"; whether gifted with divine foresight, miraculous powers, or, we would say, extrasensory perception. He has been maintained as the necessary medium between the living and the so-called dead ancestors, supposedly interpreting their will to their good or disobedient progeny.

At once we enter the realm of African beliefs in the spirit of their ancestors, in the power of "taboo," of good and evil forces. I have learned that we have to recognize that the African community includes both the living and the so-called dead, and also that there is a constant coming and going between these two worlds, for the living are always passing from the one into the ranks of the other. The spirit that assumes a material body is not confined to that body but becomes a sort of protecting aura. So the spirits are roundabout, accessible, even able to speak to the living through the lips of their mediums, for there are methods of divination by which their will can be discovered.

This is a vast subject on which I am no authority. I have gathered only scattered bits of knowledge through my friends in various areas of southern Africa, whether they were professors or judges, such as Tom Graham of Grahamstown, or missionaries, as was Edwin Smith, whose books show profound research into the psychology and beliefs of the African peoples.

We wound our way up the slopes toward the mountain where Lobezu's people had settled in the safe fastness of rocks and trees. As we passed shrubs and grasses I didn't recognize, I remembered that the commissioner had told me that the medical uses of all the natural flora that surrounds them had always been part of the culture of this tribe.

I persisted with questions to my host. "Don't we even know how long they have been here?"

"They say this settlement is very old, but you see," he explained, "we really know very little about them. They are suspicious of interference by the white man, and don't like being questioned."

"In any case, I don't suppose all this can go on much longer," I said.

"Well, the last queen is supposed to have tricked the Boer general who came to see her about some rebellion among the tribes."

"What did she do?" I asked.

"She hid herself, and let him talk to someone she sent to impersonate her. She was much too scared to mingle with any ordinary intruder," he said, laughing.

The more I heard about this extraordinary personage, the more unreal she seemed to become.

"That was the same queen," he went on, "who killed herself by taking poison, and inspired Rider Haggard to write his novel *She*."

"My father knew Haggard well," I said, "and I met him when he came to our house."

"Did you?" he said. "Then I expect your father knew it was Rhodes, with all his stories of what he had seen and heard, who really inspired Rider Haggard, urging him to come up this way."

"He went to Zimbabwe, I know. I want to get there somehow and see it all myself."

We dismounted at the base of a steep promontory, where we left the guards with the horses. At once we were surrounded by groups of children of all ages, peering at us from behind the boulders or running ahead of us up the winding path leading to the village. The bright-eyed children of the Bantu, with their smooth, shining skin, their beautiful little bodies naked to the sun, have a peculiar charm. They always seem happy, always playful; one seldom hears them crying, and, though they are very shy with strangers, they seem to have a natural courtesy.

Several elders of the tribe came to meet us, greeting the commissioner in their native dialect, which he spoke perfectly. They led us to a clearing among the adobe huts, in the center of which were three chairs placed on leopard skins. But there was no chief, no sign nor sound from the people. It added a somewhat eerie atmosphere to the place itself, remote and hidden from the world with only the queen as its pulsing heart. Around the clearing, banana trees hung out their huge, green leaves like tattered banners over the thatched roofs of the huts; around us the clouds, so important to the cult of the queen, seemed to be waiting on her will, resting on the peaks of the hills surrounding the village.

"The chief usually waits for us to be announced," said my host. "Then he will probably lead us to his own yard, where I expect he will entertain us with beer and, I hope, some dances."

Over to the side I noticed a huge drum, the bowl apparently of hollowed wood and over which a hide was stretched taut and pegged to the sides. The Commissioner told me that drums played an important part in the culture, as they do throughout all Africa, but that the Lovedu have two types of drums: some for communications only, round and played with drumsticks, and others of a narrow, cylindrical form played with the hands, for ceremonies and the secret rain dances. The drums used in the rainmaking rituals are sacred and never seen by the people; their structure is secret as well, for strips of human skin are pasted under the resonator of ox hide.

Lobezu appeared, accompanied by two of the elders who had greeted us. To my surprise, he was dressed in dark European trousers and a white coat, not, as I had expected, in royal regalia of feathers and skins. He shook hands with us in European fashion and led us between the huts to another clearing, where a large household chair had been placed in the center beside what looked like a modern washtub.

I was fascinated by the decorations, black and white geometric patterns that covered the front walls of the surrounding huts. The chief sat down as we were ushered onto a pile of leopard skins heaped on the polished mud floor. We were hardly seated when from the foremost hut a group of women crawled out on hands and knees, to sit in a long row around the circle of the clearing. These were Lobezu's wives, young, attractive, shining smooth, their skin glowing as though polished brown copper. They were almost nude except for a small apron, but their ornaments of rows of beads, countless bracelets, and anklets of copper and brass made them appear almost fully dressed. They made no sound, but knelt silent, statuesque, looking rather serious, without laughter or bright smiles. I was at once reminded of the animals of the African landscape, who partake of their surroundings, static, hardly visible, who do not seem alive at all until they move. Lovely, sinuous, these dark women also seemed at one with nature, the trees, the flowering shrubs, silent but gleaming with iridescent color, more like rare birds than humans.

Lobezu bent over the washtub, dipping a large ladle into it to withdraw some liquid he proceeded to sip, smiling at us between his gulps, and finally holding up a full ladle to me. At this gesture of welcome, two of the young wives crawled forward to kneel in front of their lord and master. Their hands folded, with heads lowered in submission, they began in low murmuring tone to recite in unison. I discovered later they were repeating a long list of compliments, with flattering similes, to the manner and looks of their guests, me and the commissioner!

"Go on," the commissioner prompted, "Lobezu wants you to drink from his ladle."

"What is it?" I murmured nervously.

"You'll see," he said. "Only kneel when he gives it to you."

As I went forward to kneel before the chief, the women started a crooning, humming song and I glanced up quickly at the sound. Each wife had crossed her long, graceful arms and grasped the hands of the woman next to her, making a chain of slim, dark arms like an undulating snake swaying back and forth to the rhythm of their song.

Even this could not distract me from the potent, sickening smell of the liquid in the ladle. Lobezu nodded, smiling a white, flashing smile as I brought the evil-smelling ladle to my lips. I was conscious that every eye was on me, so that no matter how I felt, with my insides heaving at the smell, I knew I mustn't fail, nor disgrace my kind host by offending the chief and his tribe. Somehow I swallowed, got to my feet, and managed to bow, using all my willpower not to repulse the disgusting liquid.

Now, as my host went up to accept his portion, the women began to sing a happy tune, clapping their hands to accent the rhythm. Rising to form a line again, the women joined hands and proceeded to dance with shuffling steps in tune with their song. Quite unself-conscious now, and gazing at us boldly, the chorus of wives danced a regular monotonous measure while Lobezu continued to drink slowly from his ladle, admiring the swaying, supple line of dancers.

I knew that kaffir beer, as it is called, is an essential part of all native life. It is considered the food of the gods by the Lovedu, so there is much ritual attached to the drinking. It is drunk with leisure and decorum, and, though it induces a high state of excitement among the drinkers, real drunkenness is not tolerated but severely dealt with.

Lobezu now told us that in honor of our coming, the people would have a feast and, as customary, the honored guests were to select an ox from his herd, which would be roasted for all to share. So we returned to the open square, seating ourselves in the three chairs with the chief between us, whence we could look down onto a clearing among the trees.

With shouts and yells from the herdsmen, the royal oxen were driven into the open. The commissioner, using a stick given him by the chief, went down to choose his victim from among the tall, bony beasts with the huge, widespread horns common to most African cattle.

"It is the custom," he told me, "to offer the guest an ox, but the joke is that the guest is then expected to return it to the chief for the tribe. We may be lucky to even be given a joint to carry home with us."

We soon took our leave of Lobezu, though nothing was said about our share of the spoils.

"I don't think he will forget us altogether," said my host. "Probably, when they have finished feasting, he will remember."

The day after our visit we received a small steak wrapped in a banana leaf, brought by one of Lobezu's men as a present. We had not been forgotten.

II. THE NDEBELE

I went to stay with a legal associate of my father's, who with
his kindly wife lived in a charming house overlooking the town
of Pretoria. They had no children, but when they had visited
the Cape they stayed with us. I found them kind, appreciative
people, and they seemed to like me. I was having lessons in taxidermy at the time, and I think it was our mutual affection for
the birds of the country that aroused their interest in me. Thus
it was arranged that, as winter grew nearer, the time for my
yearly exodus from the Cape, I should visit them. "You'll find
that you don't know many of our birds in the Transvaal," said
my future host. "We have some beauties," he added. "We'll
also introduce you to one of our friends at the museum, who
is painting a book on our birds. He'll teach you a lot about them."

I was excited by the thought of going to Pretoria for the first
time. To those of us living at the Cape, proud of our origin

under Table Mountain, the golden, diamondiferous aura of the cities of the north had something almost suspicious about it. There was gossip of the grasping, treasure-seeking world that had rushed into Johannesburg when gold had been discovered, while Pretoria, so prominent during the Boer War, was the center of all the "rebel" activities. It had been the capital of the old Transvaal Republic and was therefore considered to be mainly Afrikaans speaking.

But with the coming of union, when the four states—Natal, the Transvaal, the Orange Free State, and the Cape Colony—joined hands in 1910, Pretoria, founded in 1850 by M. W. Pretorius, the first president of the South African Republic, became the administrative capital of the Union, and both the official languages were freely spoken there. To effect a compromise that would satisfy the descendants of many of the early settlers, Cape Town was made the parliamentary capital of the government. This division of function still necessitates a migration each year of hundreds of public servants from Pretoria to the Cape for the session of Parliament, which still sits in the old Houses of Parliament in Cape Town.

Papa had told me some of the history of Pretoria when I began to learn about the Boer War. I read a great deal about President Kruger, that great emblem of Afrikaner history, who represented to his people all the qualities of determination, courage, and faith. I remember as a small boy seeing pictures of him, the trusted patriarch, sitting solidly in his frock coat and top hat with his hand on his Bible, radiating the fierce strength that resisted all the plans and machinations of my hero, Cecil John Rhodes. One felt sorry for "old Kruger," as we used to call him, old and in exile from his beloved land, dying in Switzerland only a few years after Britain had won the Boer War.

I have lived long enough to see his ideal for his people almost fulfilled. South Africa is indeed a republic, though torn by a dark strife even President Kruger never imagined.

As I write, pictures of three unforgettable buildings in Pretoria come to my mind. The Union Building (1913), of majestic scale and set on a hillside surrounded by lovely gardens, was designed by Sir Herbert Baker, the spiritual offspring of Cecil Rhodes, whose house at the Cape, "Groot Schuur," Baker had built. Another is the Voortrekker Monument, a symbol of Afrikaner solidarity, which rises massive and immense on a rocky ridge outside the city. It is the focal point of Afrikaner faith with its vision, its poetry, its dominating strength.

The third building I see contains within it some of my dreams, aspirations, even some of the despair of my life. Years after the time I have been recording I went to Pretoria to execute two mural paintings in the City Hall. They were so large they took me two years to paint on canvas, though they were ultimately stretched and pasted onto the walls.

The choice of their subjects was a matter of discussion between me and my clients, who were presenting these works to Pretoria to ornament the City Hall. On one of the walls, I wanted to depict the historical incident of the presentation of a Bible by the local British residents to the "trekking" Boers as they passed through on their way to their ultimate goal on the Witwatersrand. The original Bible is still to be seen in the Pretoria Museum where I found it. Instantly I decided that if I could get approval I would record this gesture of friendship and solidarity between the English- and Afrikaans-speaking South Africans. The idea was at once approved, and at the unveiling ceremony, when I was flattered by congratulations and my efforts praised before a large gathering, I offered up a silent prayer of gratitude for having been allowed to portray this historic event. It was my profound hope that in some way my work might help to heal the wounds that still bleed in the Afrikaners when any memory of the Boer War touches their hearts.

But none of these buildings existed in the days I am writing about.

As I got out of the train to first set foot in Pretoria, I was suddenly conscious of entering a different atmosphere, a world I only knew by hearsay or by reading. The voice of my host on the station platform awoke me to reality; "Welcome to *ons land*," he said. "We are so glad you have come."

As we drove to my host's house on the hill, I realized that many of the streets were lined with trees: some tall eucalyptus, some the thorny mimosa of the bushveld, here and there a *boerboom* (schotia) growing in cultivated gardens filled with flowers.

"Oh, look," I exclaimed, as with a flash of orange and black a bird darted into the hedge of bauhinia, a plant with clusters of scarlet flowers I grew to know well in the Transvaal.

"That was a bush shrike, I think," said my host. "He is a cousin of your bokmakierie. He sings duets with his mate just as yours do," he added.

Once into the garden of my new home I knew I was not at the Cape any longer by the different flora flourishing everywhere, trees and shrubs I only knew from pictures, as were the birds flitting through the underbrush. I had learned enough ornithology to know that because most of Europe is subject to severe winters there is an enormous migration of birds into and out of Africa every year. Many varieties don't even come as far south as the Cape, so there were many I had never seen or heard that choose the Transvaal as their habitat. Spring not only brings the troops of wintering birds from the Northern Hemisphere, but at the same time brings birds from tropical Africa who come south to breed. There are not many entirely indigenous varieties peculiar only to South Africa. Besides, I knew how easily I could be fooled into thinking I recognized a certain species when in South Africa there are often many species of the same group of birds that differ only slightly.

Most African birds don't sing for any length of time like the birds I had heard in Europe, or the glorious English blackbird or nightingale, whose songs can go on and on in infinite variation. I hoped that perhaps there, hidden in the shrubbery of the garden, I might hear the song of some new bird I did not know; but other than a rich ringing call now and then, or an undercurrent of brief, gentle singing, I heard nothing. There were some contributors I recognized with pleasure; the Cape robin and the ubiquitous sparrows, and some gay canaries traveling in bright-colored groups. But from my point of view I never heard a new bird song during my entire stay in Pretoria, though, as I have said, I did, as time passed, see many new species.

Staying in the house as another guest was a man I got to know well that winter, and in the end to love as a friend. Dr. Felix Brewer was a half German, English-speaking South African who had been born at the Cape and who possessed the enthusiasms that endeared him to all. I realized this from the way my hostess described him to me.

"You will grow to realize what an unusual person Felix is," she said. "Quite apart from his happy nature, as his name implies, there is nothing he doesn't know about."

How well I was to appreciate this description I only realized later.

Felix had one unfortunate mannerism that irritated terribly until one grew to accept it. He stumbled as he began to talk, as though thinking, undecided about how to begin, so that "Um . . . er . . ." always heralded his brilliant, often witty conversations. He was not tall, neither was he too short to be perfectly proportioned; he wore glasses that covered his large, innocent-looking blue eyes. He had strong, beautiful hands, which he used as Europeans do to accentuate their words. How much I learned from him, how I laughed at his wit, how deeply I missed all he gave me I only understood when he died.

At breakfast the next morning my host announced, "I am going to take Jan over to visit the Ndebele. Would you like to come with us, Felix?"

"Um . . . er . . . but of course," said Felix. "Um . . . are they very incestuous?"

The question seemed to shatter the breakfast conversation. I wasn't sure what incest really meant, except that I knew it was something that people were not allowed to indulge in.

"Far from it," was the answer. "They live by very strict moral laws."

All the way over the crouching hills that surround Pretoria my two companions talked of the unusual tribe we were going to visit. I learned from their conversation that the Ndebele come from Nguni stock out of the valleys of Zululand, but had broken from the main stream of that family to which both the Zulus and the Xhosas belong. By moving they had escaped the subjugation, the merging influences of domination that Chaka, the great Zulu chief, had enforced upon all his vassal tribes. These he had welded into one huge nation that in his vanity he had named the Amazulu—("the people of heaven"). The tribes of the Ndebele, scattered though they were, clung tenaciously to their Nguni culture despite their contacts with people of another stock. Thus, perhaps they had preserved customs and rituals that the Zulus themselves, thundering through the land in battle and bloodshed, had lost long ago.

Whatever the truth of their inheritance may be, the fact remains that, although mural decoration is characteristic of other African peoples, nothing like the invention or variety seen in the paintings of the Ndebele is to be found elsewhere. Their techniques are the same as others; they use paints made of the same colored clays and earths found locally, but the terraces, courtyards, and steps that are their architectural expression are unique when covered with the vivid designs they paint on the plaster surfaces. There is a grandeur about the scale of the rising walls and platforms they build that is surely reminiscent of something lost in the past, perhaps cities of great fortifications, of public areas walled around by decorated plaster. Huts or terraces are all made of the same mud and dung mixture, resulting in a sort of "adobe," as we know it. Their villages suggest order and dignity, the expression of an organized people. Everything is tidy, neat; their designs are precise, the paintings highly finished, the balance conceived with knowledge, one might even say sophistication.

"The strangest wonder of it is," said my host, "that the artists are all women. The men can't paint."

"Um . . . er . . . a thoroughly matriarchal system," agreed Felix. "They paint, design, or thread their lovely beads with an inherited talent they themselves cannot explain.

"After all," he went on, "women began by being the original artists of the world, the music makers, the singers, the craftsmen, until the twilight of the goddesses."

"I don't know about that," I said. "What happened?"

Then Felix in his inimitable way told us of the rule of women, first as mothers, the bearers of life, the magical daughters of the Moon. They were then the authority over religion, music and the arts; of their goddesses, who were worshipped by both sexes, of Isis, Artemis, Demeter, and Cybele. Whatever their names in whichever part of the then-known world they were worshiped, they represented woman power as the active, beneficent principle of all life, mothers of all things, generators of all creative power.

"Remember," Felix said, interrupting himself, "the Greeks chose Athena as the guardian of Athens."

"Then what happened?" I asked impatiently. "What was the twilight you mentioned?"

"Um . . . er . . . ," he said, "it was about 500 B.C., and supposedly commenced with the Chinese, who say that real civilization began when men determined to know who their own children were, and to assume responsibility for their care and education. Men began to take over, assuming the women's religious rites, even dressing as woman so as not to make the change too obvious. Apollo usurped the leadership of the Muses, taking the lyre from Artemis; Zeus became lord of the universe, subjecting Hera, who had ruled by her own right, to the subservient role of a wife; even hymns formerly sung to the Mother of the World began to invoke the gods."

Men were in the ascendant. The Jews, who altered the pattern of the world, disposed of the goddesses by banishing them; even Ishtar, one of the most powerful Semitic deities, became superseded by various male-female divinities of the mythology of the Near East, where the Sumerians and the Hittites had previously established goddess worship. In 3000 B.C. Yahweh was god of the Hebrews; he was then worshiped as man-woman together.

I was so hypnotized by all that Felix was telling us that I was quite unconscious that we had crossed the hills and were approaching the village. Still trying to absorb all Felix had said, I could hardly believe that it appeared exactly as it had been described. But there were the decorated walls like ramparts, with steps leading through an opening into a smooth, cleared courtyard, surrounded in turn by decorated walls. Most of the designs, bold in concept, some quite abstract, were painted in black, terra-cotta, or ocher on white surfaces, the whole effect vivid and powerful.

There was no one about, no sound other than the bleating of goats herded in the background.

Walking through one of the entrances I caught sight of a woman, seated facing an unfinished painting on a wall, her baby and her paints beside her. As I walked toward her she leaped up like some wild animal, and, enfolding her wide-eyed baby in her arms, she rushed into her hut nearby. Only the slow flattery of my host, who was able to converse with her in her language, and the sight of money lured her out again into the blazing sunshine, where I was able to photograph her.

"Please ask her," I said, "whether she knows what she is painting?"

She dropped her eyes and slowly shook her head.

"Where did she learn what to paint?"

"From my mother," came the reply.

"And do you know where she learned?"

"From her mother," was the immediate answer.

"Don't your brothers or any of the men paint?"

At this she flashed a wide smile that illumined her whole face, but, shaking her head, "Only my sisters," she said archly.

Here then was the true matriarchal structure, where the inherited knowledge, in which men had no part, was handed on from mother to daughter, just as it had been in the days Felix had told us about—the arts originating no one knows where or when, being carried on only by the women, who alone retain the old traditional customs of their ancestors.

In the past the men had their own responsibilities—warfare, obtaining food, care of the livestock—but now they all wear European clothes and are off to work on the farms or in the neighboring town. The women still design and paint their walls or sit like dark birds, vital and iridescent, threading their beads into patterns for bangles or necklaces. These they wear on their arms and ankles, together with countless others of brass or copper that glint and sparkle as they move. Over their shoulders, covering their short petticoats of soft hide, they drape a colored woolen blanket. Like most African tribes, this one has found the imported blanket the answer to their needs, serving as a protection against both heat and cold.

We approached a group of women working in silence on a raised platform, seemingly quite unconscious of our presence. There was an animal grace about their movements, the turn of their closely shaven heads, their slim necks with the light gleaming as brightly on their polished skin as on their necklaces. We asked if we might be allowed to visit one of their huts, whose thatched roofs I could see beyond the painted walls. Depending on the number of his wives, a man may own several huts. The more wives a man has the greater his esteem among the tribe; their number depends in turn upon his ability to purchase them in terms of cattle, the usual medium throughout Africa. Each hut must be "doctored" with traditional ceremony by a witch doctor. Before the foundations are laid, pegs smeared with medicinal ointments are buried at the corners and center of the site, to protect the inhabitants from evil forces exerted upon them by their enemies.

We were invited in by one of the older women, who led us up the decorated steps into the shadow of her hut. Each hut is surrounded by a smooth mud-floored yard, which in turn is bounded by a high wall. Along the base of the interior wall runs a low, projecting seat with the upright surface painted, some of it with a repetitive design of white lines on an ocher ground, or black on the natural clay. Sometimes the designs are scratched into the damp clay with a sharp stick, though most of them are painted.

I was impressed by the fact that very few designs included a recognizable object. Unlike the Bushmen paintings, there is no attempt to portray people or animals or environment; nothing but an intellectualized mural decoration surrounds them. They are essentially decorators, not painters in our sense, yet the effect they create is one of gaiety, vitality, shadow, and light with a precision at once fascinating and satisfying to the eye.

The subtle smell of the warm thatch permeated the gloom inside. There was just enough light to I could see that the Ndebele build a lower inner wall running parallel to the outer wall of their huts, creating a corridor around the inner sanctum. In this space they keep the simple stores and possessions, the drying heads of corn, some earthen cooking pots, and in neat rolls the straw sleeping mats of the family. The inner area was completely empty and lit only by the one entrance where we stood, though a small aperture in the center of the roof through which the smoke from the fire escaped let in a shaft of sunlight. I could see that the floor was scrupulously clean, with a hollowed-out circle in the center for the fireplace; around this one could imagine the whole family sitting on the polished floor, encircled by their imaginative paintings, waiting for the great pot on the fire to cook.

Having thanked our hostess and said good-bye to the now smiling ladies, we walked back to the car.

"What do you think it is," I asked Felix, "that makes these people decorate every square foot of wall space?"

"Um . . . er . . ." He thought for a moment. "They don't like all that bare plaster, I imagine," he said, "any more than the Japanese, who hang kakemonos on their walls, or we, who like pictures to look at."

"Perhaps you are right," I said, "but another thing puzzles me," I went on. "If it is the memory of something lost in the past, why is it only this tribe that remembers?"

"Er . . . that no doubt is puzzling all the anthropologists," he answered.

Perhaps a closer study will yield the ethnological information needed to answer this mystery, which, like many others that puzzle the white man, lies obscured in the dark, pulsating heart of native Africa.

III. ZIMBABWE

How many of us believe that old buildings or ancient habitations throughout the world retain within their walls an atmosphere that radiates from the structure itself? This atmosphere can only be sensed by those who have highly developed nervous systems, or have what is known as extrasensory perception. It is argued that the history associated with a particular area or room can account for this sensation, that the imagination itself creates this feeling. Places whose background is lost in antiquity convey to certain people a mysterious message of something out of the past, particularly if violence and bloodshed were involved, hence the persistent idea that certain places are haunted. Does one believe that crime or torture of the human spirit can exhale an influence that remains hanging in the very air to be felt by those sensitive enough to capture this "air of the unseen," which even sightseers or relic hunters fail to disturb?

In Africa, two hundred miles inland from Sofala, a port on the east coast, lies a ruin, a temple, a citadel, a ruined city. To date it remains one of the great archaeological mysteries of our time, in that no one can say who built it, exactly for what purpose, or at what date. Despite countless theories, some quite fantastic, little can be substantiated. Archaeologists have come and gone, books have been written, theories tentatively presented, but the mystery of Zimbabwe remains as silent and mysterious as when it was first discovered in the African darkness by Adam Renders in 1868.

I have told earlier of how my interest in this place was aroused by Cecil John Rhodes himself when he described it to me in his great room at "Groot Schuur." And, since Papa took me to Zimbabwe when I was very young, the impression of that first experience has never left me.

My father had legal business in Salisbury, capital of Rhodesia, which offered an opportunity to take me over to see the place that had filled my mind from the moment I had been told about it. Indeed, I had never ceased to worry him to find some way of allowing me to go there. Though we only spent a few hours at the ruins, it was enough to whet my appetite.

At the entrance to the ruins we found a native guard who spoke English and warned us not to go up to the acropolis without him. But we were allowed to wander through the temple areas unaccompanied. So with Papa as my guide, giving me bits of information as we went along, my excitement grew, until I silently vowed to myself that somehow I would return when I could have more time to study the whole extraordinary enigma. Everything I had read by then only added to the mystery surrounding the area, so that, when I actually saw it, walking down the corridor between the silvered walls of the temple, I was tingling with an excitement I could neither explain nor control.

On our drive back, Papa told me all that had been deduced about the origin of the ruins, the contradictions, the arguments as to the date, the builders' purpose for their existence.

"You know," Papa said, "the Phoenicians were great sailors, so it wouldn't have been very difficult for them to sail down the African coast to Sofala."

"But I thought they were in the Mediterranean?" I asked, puzzled.

"They were, but many of them were experienced sailors, working at the Red Sea port where Solomon was building his navy," Papa replied.

"What did Solomon want a navy for?" I persisted.

"He was building the Temple in Jerusalem. You've read all about that—he got cedar wood from Lebanon, but gold came from Africa, though no one is sure from just which place he got it."

"But where was his seaport?" I asked.

"At the top of the Red Sea on the gulf of Aqaba. It was called Ezion-geber—we'll look it up on the map," he concluded.

"Were there lots of gold mines down here?"

"Scattered all over what is now Mashonaland," Papa said.

"No wonder Mr. Rhodes said Zimbabwe was the great secret of southern Africa," I reminded him.

"It still is," said Papa.

"But how do we know about this?"

"It's all in the Bible, my boy," said Papa, "you can read about Solomon's association with Hiram, who was king of Tyre, the great center of Phoenician trade."

"Please tell me where to look."

"I'll have to check that," Papa said, "but I think it is in Kings somewhere, or Ezekiel, and they tell us how Hiram's navy sailed every three years to collect 'gold and silver, ivory, apes, and peacocks,' but where from is the mystery. Ophir is mentioned, and Punt, but no one knows where these places were."

It seemed to me that Zimbabwe floated in a world of its own

between fact and fantasy, lost in a world of suppositions, few of which could be substantiated. The impression the ruins had left upon me almost made me wish that nothing more would be discovered about it, but that men would leave it buried in the darkness as a perpetual puzzle for generations to come.

From that first experience, when Papa out of his own theories suggested the idea that the temple complex together with the many scattered ruins in the area were all part of a colonial mining center established by the Phoenicians, I have never ceased searching for more evidence to prove it. Archaeology notwithstanding, with many illuminating arguments, my father was never convinced that the "brains" behind the settlement resulting in the ruins could have belonged to a people other than one sophisticated and experienced, with knowledge both cultural and religious.

The whole concept fitted only one people, especially when it is remembered that the Phoenicians, besides being the great sailors of the then-known world, were traders, miners, and craftsmen settled in such scattered parts of the world as Greece, Sicily, Tunisia, Egypt, Spain, and the Scilly Islands, to mention only a few.

Coupled with their mining intelligence is their obvious religious involvement. They were a Baal-worshiping people. The sun god, Baal, and his opposite feminine principle, Astarte, were both symbolized by their great and small conical towers found within the "sacred" precincts of the temple, and repeated in various areas throughout the ruins.

This whole theory, which I was told Rider Haggard subscribed to (though I don't know about Rhodes), leads into a vast research on the early history of the Sumerian, Hittite, Egyptian, and Greek civilizations, which is not within my province. But the theory presupposes a date, which I repeat has never been established. Between 1400 B.C. and A.D. 632 there were no people capable of establishing, nor more likely to have established, such a colonial, mining, agricultural enterprise on the African east coast other than the Phoenicians. Since then, there has been much evidence produced to support this theory: the efficiency of Phoenicia; her glass bead-making, required for barter with the African natives; the pottery taught to the Greeks; the delicate work in bronze and precious metals; all place this extraordinary people in a position superior to any other contemporary.

Besides, who else, except perhaps Solomon and the Queen of Sheba, bothered about the problems of gold mining?

However, there is no historical record of a Phoenician colony on the African coast with Zimbabwe as its capital, for history only begins with the Arab traders, who were never slow to take an advantage. It is known that the Arabs, later followed by the Portuguese, obtained ivory and gold from the tribes inhabiting the area. Their chieftain was called the Monomotapa, who at one time held court at Zimbabwe. Tales of the wealth of his kingdom even reached the ears of the first Dutch settlers at Cape Town. His people, aquiline in feature it was said, were called the Makalanga and were known as the "children of the sun."

Their descendants were subjugated by the fierce Zulu chief, Moselekatse, who with his rebellious thousands marched out of Zululand, swept across Africa into what is now Rhodesia, where they established themselves to become known as the Matabele. It was from their chief Lobengula, the son of Moselekatse, that Rhodes made the now-famous purchase of Matabeleland with its wealth of minerals, which he was determined to obtain for Great Britain.

Perhaps it was the Makalanga who copied the temple with very inferior workmanship found in the ruins scattered through the valley. But nothing of the scale or sophisticated design, or built in the elliptical form with such consummate skill, as the great Zimbabwe, has ever been discovered in Africa.

That was a youngster's dream. As time passed, I searched for more information about this extraordinary enigma. Then at long last I was able to return, through the kind invitation of a couple who were friends of my parents. They were both interested in the questions concerning the ruins. She was an amateur painter with a romantic streak in her nature, and he had a practical desire to see a mystery solved logically to his own satisfaction. We had talked of the ruins, and though they had been there before they were not very well informed, having read much less than I had in my passionate research for information on the subject.

Though that first impression remained, my approach to the ruins was more mature. If one has any interest in archaeology, the place itself sets one's imagination on fire. Obviously, there was much more to be discovered, perhaps the riddle even solved during my lifetime.

As we walked through the western entrance of the temple, with the massive silver granite walls rising thirty feet above us, I was able to tell them that at that point the walls were 16 feet thick, and the "parallel passage" created by an inner wall was 220 feet long. The purpose of this passage has never been explained, for at one end it is so narrow that it allows only one body to pass along it in single file. It is thought that it provided a secret access to what is known as the "sacred enclosure" in the center of the temple, in that it has no communication with the interior of the building along its entire length. However, where the passage ends, it widens to include a platform and steps, now ruined, as well as two strange stone towers. These suggest that possibly some fertility rite or perhaps circumcision ritual occurred in that area; the idea is supported by the number of phallic objects found there.

The larger of the two conical towers varies from 31 feet to 26 feet, where the topmost courses of the stones have fallen. The base measures 57 feet 6 inches in circumference. One can imagine some mystical ritual being performed in front of these amazing cones on the once-existent platform, possibly involving the sun or more probably the deities.

The now famous chevron pattern that decorates the exterior of the northeast wall puzzled the first white men to see it into thinking it was "an inscription in unknown characters." Later it was decided to be a fertility symbol found in many varied parts of the world; executed in bold style and extending for 265 feet, it is made by narrow granite bricks that project beyond the smooth surface of the wall itself. The design resembles the delicate ornamentation of Dhlo-Dhlo, Nanatali, and other ruins in the valley. One fact that may prove significant is that the only part of the wall decorated by the design receives the sun's first rays at the summer solstice. Who knows whether this is intentional or not? But not one stone cut by a word of any kind of writing has ever been found in any of the ruins, though it is known that before 800 B.C. the Phoenician alphabet had reached Greece. One would think that some word, whether of praise to their gods or warning to their enemies, might have been set up somewhere in Zimbabwe.

There are a number of these ruins throughout the valley that we did not visit but that in later years I had the opportunity of seeing. One, situated on the property of Cecil Rhodes, is called Inyanga, and is thought to have been inhabited by a prosperous agricultural population, judging by the innumerable irrigation canals and terraces, with forts built on the heights above to protect the people against raids by other tribes. If the ruined city around the temple housed the workers of the great mining enterprise at Zimbabwe, then the countless terraces, water furrows, and grain pits found at Inyanga, with its mountain streams and fertile valleys, were the heart of an agrarian development of 2,500 square miles needed to feed these workers. There at Inyanga the grain was grown, reaped, and stored in the beautifully stone-lined pits that were sealed at the top once the grain was stored. Such underground silos, according to J. D. Evans in his book *Malta*, still exist in Mediterranean countries.

The other groups of ruins, by now studied and documented by various archaeologists, are, namely, Dhlo-Dhlo, Khami, and Nanatali, each of which has yielded further evidence by investigation. Particularly Nanatali, which stands on a high *kopje* with a superb view of the surrounding, wild country. The outer wall of this fortress-habitation is ornamented with the characteristic designs of chevron, herringbone, cord, etc., in perfect condition, and positioned almost entirely around the enclosure.

One other ruin I must tell of for obvious reasons. It was found in the year 1868 when George Phillips, an elephant hunter, was visiting Renders at Zimbabwe. It is said to have once possessed a conical tower, and still has a curved wall in fine condition that was originally ornamented by carved soapstone monoliths. In 1903 one of these monoliths was discovered by Mr. R. N. Hall, the first curator of the ruins. On the beam was carved the now-famous vulture, together with the figure of a crocodile. On seeing this beam in the Curator's House my mind flashed back to "Groot Schuur" and Cecil Rhodes's bird, which had brought about my interest in Zimbabwe. I still wonder whether it is the vulture of Astarte.

Later that day I could not resist walking alone along the passage curving into the shadow. In some places this corridor, almost dark, and secret between the two walls, was only just wide enough to pass through. I was conscious of my footsteps echoing into the silence, the utter, impenetrable silence that seemed to hang over the temple. Was I perhaps walking down the very corridor reserved for the condemned who would meet their fate at the sacrificial altar?

When I emerged into the "sacred enclosure," would I find a mass of the people, shiny, black, and terrifying, spattered with the blood of other victims, reveling in some wild orgy? Or would I see only reserved, thin, brown-skinned priests offering up their tribute of gold to some unknown god, bright with transmuted golden light? I was suddenly afraid to move forward and retraced my steps out of the dark shadows.

Lastly, we visited the acropolis, as it is called, a hill 320 feet high dominating the whole valley of the ruins, with the temple itself below it. The ingenuity shown by the builders of this stronghold is shown by their ability to make use of all the natural rock formations. The oldest ascent is 1,250 feet long, and winds in and out between rock fissures so narrow as to allow only one person at a time to pass through. One is left breathless by the steepness of the climb and by the vision the whole structure conjures up. The colossal walls, the maze of fallen rocks scattered down the valley that was once the city site, all seemed to belong to the barbaric landscape that fills one with a feeling that is almost fear. In my imagination I could see the long lines of dark slaves, each carrying a load of golden ingots, being herded down the jungle track to Sofala on the coast. Perhaps their overseers were thin-lipped Sabaeans, or hook-nosed traders from Phoenicia, following these "beasts of burden" through the jungle until at Sofala the navy of Tarshish, carrying "gold and silver, ivory, apes, and peacocks," would hoist their brightly colored sails and slide up the coast to Solomon their king.

Whether it was they who brought the vultures of Astarte from Syria or not, it is surely certain that the skill required to build the elliptical walls and conical towers must have come from a people with a culture far advanced beyond the smiling, black-skinned "children of the sun." But it was surely these same enslaved thousands who were used for the tremendous labor required to build the complicated structure for their masters. For the walls are made of countless granite bricks, cut and exactly squared to size, which must have taken endless patience and experience to lay. Yet there are no signs of any quarry nearby, though it is estimated that for the circular walls of the temple alone 100,000 tons of stone were required. Where are the chippings, where were the bricks cut and hewn to size?

In the First Book of Kings, chapters, 5 and 6, is a description of the building of King Solomon's palace that is interesting in relation to Zimbabwe:

> And Solomon had three score and ten thousand that bare burdens, and fourscore thousand hewers in the mountains . . .
> and the house, when it was in building was built of stone

made ready before it was brought thither: so that there was neither hammer nor axe nor any tool of iron heard in the house, while it was in building.

The millions of hewed stones squared and fitted exactly for the Temple walls must certainly have needed fourscore thousand hewers, and it is possible that these also made ready the granite bricks before they were brought to put in place. This would explain the lack of any quarry, or any piles of the millions of resulting chippings to be found anywhere in the area. If this was the case, from how far the hewn stones were transported is another question no one can answer.

As we saw no guards or anyone official to prevent our wandering about, we walked up the carefully hidden pathway between the rocks to the summit of the acropolis. There we found an old man who looked like a white hunter, gray-bearded, wearing a wide straw hat, examining the precise construction of the walls.

"Good day," we said instinctively in English.

He seemed too engrossed in his work to be aware of us.

"Excuse me," said one of my companions, "I wonder whether you know for what purpose this area was used?"

He turned slowly, giving us a broad grin.

"I don't think anyone is sure of that," he replied.

"But there was originally a smaller temple up here, wasn't there?" I asked.

"They think so," he said, "but I believe it is a lot of guesswork, in spite of all the archaeologists we have had here."

"Have you read all their varied opinions?"

"Not all," he said, "but I've been coming up here on and off for a very long time and I've got a few theories myself, but I go on hoping that I'll come upon something—you know—something that will help to solve this riddle."

"What sort of tools do you think they used?" asked one of my friends.

"They found some, you know, down there in the temple, all

made of iron," he replied, pointing to the temple ruins below.

I remembered that iron smelting was known to the Greeks as early as 1000 B.C., and no doubt the Phoenicians had learned it from the Hittites long before that. The earliest method of breaking up the enormous rocks was by fire and water, inasmuch as they had no dynamite; the rocks were heated by tremendous fires, then split into portable sizes by pouring cold water onto the steaming surfaces. This method accounted for the ventilation shafts found in the mining areas. They had to use fire and needed to create a draft as well as an exit for the smoke.

"Come with me," said our newfound guide. "I'll show you where the gold was smelted."

We crawled through the protected entrance.

"You see how carefully they hid their operations," he said as we entered the furnace area. "No African native could have thought so logically, or so far ahead," he concluded with a finality that seemed to allow of no argument.

The acropolis is thought to be older than the temple, though the curving walls of dovetailing into the immense boulders with amazing ingenuity, the hidden defense of the mounting pathway, the huge rocks hollowed out for the smelting furnaces, don't help to date the extraordinary structure. There is a maze of walled areas on the summit, much destroyed by years of Bantu occupation, by gold hunters since the very discovery, and later by amateur archaeologists. We are told it was the high point of the caravan route from the mining areas to the port of Sofala.

Here, certainly, the gold was smelted for transport by the countless slaves, but here also the deities presided. Their monoliths, planted with precision on the stone walls, as well as the ever-present "bird" stelae—the vulture of my first acquaintance at the Cape—all were there, no doubt to safeguard the lives of the miners and the goldsmiths, but also their precious product.

Here, too, was the reason for the acropolis, the treasure

house—secret, guarded, and unassailable—which the builders of the ruins set on the hilltop. The whole wide panorama of
the country could be scanned from these high walls, and anyone
approaching the citadel from any direction could easily be seen.

Of all of this amazing activity by thousands of people involved there is not a trace left: no word, no skeletons, no
graves, not even the tons of granite chippings, just silence—
which has stirred and has continued to excite man's imagination ever since the discovery of the mystery in 1868.

There is a theory, among others, that when the followers of
Muhammad began their fanatical invasions after the Prophet's
death in A.D. 632, the whole structure of the Phoenician colony
in Southeast Africa collapsed. Later, when the Islamic Arab
traders renewed their trade with the Sofala coast in A.D. 732, the
nature worship of the Phoenician colony was doomed. So indeed were the Phoenicians, who had to submit to Assyria, Bab-
ylonia, Persia, Macdeonia, and Rome, in that order, according
to Professor Rawlinson.

But annihilation by the invasion of unknown tribes of Bantu
sweeping down through Africa seems a more likely explanation
of the total, unrecorded disappearance of the gifted builders of
Zimbabwe.

The bibliography at the back of the book lists titles for those
who may want to read further.

6. Domestics

In my youth, there was no race problem such as we now have in South Africa. The people who were either black, brown, or coffee-colored were simply not "white people" and as such, therefore, were considered inferior. Instinctively they seemed to understand their relation to the whites and seldom if ever attempted to assume any other position. As children we were surrounded by people of all shades of color from the dark, often handsome Bantu—Basutus or Xhosas—to the slim brown Malays who, by their culture and Muhammadan faith, kept very much to themselves. The most unfortunate minority, who have since grown in such numbers as to become an individual political problem, were what were known as the "colored" people. They were the product of the haphazard relationships between the earlier white settlers—English, Dutch, and French, the men of the ruling white world—and the dark, indigenous people of the country. Their coloring ranged from very dark to almost white, but they belonged neither to the white world nor the dark, and occupied a sort of shadowy position between the two as domestics, shop assistants of the most menial category, or, in the case of the men, as gardeners or scullery help.

The Malays, as we have already noted, were either the descendants of the slaves brought to the colony by the Dutch from the Spice Islands about 1710 or of the many political exiles given sanctuary by the Dutch government. Some of these were artisans, others men of certain learning and culture whose abilities fitted them to work as carpenters or builders, teachers or priests in their own mosques, around which their co-religionists clustered in close communities. Others again became fishermen, fruit sellers, or grooms, for they were particularly understanding of horses. Their womenfolk, still wearing their *doeks* * with their national dress, were washerwomen or domestic help. In my day, even the men still wore the little red fez of their faith and *kaparrings* or wooden sandals on their delicate brown feet.

We had a Malay washerwoman named Gahdia who took in laundry for a few selected families. I shall always remember her as courteous, handsome, and thoughtful to us children, often bringing us little presents of sugared figs or oriental sweetmeats, delicious delicacies from the East, smelling of spices and herbs, which we relished. She would arrive with huge baskets of snowy white laundry in an open Cape cart driven by her son Abdul, wearing his red fez, or sometimes in the hot sun his "toering," a pointed straw hat perched on a scarlet handkerchief wound close to his head as a turban beneath it. Gahdia would unwind her *yashmak* and bow gracefully to us before giving us our gifts wrapped in cool vine leaves.

On Saturdays Abdul called, the back of his cart filled with a mass of multicolored fish caught by his many relatives in False Bay. I used to climb up into his driver's seat to look at the

* Head handkerchiefs, swathed like a *yashmak*.

mound of fish: the snook, the *kabeljou*, silver, pink, and iridescent gray, the harvest of the blue waters of the bay. Abdul would announce his wares by blowing, on a small tin horn, a loud "toot toot" to all the cooks in the neighborhood. Nannie told me that the tin horn had taken the place of the conch shell, which the Malay fisherman had used since the earliest days of the colony. Fish had to be eaten on the very day it was caught, as we had limited means of refrigeration, and ice was considered a great luxury in that part of the world.

Our cook was colored, more light than dark, an attractive, dissolute woman who, though a Christian, had her own ideas of morality. We knew she had several children, though she was supposedly unmarried, but, when asked by my mother as to why she did not marry their father, invariably replied (naïvely), "But, madam, I doesn't know him well enough to marry him." She continued to receive her lovers when my parents were out to dinner and we children were left at home. Although she never knew it, I was well aware of her "callers," a custom strictly forbidden by Mama.

The butler, John, was also colored, and rather darker brown than the cook, while our housemaid might easily have been mistaken for a white woman by those who did not know the distinguishing marks of the colored strain. Each of these three—the cook, the butler, and the maid—came from a slightly different class, yet in most white eyes would have been thought of simply as colored people. The kitchen or yard boy was much darker, having a strong strain of Zulu blood in his veins. He ate his meals alone, not being considered equal to the colored domestics, although I think they were kind to him despite this distinction.

John was an exceptional human being. As a very young man he had been trained in a superior white household; he had beautiful manners and control, coupled with a good sense of humor. I remember thinking his opinions of the various rather dull people my parents had to entertain were often pertinent and humorous, and I used to laugh with him about certain of these visitors I did not like. But he had a passionate admiration for my mother and would do anything in the world to please her.

However, there was one cross that he found hard to bear, even for her sake. That was her lady's maid, one of many imported either from England or Scotland. They came to the Cape on a contract for three years, but seldom stayed any longer in spite of their much happier, freer position than in Great Britain. "Home" was what they all longed for; some were inclined to suggest to us children that we were very unfortunate to be "colonials," living so far from civilization! Coming generally from a certain class in Britain, these women usually had preconceived ideas about South Africa and the dark people. Often they were condescending, even very rude to the other domestics, intolerable in their attitude of superiority. Mama's maid naturally ate by herself, waited on by the cook, who invariably disliked every maid in turn.

But the most important person among the domestic staff was Nannie, who was coffee-colored, passionately Christian, and possessed of an extraordinary philosophy that seemed to solve all the problems in a multicolored household. She was a strange woman, uneducated yet gifted, whose character was a combination of the traits of her forebears. She was a half-caste, her mother a Malay of breeding and dignity, her father a renegade Irishman, attached in some way to the governor's household at the time.

Ouma, as Nannie called her mother, traced her family back to one of a group of Eastern noblemen who had been sent as political prisoners to the Cape of Good Hope. There they had settled under the gracious shadow of Table Mountain, some to become teachers and establish a little colony of the faithful.

As I grew older and heard the story of her background, I used to picture in my mind the black-haired, romantic young Irishman escaping from the high-walled garden that surrounded Government House, wending his way through the avenue of dark oak trees to the flat-topped, Oriental-looking houses of the Malay district, to meet his almond-eyed mistress with her slim, cinnamon hands.

There he must have spent long hours, while Ouma told him, in her quiet voice and halting, studied English, of her people and their vivid Oriental land, whose colorful customs were perpetuated in the seclusion of the colony under Table Mountain. She must have pictured for him that land of towns with queer-sounding names that shimmered in the clear air; a riot of color-washed houses and narrow, winding streets, with the quiet, feline people moving gracefully to market in their bright-colored clothes; with parakeets whistling from the treetops and monkeys scampering along the vines of rich, waxen flowers. It was a land of markets, of spices and rare fruits, silks and satins that came in strange-looking ships from China and India of the mysteries, gliding into the azure waters of the harbors, manned by brown men or black men from Africa; Arab traders, with their bright turbans, or soft-spoken yellow men from China, bringing materials woven of the silkworm silk into a myriad intricate designs. She would sing him a little plaintive melody with all the sorrow of the East in its harmony, full of the world's old melancholy.

How it must have appealed to an Irishman, with his quick response to legend and his own Celtic love for the romance of a strange country.

Of course, he never married Ouma, and, when she bore the little dark-eyed girl called Maria who later became my Nannie, she never told how she arranged to become the wife of a half-colored gardener on a nearby estate and bear five more variegated children, some pale, some dark brown.

But Maria, her firstborn, the love child of the illicit romance, had all the qualities that her father and mother possessed—the mixture of Irish and Malayan blood that gave her the smooth, dark skin of her mother and the romantic, sensitive imagination of her father. She brought to me the untutored influences of both in her complex, dominant personality. I remember particularly her long, tapering hands and the wide, enveloping smile that showed her straight, white teeth in even array.

We knew very little of Nannie's own life except that, after an unhappy childhood with brothers and sisters of an obviously different class, she had been engaged as a nursemaid by an English family who boasted a Scotch nannie.

I am quite sure she was conscious of the differences that distinguished her from the rest of her family, who were younger than she was by several years, but whether she ever knew the true story of her birth I never discovered. When, years later, after old Ouma died, I was told it by Nannie's sister, who loved her deeply, I was sworn to secrecy, for her mother had only confessed it on her deathbed and Nannie was never to know!

Maria had become a devout convert to Christianity, though her mother had kept strictly to the faith of her own people. The hymns she taught me were the prevalent Sankey and Moody favorites of the time. She also knew a collection of children's songs, some of the words of which she pronounced in her curious English so as to make them almost unintelligible. She used to murmur one about a "dawggie" that went like this:

> *I had a little dawggie*
> *That used to sit and baig*
> *And dawggie tumbled down the stairs*
> *And broke his little laig.*
>
> *Oh! dawggie, I will heal it*
> *And try to make you well,*
> *And then you'll have a ribband*
> *With a golden bell.*

When I needed cheering or had had long, restless days in bed, she would break into something brighter, with a gayer rhythm, to encourage me as she pottered about my room, dusting or arranging my toys:

199

BACKGROUND IN SUNSHINE

The appels are ripe and ready to drawp
Hm—ha—ready to drawp.
There came an old woman to gather them op,
Hmm—ha—gather them op.

This song had endless verses and, finally, when she and the song were both exhausted, would come the final moral:

The appels were picked and put on the shelf
Hm—ha—put on the shelf.
If you want any more, you can sing it yourself,
Hm—ha—sing it yourself.

She would end with a broad grin and stop whatever she was doing to say, "Now you sing, Master Jan. It will make you well to sing. Remember, de Lawd likes a cheerful sinner!"

"But I'm not a cheerful sinner, Nannie," I would protest. "You said sinning was ugly."

"Well," she would add, confused, "you won't sin if you sing. Think of the birds you love so much. Dey don't do nobody any harm."

I would ponder at this mixed simile and wonder why, then, the birds caught my favorite yellow butterflies, and whether that was considered "cheerful sinning"!

But sometimes Nannie would hum a sad, queer-sounding melody that would arouse me in a way I didn't understand.

"What's that you're singing?" I would ask.

"I don't know, Master Jan—something Ouma used to sing to me." It was probably something that her mother, in her young days, had sung to her white lover to remind him of his own island of the blue mountains, where the sun slanted between the clouds onto the little thatched cottages standing lonely, like white gulls, on the wet peat bogs.

Nannie's philosophy was partly Christian, partly pagan, but everything in life seemed in her mind to fall into two classes: the "ugly" and the "beautiful" or "pretty." She used the words indiscriminately and applied them to everything, so that, if she found me sitting on the damp flagstones, my hands and clothes dirty, it was not surprising to hear her say, "No," Master Jan, that is *not* pretty."

When my embarrassing misdemeanors would necessitate a hurried rush up the stairs to my bedroom, Nannie would explain the situation to anyone we passed en route by saying, "Master Jan has had an ugly accident!"

Life to me became divided by these two words; for years I thought of things as either "ugly" or "beautiful" without troubling to define what either of the words really meant. Gestures, incidents, people's natures or their remarks, partook of the same quality as the tall majesty of the pine trees or the mass of clouds that gathered on the mountain.

Dr. Smith, one of my godfathers, who used to snap a curt reply to his submissive wife, was really "ugly" to me, and I had named my two favorite pigeons Dr. and Mrs. Smith because of their extraordinary resemblance to my godparents. I realize now how deeply I embarrassed Nannie and shocked my parents and their friends one day when, describing a scene near my pigeon house that had fascinated me, I said, " 'Dr. Smith' made such an ugly gesture, Mama. He treads on 'Mrs. Smith' and I know she doesn't like it." I was hurried out, protesting that it wasn't "pretty" of him at all!

I don't think that I ever quite lost this feeling of the classification of things in life. In later years, some subconscious voice from within would almost pronounce the words and apply them to the situation I was facing. From somewhere beyond the reach of sense or argument came the word "ugly," which made me recede, or the consolation of "beautiful," which somehow put me at ease.

"Don't be afraid, Master Jan," Nannie would counsel. "Expect people to be nice and kind and dey will be and, if dere tempers are ugly, just don't take any notice and dey will go away."

She must have been an enigma to the nurses of my various friends. Both the stiff, superior white nurses imported from England or Scotland, with their fixed ideas and imperial opinions, and the colored nurses of all shades were afraid of her, sensing something they didn't understand about her.

She would confuse them by her directness, her obvious belief in justice and the triumph of right over wrong. When the red-haired boy who lived across the road would snatch my favorite toy, Nannie would say, "Give it to him, Master Jan. Let him take it away. It will come back to you—perhaps in some other way." I didn't understand the truth of this until I had grown old from experience, but my childish nature rebelled against a generosity I didn't feel at all.

She would take me for walks and, naturally, I developed a taste for certain places or vistas that became associated in my mind with a story she had told me, or a song she had sung there, or even some incident that had set me imagining childish ideas of drama or romance.

There was a steep lane near my home that led down the hill to an old Dutch colonial house. This was one of my favorite walks, for there was a tiny stream that flowed down one side along a low stone wall, while the other was bordered by a hedge that sheltered every conceivable wild flower that delighted my young heart. Here we found the pink and yellow sorrel—the oxalis of botanical fame, and, in the deeper shade, the wild orchids, growing on stiff stems from a rosette of purple-veined, fleshy leaves. Along the stream's edge, one could find ferns, too, and in some places the moss was deep and bright green, then again golden or russet. Where the water tumbled into little brown pools, sometimes I would see a big green frog on the bottom, with large pop eyes that reminded me of our minister, who rather frightened me. Sometimes, if it was spring, the dog roses would trail their white, untouched beauty along the hedge.

There was a gap in the hedge where a steep stile led into the fields bordering the lane. Here we would always stop and climb the steps to look out across the hazy valley to the blue curve of the bay or watch the sunset light up the peaks of the far-off Blaauwberg ("blue mountains") that bordered the horizon to the north.

"That is where he wanted to cut the canal," Nannie would say, gazing into the distance.

"Who wanted to?" I asked.

"The governor who lived in the Castle in Cape Town."

"What's a canal, Nannie?"

"A stream of water, like a river, I think."

"What did he want to cut it for?"

"To join the two bays—dere, Table Bay, and dere, False Bay—you know, Master Jan, where the beach is." She would point vaguely to the horizon.

"But what for?" I pestered.

"For the boats to go through," she replied. "It's a long way right around the Cape."

"Why didn't they make the canal?"

"I expect it was too expensive."

"Even for the governor?" I asked.

"Or, perhaps, too difficult," she added.

"How d'you know, Nannie?"

"Ouma must have told me. Dey began to cut the canal— right across dose sandy flats—but the wind blew the sand back and the tides swept all the work away. I expect he thought it was just as well—that God never meant it to be built."

Conversations frequently ended with that finality. If a thing didn't happen, well, it wasn't meant to happen. To Nannie, the pattern was clearly defined; there was no use worrying or grieving, the design was preordained. It was to be accepted, no matter how unpleasant or how contrary to one's wishes.

Nannie saw the hand of the Lord in everything.

"Look, dere are the animals," she would exclaim. And there they were, as always, in the green meadows of the big house:

the woolly, dignified sheep, the golden-brown horses, and the little gray donkeys.

"D'you see de cross of Christ on their backs?" Nannie would ask, pointing at the donkeys.

"Why is it there, Nannie?"

"Our Lord gave it to dem as a sign of blessing after He rode one into Jerusalem."

"Am I blessed, too?" I inquired.

"If you are a good boy," she would say, "but not if you get into an ugly mood."

"Are you always good, Nannie?"

"I try to be—Ouma taught me how to be—but no one can always be good."

"Then it doesn't matter if I get an ugly mood."

"Oh, yes, it does, Master Jan, for God always remembers— even if I forgive you!" She smiled one of her broad, wide smiles.

The white house to which the lane led was one of my favorite playgrounds. As I grew older, it became a center of interest to me—its graceful architecture, its kindly inhabitants, and even its ghosts. But it was Nannie's stories, half truth, half fantasy, that gave to it an added atmosphere of romance.

In the teak shutters of one of the large windows looking out onto the yard were cut two holes in the shape of hearts—or were they lily buds?

"Those were cut to remind de owner of his lady," Nannie would state.

"What happened to her?"

"She went down to the lake, dere at the bottom of the field, you know, Master Jan, to pick lilies. Not 'pig lilies,' but the big, blue lotus that grow so thick and float on the water. She waded out and got caught in dere long stems and sank into the mud. Dey say de lilies drowned her, pulling her under slowly, before anyone in de house missed her.

"An' if you go down to de lake at sunset, dey say—" and

Nannie's voice would drop almost to a whisper—"you can still hear de poor lady call."

"When did that happen, Nannie?"

"Years and years ago, but I expect it taught de master a lesson—and he so cruel to her, dey say—because, when she died, he had the two holes cut into the shutters, one into each to make a pair, to remind him of his lady, out dere calling among the lilies."

Behind the house were the slave quarters, built of thatch and plaster in a large square. In the center, supported between two elegant plaster columns, was the old slave bell used to summon the slaves from their labors in the fields and orchards. There, too, were the open stalls for horses and cattle, where the swallows nested.

Nannie used to sit under the bell with her sewing while I played in the shade of the oak trees or visited my Chinese friend, the slim, little yellow manservant who lived in one of the slave houses.

He had a truly Chinese name, but I had nicknamed him Ting-a-ling because he was summoned by the ringing of a little temple bell of ancient Chinese bronze that his mistress carried with her wherever she went. Ting-a-ling wore a dark-blue, close-fitting silk jacket and plum-colored trousers that showed his little feet in black slippers edged with blue, and, on his head, a black Chinese cap with a coral bead on the crown.

He talked broken "pidgin" English, which I grew to understand, and, on hot summer afternoons, used a neat, small brown fan. This fascinated me, for I had always associated fans with women. I used to stare at him, fanning himself as he moved about the rooms silently and smoothly as a cat.

"Velly hot Ting-a-ling," he would say, and I would picture him at home in China, as Papa had described it to me, in a cool house of paper screens with wisteria falling in cascades from the roof and little, silent, slant-eyed women carrying him trays of tea in tiny celadon cups.

BACKGROUND IN SUNSHINE

I found him one day on the wide veranda that bordered his house on the garden side, kneeling in front of a low table, on which was a carved Chinese vase. He was arranging flowers, which he chose with thoughtful precision from a bunch he held in his left hand. I stood quite still, fascinated.

"Good day, massa," was all he said, as he went on with his task.

I watched him select an iris with a smooth, curved stem, two sprays of peach blossom that he bent and twisted into his design, another tall, straight bud of the iris with the three sharp, pale green leaves that sheltered it.

"Pretty, massa?" He smiled at me.

"Why d'you do it that way, Ting-a-ling?" I asked.

"Making speech," he said.

I didn't understand, but I asked Mama later what he meant. She told me of the oriental ritual of flower arrangement, with the significance of each flower in relation to the curve or line it took.

I became inquisitive and used to escape from Nannie to call on Ting-a-ling. I would get him to show me, first, which flowers to pick and then how to subtly bend the stems. Some wouldn't do, some were too stiff or naturally curved the wrong way. But his narrow, enigmatic hands would weave a pattern of forms that would delight my eye. He taught me some of the first elements of good design.

One day, I found him ill in bed, with his little black silk cap still on his head, dark against his pillow.

"Ting-a-ling velly sick," he murmured.

I went into the garden, chose a few flowers, arranged them in his favorite porcelain bowl, and triumphantly placed it at his side. He smiled widely, staring at the flowers.

"Better now," he said nodding.

I never saw him again, for he died a few days later, and I cried alone under the oak trees for my lost friend.

With her usual philosophy about life and death, Nannie tried to comfort me.

"You mustn't cry, Master Jan," she said. "Remember, de Lawd giveth but He taketh away."

"But why did He take Ting-a-ling?" I asked, annoyed at my loss.

"I expect he wanted the Chinaman. You wouldn't want to keep Ting-a-ling from His heavenly pleasure, would you?"

"No," I said, uncertain, but anxious to appear generous.

"If de Lawd is ready to take you, you mustn't try and change His mind by nudging Him; just be thankful He don't want you yet."

But even her philosophy deserted her one day, for she received a telegram that obviously disturbed her.

She dressed me in my best suit, silently, nervously.

"Where are we going?" I asked.

"We're going to see Ouma," she replied.

I was delighted. I always enjoyed my visits to Nannie's family, who gave us an excellent tea, sometimes with home-made ginger cake, served with thick cream, and various fruit preserves or *konfijts*, as the Dutch call them. Ouma had taught her daughters how to prepare the juicy green figs in a honey-sweet syrup or whole tangerines with a little brandy mixed with their pungent juice. But, most of all, I relished the watermelon *konfijt*, which was more complicated to make, for the squares of the thick rind were laid to soak in some subtle mixture of bay leaves and lemon rind that gave them a delicious, spiced flavor. I usually returned home with a special gift from Ouma—ripe pears from her favorite tree, or fresh guavas in a little wicker basket lined with vine leaves.

I never discovered why Nannie's mother was known as Ouma, which is Dutch for "Grandma," but she was called that even by her two other, highly respectable daughters, who lived with her not far from my home. One was a postmistress, much paler than my nurse, but neither of the sisters had any of the charm or oriental quality that Nannie seemed to have inherited from her mother.

Even at my age, I could sense the matriarchal domination that Ouma exerted on her daughters from her bed or wheelchair. At that time, I didn't know the romantic story of her past and had merely been told she was a Malay by birth, brought from an island far, far away to live in Cape Town. But the drab, ill-fitting clothes in which her daughters dressed her did not hide the beauty and breeding that still radiated from her. Her thin hands, her slanting, velvet-dark eyes, her slow, enigmatic smile always fascinated me.

I can still see her, sitting static, mysterious, surrounded by her large daughters, her two hands folded on her lap. Her cottage was filled with a variety of hideous objects fashionable at that time: a palm in a yellow pot, a huge portrait of Queen Victoria, knitted antimacassars on every velvet-covered chair. Only here and there was there any reminder of her background: a magenta silk scarf that smelled of spices, draped over one chair; a photograph of a Malay wedding, the women in their dazzling headdresses of spangles and satin; a little copper pot of Eastern workmanship. All else had been suppressed by middle-class respectability.

Nannie was so silent all the way to the cottage that even my endless questionings did not rouse her. We were met by the sisters at the gate, very serious and sad-eyed. As Sophie, the younger, kissed Nannie, she burst into tears and went hurriedly into the house. Nannie told me to stay in the garden until she fetched me.

I sensed something very unusual about the whole situation and wondered inquisitively what was the matter as I wandered under the peach trees to watch my special friends, the tiny bantam cock and hen, golden brown and delicately made, with their brood of minute chickens.

Presently, I heard voices in the back room leading into the

garden. Consciously but, I hoped, seemingly innocently, I drifted nearer and nearer the window. Sophie, the postmistress, was talking.

". . . and it was only a tiny black spot when we first noticed it—as big as a pinhead. But Ouma wasn't ill. She wouldn't let us send for the doctor and now it's spread and it's too late. She will have pain, bad pain, and it can't be cured, the doctor says. Whatever shall we do?"

I was beginning to understand now.

"I'll help you," said Nannie. "We'll manage. But how long will it be?"

"Perhaps months, but—perhaps—only weeks . . ." Then, the sound of sobbing through low-murmured words of comfort.

Nannie fetched me and we had tea on the veranda. Only Sophie joined us. No one spoke, and I was frightened deep down in my stomach by a sense of foreboding.

"Can't I say good-bye to Ouma?" I asked.

Sophie turned away rapidly, her handkerchief pressed to her mouth. Nannie took my hand.

"She is very ill, Master Jan," she explained gently. "She says good-bye to you, though."

We walked home in silence.

"Will she die, Nannie?" I asked suddenly.

"Yes, Master Jan, but I wish I could save her de suffering."

"Couldn't we pray, Nannie? You told me we can do anything by praying."

"Only if what you ask is also God's will."

I thought and thought as I lay in bed that night. I had said a prayer for Ouma, Nannie sitting beside me, and, when she had turned out my light, I could hear her, as she sewed, singing one of my favorite hymns.

"God's will—God's will." I wanted to understand about death. Was it like the withering of a flower after a scented, colorful period in the sun, a withering to a brown nothingness and dust? Or was it an opening, like the bud unfolding into a full flowering of life, with the Hosts in the high blue dome of the sky all around us? Was it always God's will that took us— that had taken Ting-a-ling and was taking Ouma—or just that she had been long enough in her little cottage and it was time to finish her allotted days? Nannie had always told me everything was God's will. Did He have a scheme, a pattern into which we all fitted—I and Mama and Papa, Nannie and my friends—and would we go on to somewhere else where there were no tears, no suffering, nothing "ugly," only everything serene, full of "beauty" and peace?

A few weeks later Ouma died. Nannie told me quietly one morning. She dressed herself all in black, with a black veil that Mama gave her for the occasion wound around her hat and hiding her face. She was very still and resigned. I picked a bunch of flowers for her to take "to give to Ouma."

When she returned, she brought me a wicker basket, the lid tied with straw. Inside I found the little bantam cock and hen I had always envied.

"Ouma sent you these," she said simply.

I was too excited to do more than murmur my thanks.

Later that evening I tiptoed into Nannie's room. She was on her knees, her head buried in her arms, her body wracked with sobs, and crushed in her hands was the magenta silk scarf, smelling of spices and sandalwood, her only bond now with the romantic land of her mother's people.

Nannie's philosophy also had its practical aspects. At the various birthday parties given by my friends, she would hover near my chair, murmuring to me sotto voce, "Put it in your pocket if you can't eat it." This I soon discovered was a most embarrassing piece of advice, as cakes would crumble and jelly sandwiches disintegrate in my small trouser pockets only too easily.

But on the days when my dog was perhaps ill or my favorite bantam chicken had died, Nannie would overwhelm me with consolation, trying to cheer me up with some sympathetic remark, such as, "Now, don't worry, Master Jan, dey is more happier where dey has gone. Remember God looks after every sparrow. I expect your bantam cock is crowing to de Lawd right this minute."

To Nannie, the Lord was everywhere and in everything. Having left home and Ouma's Muhammadan care at a very early age, she had embraced the Protestant faith of her employer with all the fervor of a convert. So, although she never criticized Ouma's pagan faith, she used to confide privately how sad she was that her mother had never found "de real Lawd."

In the domestic hierarchy, in order of long service next to Nannie was Peter, the gardener. Friend to us all, jack-of-all trades but never a master of any one, he was the source of continual irritation to my father, but a great help as well as a consolation to the rest of the family.

Peter was a soft-spoken, gentle colored man of doubtful parentage with an uneducated natural love of nature and an undoubted loyalty to the family he served. I think of him now as standing for hours through the long, hot afternoons of the summer, holding the hose and watering the growing annuals, while singing in a low, humming voice a series of his favorite hymns. This at least helped to keep him awake on his feet, even though, forgetfully, he often swamped the flower beds. Peter was expected to do a great many things, none of which he did very well, but his willingness made up to some extent for his inefficiency.

If, in carrying out Mama's copious orders, he made some fatal mistake, he would always try to retrieve the situation by saying, "But I thought Milady would prefer it done that way," to the utter confusion of my mother, who later reporting the matter would add, "Poor Peter is so stupid, but I suppose we must be thankful that he has any ideas at all of his own." My father was less tolerant, especially when he found his annuals planted in the wrong bed, or in the wrong color. "Dey all looks alike," said Peter in self-defense.

He had a colored wife, paler than he was, and a great many children. They lived with relatives in a crowded little cottage not far from our house. Though we seldom saw them, it seemed we were always hearing that Mrs. Peter was going to have another baby.

"And how many have you now, Maria?" I remember hearing Mama ask.

"Oh! Milady, I has to count them every time. I'se got a porch chile, and a creeper, den dere's a lap chile and a suckling, and now I'se got a hot bun in de oven." But Peter seemed quite resigned to his fate.

I know he must have been a kind father because of his courtesy and consideration for me. He had been with the family ever since my birth, so he had seen them through the long period of anxiety when my life hung in the balance. His thought for my mother through those anxious days had so endeared him to her that she supported him even against my father, who I am sure would otherwise have dismissed him in favor of a better gardener. But Peter remained, working very hard, trying to please, yet apparently the butt of everyone's annoyance. John, the butler, who was jealous of mother's fondness for Peter, never lost an opportunity to blame him for any little thing that might go wrong—the flowers cut too short, the wrong ferns brought in from the greenhouse, dirty boot marks on the polished floors—always poor Peter, who never answered back but accepted blame as though it was his fate to be the scapegoat.

But he knew how to please Mama. When things had gone badly against him, he would appear with the first opened gardenia, or a basketful of green almonds in his hand especially for "her ladysip."

He took correction from my parents in hurt silence, but with a look of such suffering that it was difficult to blame him. But even his nature rebelled against criticism from our governesses, especially one who, being very thorough in everything, did not hesitate to correct his inefficiency. He used to call her "Miss Boss" behind her back.

He had another problem in social relations that worried him a lot. For twice a year at least, there descended upon the garden six, usually portly colored women hired to weed the grass lawns. They came chatting gaily, armed with old forks or knives, to settle in huge clumps to dig the copious weeds, dandelions, and other pernicious plants that would sprout after the rains to strangle the finer grass sown on the croquet lawns. Their efforts were accompanied by much happy laughter, giggling, or jocular talk, and sometimes by songs that, if they became too raucous, had to be stopped by Peter with severity. He knew Mama forbade too much garrulity, but how to control these boisterous, gay females who could have picked him up in their motherly arms, he could never discover. He would be exposed to all the teasing and leg-pulling (no doubt often indecent) of the six large ladies, whose banter he could not suppress, since they swept his authority aside in gales of laughter.

I used to watch the scene from my window, the women with their bright-colored headkerchiefs like strange birds squatting on the grass, with Peter, self-conscious, small, beside them, quite unable to restrain them.

Years after our house was sold and my parents dead, I returned with my wife and stepdaughter to the Cape. I took them out to see the old house that had been my happy home. I asked a colored man we found working in the garden if he knew what had happened to Peter, who had worked so long for my family.

"He still works for de lady next door," the man said.

We sent for Peter. He came, gray-haired, limping, his eyes full of tears at the sight of me.

"Master Jan, it's Master Jan," was all he could say between his gulps. "I used to hold Master Jan in my arms," he said to my wife, "when he was a baby."

His children grown, his wife dead, Peter lived with a daughter, an old man full of memories, he told us, of the gay, entertaining family he had served through the long years of his life.

Thus we had black, brown, and white employees around us in our house, with the same variation among the outdoor staff. While Peter, the gardener, was colored brown, Taylor, the coachman, was white and very proud of his English background, though he had married a colored woman, a disgrace in those days, and produced a number of children of all shades from brown to white.

Kosi, the groom from Basutoland, who taught me to ride, was black—shiny blue-black—with the whitest rows of perfect teeth ever seen. He was quite young, wore a tattered straw hat, and seemed to be the happiest person in the world, judging by his ever-smiling face. He lived in the groom's room above the horse stalls of the stable, but he seemed to spend his whole life with the animals. Only on his day off and Sundays did he appear tidy, wearing his untorn straw hat, for he was a Christian and went to church on Sundays.

Papa had brought him from Basutoland to look after our horses under Taylor, the coachman, who was apt to scorn the obvious ability Kosi showed in managing them. But the Basutos were famous horsemen; besides, Papa had another idea.

We then had four horses. My two sisters at home each had their hunter and Mama her handsome pair of carriage bays, who were the pride of the stable. They were well bred of Arab stock, a perfect matching pair; Kosi polished their shining coats until they literally shone, a golden bronze. When I graduated from a bicycle, Papa gave me a birthday present of a Basuto pony, as dark and handsome as she was surefooted. She came from the same part of her native land as Kosi himself, and I shall never forget his huge, white smile of pleasure when she arrived to join our stables. She was fourteen hands, dark as a blackberry, with a pale belly and a bright white star on her forehead.

"She's lovely, isn't she, Kosi?" I said.

"Yes, *baas*," he answered smoothing the dark rump of the pony.

"But quite small," I added, "just the right height for me."

Kosi grinned. "Horses all same size, *baas*," he said emphatically, "don't grow no bigger."

"Could you ride when you were my age, Kosi?" I asked.

"Since I was piccanin, *baas*," he replied, putting his hand to the height of about three feet from the ground. "All ride horses in Lesuto," the name I discovered the Basuto call their own land.

I told Papa what Kosi had said.

"It's quite true about their size," he told me. "They are all small, maybe from the climate or simply because in winter they don't get enough of the right food to eat. Anyway, there are no horses in the world to equal them. They are more surefooted even than mules, and very hardy."

Papa had been to Basutoland quite often. He used to tell me a lot about that very individual tribe among the Bantu who had settled in the high mountain fastnesses. It seemed that, just as the Basuto had sprung into being as an individual tribe among the Bantu in only about a hundred years, so had their horses evolved into a breed entirely suited to their mountainous environment. The forebears of this sturdy breed of horse had been brought to South Africa from Java by the Dutch East India Company; they were of Arab and Persian origin. Through the early years of the company's government of the Cape, horses were often imported to replenish their stock. Thus, in 1778 a variety of mixed Arab blood was brought from Andalusia, while a few years later the first blood stock arrived from Britain.

I remember Papa telling me the story of these horses, for the Basuto, among all the tribes of the Bantu, is the only one known to either ride or even possess horses. Naturally, I asked the obvious question. How, if the horses were imported originally by the Dutch to Cape Town, did they ever reach the Bantu tribe living far inland in a mountainous area totally unsuited to the use of horses?

"It was their own chief, funnily enough," said Papa, "the great Moshesh himself, who introduced them to his people."

"How did he ever find them?" I asked.

"By raiding other tribes, among whom were the Griquas, who in turn had stolen them from the Dutch settled nearby along the Cape frontier."

"But the Bantu never owned horses, did they?"

"Of course not. They were scared to death of them at first, and thought they had come out of the sea. It took a long time for the Zulus even to go anywhere near a horse, but old Moshesh asked his witch doctors how to ride them, and, finding them quite simple to handle, he established an easy form of transport for everyone. The whole nation took to riding whenever they could find a horse."

"But what made the animals become so different, to other horses, I mean?"

"Only by inbreeding, I imagine, up there in the mountains. Animals adapt themselves very quickly to their surroundings," he added. "But it isn't only horses that make the Basuto so unique," Papa went on. "Their blankets and hats are just as unusual."

I laughed as I remembered that Kosi always wore a torn straw hat unlike any of the other Bantu boys who worked for us. A strange hat it was, too, pointed somewhat like the Malay hats but made of mealie (maize) straw, casually woven, with serrated edges.

"Why d'you think he wears a hat all the time?" I asked Papa.

"They all do in Basutoland," he answered. "I suppose to keep dry from the heavy rains and snow in their mountain ranges."

From what Papa said, it was the climate that was also responsible for the Basuto use of blankets, in which both men and women constantly draped themselves. What they did before the coming of the blanket I never found out. But it seemed that there were firms in Bradford, England, that had been making blankets for over a century in the vivid color schemes beloved by the native—red and blue, cerise and yellow, orange and green—entirely for the Basuto trade.

Some years later, I went to Basutoland and saw it all for myself: the high dramatic mountain ranges often covered in snow, the magnificent valleys green from the ever-silting snows, the people, draped in their brilliant blankets, looking like huge tropical birds, working in the fields or seated on their nimble ponies. There were few carts and fewer cars, since the roads were bad, water eroded and obviously little used; yet everywhere through the countryside were these gaily clad people riding their handsome horses, adding flaming accents of color to an already extraordinary landscape.

I soon found out that Basutoland is only about twelve thousand square miles of mostly mountainous country to which Moshesh had led his followers when he broke away from the Zulu empire. Moshesh led them over the ranges until they stood before Thaba Bosigo ("mountain of night"), the high, towering peak that was to become their citadel. From there Moshesh ruled, resisted, and conquered his enemies through numerous wars and frequent raids by jealous neighbors until, gradually, the Basuto, men of the mountains, became a nation. It has been administered by Great Britain together with Bechuanaland and Swaziland ever since Moshesh, the father of the nation, asked Queen Victoria in 1868 to include his people "under the Queen's blanket."

Now I had one of the famous horses of the Basuto for my very own.

"What shall we christen her, Kosi?" I asked.

"Don't know, *baas*. *Baas* wants Basuto name?" he asked incredulously. "I'se got a girl, *baas*, not Basuto girl. She's called Daisy."

I could hardly control my impulse to laugh, remembering the millions of daisies all over the world as white as snow, but I was the first to find a black daisy.

"Wonderful, Kosi," I said, laughing at last. "For you and for me she shall be called Daisy." He looked at me with his huge obsidian eyes limpid, like a loving animal.

"T'ank you, *baasje*," was all he said, leading Daisy back to her stall.

I have said that Kosi taught me to ride, not in the best European style perhaps, but he taught me something much more important, which was to really understand my horse. As I grew older, I learned to appreciate the secret communication between man and animals. I already had a wonderful intimacy with my dog Scamp, but I had never had a horse before.

Kosi knew all about horses. Papa used to say that the native peoples, not so far removed from the jungle laws as the white man, had retained an awareness that gave them an affiliation with the animal world. He told me that the Bushmen could smell animals from a long way off without being able to see them, and that by putting his ear to the ground the Bushman knew exactly what sort of animal it was that he could smell. Daisy and I developed a secret understanding whereby she forestalled my wish, foresaw my intention.

"You mus' talk to her, *baas*," Kosi would say, "speak close to her head, she will understand you." Gradually she did, until I didn't need to speak except to flatter or encourage her.

Kosi began by teaching me to ride bareback in the field below our house.

"No saddles in Lesuto," he said, "but Basuto ride any horse."

I remembered what he had said when I saw them in Basutoland, scrambling up their steep mountain passes, leaning forward like jockeys to help their horses, or tearing in full canter down the sharp inclines into the valleys, the riders in perfect balance, at one with their surefooted mounts.

Once I could ride I was allowed to go out alone without Kosi at my side; I would escape and canter, sometimes for hours, over the flats, as the wide, windy moors were called. These flats stretched beyond the fringes of the suburbs across the narrow corridor of the peninsula between the two seas, the Indian and Atlantic oceans. Planted with imported mimosa trees to hold the shifting sands, the flats were covered with an infinite variety of the loveliest indigenous flora for which the Cape has now become famous. Here and there an intrepid Dutch or German farmer, struggling against wind and sand, grew fruit and vegetables for the local market. But Daisy and I liked to gallop, undisturbed under the immense skies, stopping only to admire a drift of brilliant flowers or to cool ourselves in the water of one of the ponds. Sometimes these were covered with the scented blue lotus lilies or the white "water *uintjie*," as the Dutch called a lily-like water plant, the roots of which the colored folk cooked and ate. Sometimes I would be given a glass of fresh milk by a kind German *Frau*, or, leaving Daisy to crop the grass, standing in one place as she had been taught to do, I would pick a great bunch of wild gladioli to take back to Mama. Then for a wild gallop home in the setting sun, breathless and glorying in the smooth gait of my horse, who loved these outings as much as I did.

Indeed at all times of year, the flats were my favorite haunt.

Kosi had taught me to jump at first over the wide ditches running from the lakes, then later over low hedges of shrubs until he thought I was skilled enough to take the fences. My pony never hesitated, but seemed to enjoy jumping as much as I did.

7. *Flowers in South Africa*

FLOWERS have fascinated me from my earliest years. Mama used
to say it was my Dutch blood that explained it. But whatever
the reason, the fact that I was born and raised at the Cape of
Good Hope, one of the natural wild flower gardens of the
world, is something for which I have never ceased to be thankful.

The indigenous flora of that tip of the African continent has
grown to be recognized by botanists the world over, and it is no
wonder that the first Dutch pioneers exclaimed in ecstasy at the
miracles of natural growth they found on their arrival in 1652,
plants and flowers that no Dutchman had ever beheld before
then. Indeed, there were places on the Cape Peninsula that by
my time had become famous as centers of wild flower growth.
In fact, botanical experts have said that few areas in the world
of such a limited extent hold such a prolific flora.

By the time I was old enough to appreciate both the variety and natural beauty of the flowers growing around us in the lovely setting of my home, I had heard of the extraordinary profusion to be found in such places as Tulbagh, Ceres, and Caledon, the last of which I had seen for myself on my trips to the thermal baths there with my mother. But friends and travelers had returned from the hinterland of the west coast, north of our peninsula, known as Namaqualand, with tales of seeing such a profusion of wild flowers that my determination to see it all myself became an obsession and a bore to my family.

Papa had told me stories of the early days of Namaqualand, an area extending six hundred miles along the west coast and divided in two portions by the Orange River. The original inhabitants were thought to be the purest surviving type of Hottentots, some members of which tribe had finally found their way right down to the settlement on Table Bay. Thus it was that in 1661 van Riebeeck, the first Dutch governor of the colony, sent out several expeditions to explore this unknown area, one of which actually reached the Namaqua tribe, who sent back to van Riebeeck "a small buck, the first of its kind we have seen here." There were countless difficulties and hazards to be overcome on these expeditions but, nothing daunted, one Peter Everhardt was sent off with many gifts for "the King of the Namaquas and his family," according to C. L. Leipoldt's book, *J. Van Riebeeck*. The present for the king consisted of several strings of gaudily colored glass beads, a copper bracelet set with "an emerald stone, a red serge cap, and some pounds of tobacco, pipes and two small mirrors." After nearly two months, the expedition returned without having achieved their object, the Namaquas having retired further inland "beyond a large expanse of dry, salt, sand waste without the least drop of water."

No mention was made of the rich copper deposits that had not then been discovered by the white man, nor indeed of the fabulous flora, two most dissimilar assets that were to make Namaqualand famous in the years to come. Papa, being a Hollander, was more concerned with the flowers than the mineral wealth, and seemed anxious that I should go north to see them on one of my holidays. "The area has its own indigenous flora, unlike the rest of the country," he told me.

As early as 1772, two Swedish botanists, Andrew Sparrman and Carl Peter Thunberg, landed at Cape Town to be joined later by a third, Francis Masson, an Aberdonian who had been sent plant hunting in South Africa by the director of Kew Gardens, Sir Joseph Banks. A berth was found for him in Captain Cook's ship *Resolution*, which, sailing from Plymouth in June 1772, put Masson down at Cape Town. Here he found over four hundred species of plants new to the scientists of Europe, and with these, Kew Gardens attained eminence in the botanical world to become one of the richest institutions of Europe.

It was Masson who corrected the botanical world about the flower called *Nerine sarniensis* when he found it growing on Table Mountain, where it rightly belongs, though for most of a century people accepted it as a product of the Channel Islands. This was because in 1659 a Dutch ship, homeward bound via the Cape from the Far East, was wrecked on the Channel Islands. There were boxes of bulbs from the Cape on board consigned to Holland. The bulbs washed ashore on Guernsey and took root there, where later they burst into radiant flower, to the delight of the inhabitants. There they flourished, and in time bunches of the lilies were shipped to Covent Garden in London, where they naturally were called Guernsey lilies, until the botanists came to classify them, naming them *Nerine* and *sarniensis* from Sarnia, the Latin name for the Channel Islands.

The two Swedes collecting at the Cape were naturally hovered over by the spirit of their master, the great Carl Linnaeus who, though he never visited South Africa, is responsible for having named a large number of native plants sent him by his two eager pupils. He once referred to the Cape of Good Hope as "that paradise upon earth," and was at the peak of his career during the governorship of Ryk Tulbagh (1751–71), with whom he carried on a correspondence in Latin. He used to send to the governor the names he had given to the new plants sent him from various sources in South Africa, with details of "their genera and distinctions." To honor the governor, he named one of his new acquisitions "tulbaghia," a member of the lily family having more than twenty species in South Africa. He wrote that he would have given up all his good fortune to change places with his correspondent, the governor of the country, "which the beneficent Creator has enriched with his choicest wonders."

Tulbagh died seven years before Linnaeus and only one year before our two great Swedes, Sparrman and Thunberg, landed at the Cape. Masson spent more time at the Cape than either of his contemporaries, for, after returning to Kew and exploring Portugal, the Canaries, and Madeira, he went back to the Cape in 1785 and stayed many years.

I had been to Madeira many times as a child, as it was the one stop on the sea route between Cape Town and Southhampton, and as I traveled with Mama back and forth to England, I had grown accustomed to looking forward to our regular stops at the island.

As history always surrounds any place of interest, so Papa had told me in his inimitable way, making history into a romantic tale by the manner of his telling, about the discovery of Madeira by the intrepid sailors sent out by Henry the Navigator of Portugal. Madeira had been one of the first Portuguese discoveries as their ships crept down the African coast searching for a way across the enormous continent, or at least for an end to the tremendous obstacle this land mass created, barring their way to Prester John and the unknown Indies.

Henry had set himself the task of somehow finding Prester John, that elusive monarch whose very name had sent shivers down the spines of the courts of Europe since the twelfth century. Rumors of his power and fabulous wealth had reached Henry, encouraging him to think of Prester John as an ideal ally against the Moslems, whose sweeping conquests threatened to engulf the Christian world. For Prester John was known to be a Christian, and it was said that his whole nation had been converted and baptized as early as the third century A.D. Fanatical Portugal dreamed of such an alliance, which would resist the pagan invasion and undoubtedly add glory to the kingdom in the eyes of Rome. Besides his wealth, John supposedly had a vast number of men at arms. Henry had visions, not only of a conquest of the infidels, who constantly threatened the Portuguese coast from North Africa, but of a trade in gold, ivory, and precious stones that would enrich Portugal's throne.

No one knew where Prester John or the Indies were to be found—the Moors held that secret—but Henry, on his knees in burning faith, believed he was destined to discover it for the glory of God. There was no traffic across Africa from the Orient except over the camel trade routes of the North African deserts, and, since these were all controlled by the Moslems, no Christians dared even venture to find a way across the continent. But Henry was determined, and sent his ships further and further down the African coast until his captain, Bartholomeu Diaz, discovered the end of the continent literally by accident in a storm, when he found himself sailing north instead of south and knew he had rounded the then unknown cape of "Bon Esperanca."

By the time I visited the island of Madeira, it had become famous for several products. Most renowned was the Madeira wine made from the grapes Henry had introduced and the English had adopted almost as their own; the embroidery, at which the women of the island were particularly adept, sold successfully in England; and the cane furniture, sturdily woven and light to handle. Mama used to buy a regular supply of each of these commodities on our return sailings south, especially when Papa was with us.

But as often as I could, I would escape into the open parks or the terraced gardens of Reid's Hotel, where flowers and shrubs brought back by the Portuguese from the mysterious East flourished in abundance. Many of these were carried later to the Cape by the Dutch, who followed in Portugal's footsteps to the Spice Islands of the East, and I recognized them as old friends, remembering just where they grew at home under Table Mountain or on the flats between the oceans. But on the island were varieties I had never seen, and finding a possibly new species gives me a thrill that only someone botanically minded can understand.

I knew I wasn't a botanist, but I was beginning to keep a record of my finds, especially those in odd, unexpected places, like the rocky, windy promontory on Cape St. Vincent, where Henry the Navigator had built his "college" of navigation and where I found the white spider lily, the Ismene or Peruvian daffodil, as it is called, growing by the thousand between the rocks with apparently no soil for their roots, but scenting the air with their perfume. I found them again much later on the island of Corsica, growing on slopes under the chestnut trees, a strange, unforgettable flower.

On the island I remember once finding the lovely datura lily, not virginal white as usual, but pale yellow, the color of a primrose; an hibiscus, which grew flaming scarlet in Papa's garden but there was a rosy pink; and on one voyage I came across a thunbergia, named after our early botanist at the Cape by his teacher Linnaeus, not lavender-blue, which I knew well, but tumbling in white cascades over the pink-washed walls. From tall trees I didn't recognize I used to pick up fallen blossoms, some lilylike flowers of pale pink with a thousand stamens, and take them back in my handkerchief to Papa on the ship. He invariably knew their country of origin, their name, and their botanical classification.

To my delight, I also found there the velvety white arum lily that flourished in the fields around my home. Its elegance never suffered from its common name at the Cape of Pig Lily, so named because the pigs were said to enjoy the fleshy roots. Tall

vases of them backed by their large pointed leaves added much
to the decoration of our house. They, too, seem to have traveled
the world: in Mexico they grow in the streams along the road-
sides, though I have never met the golden variety anywhere
other than South Africa, where it is native to the Transvaal.
Our American friends knew it from their florists and always
called them "calla lilies," the name Linnaeus had originally
given them, but we stuck to the "pig lilies" of the vernacular.
On Madeira, they seemed quite small compared to the giants I
had picked at the Cape, but the velvet texture of their curved
trumpets distinguishes them from all other lilies.

"Aha," Papa said one evening on my return to the ship, "that
one comes from India," as he took the large, heavy-petaled flowers with their thick, short stems. "I don't know its name," he
had to admit, "but I know it's Indian." It is indeed found all
over India, and is commonly called the red silk cotton. A tall
handsome tree, it has prickly horizontal branches from which
spring small wrinkled twigs that carry the big, ruby-colored
flowers. Years later, I found the same tree in Mexico, when the
pointed fruits had been split open by the bursting fluffy cotton
within, floating down to earth like gossamer, carrying the small
black seeds.

When Papa said "India," my mind jumped at once to Henry's sailors, probably bringing back the seeds from Goa after
planting their Portuguese flag on Indian soil. "Wouldn't Prince
Henry's ships have stopped here on their way home?" I asked
Papa.

"Of course," he said, though I am sure he was quite uncertain.

The island seemed full of trees I knew; the jacaranda, droop-
ing its deep blue-mauve clusters as gracefully as I had seen them
in South Africa. They, too, came from Malaysia, though years
later I found them in Colombia as well.

But the greatest pleasure of all was to pick up the exquisite,
sweet-scented blossoms of the frangipani, the temple tree from
India, where it is revered by both Buddhists and Muhammadans

alike, and who have put it to various medicinal uses. I had seen it in the Transvaal when traveling with Papa on one of his circuits as the presiding judge. There the color of the waxy flowers was more crimson and pink; but on Madeira there seemed to be several varieties, though as always the ground beneath the trees was covered with a scented mantle of immaculate flowers, which fall soon after opening.

This traveling of trees and plants from land to land never ceased to interest me. As I grew older and had the opportunity of moving about the world, I kept a record of my botanical friends that I found in place after place, noting how in many instances they adapted themselves to varied environment. But, over and over again, I would find to my secret joy one or other of the plants I had known in their home setting in South Africa. As one reads of how their reputation grew, and of the many botanists or naturalists from all over the world who came to collect for their different countries, spreading varieties by the thousand to almost every country on the globe, it should not be surprising to find them, in the most unexpected settings as I so often have done.

I think back to the history of the Cape, when in 1797, under the governorship of Lord Macartney, my lovely heroine Lady Anne Barnard, to whom I constantly refer, the wife of His Excellency's secretary and one of the witty Lindsay family, accompanied her husband to his new position in Cape Town. The record of this lady's life in South Africa is told in the many amusing, though often serious letters she wrote to her sisters in England and to her dear friend, the Right Honorable Henry Dundas, secretary for war and president of the Board of Control in Pitt's first administration. These letters, tied together and carefully preserved among his most cherished papers at Melville Castle, show that "the great Minister, through all his many vicissitudes, kept a soft corner in his heart for Lady Anne."

Her interest in the flora of the Cape resulted in her close association with Mr. Barrow, the naturalist attached to the governor's staff. Between them, they collected seeds and bulbs of many of the native plants which Lady Anne sent to Lord Melville in London, tied up in little muslin bags, docketed and described with meticulous care. Since her day, a great many exotics from other countries, most prominently Holland and the East Indies, have been brought to find a happy home at the Cape; but, nevertheless, we are told that over two thousand indigenous wild flowers are still to be found scattered over the peninsula alone.

I cannot forget the Adderley Street of my youth in Cape Town, where the flower sellers gathered in front of the old Post Office Building, selling bunches of a hundred varieties of heaths from buckets and baths for only threepence a bunch. The flowers made a vivid array like a rainbow down the busy street, for there were all sorts on sale, picked ruthlessly on the flats and mountainsides. In those days, there were no "controls" over the sale of our wild flowers, and every housewife would return home after a morning's shopping in the town laden with bunches of the colorful blooms—now strictly controlled.

I did a painting of these flower sellers, reproduced in my sister's book, *The Cape Peninsula*, and later exhibited in the annual show of the Society of South African Artists, at which I was the youngest artist exhibiting that year.

One could not write of South African flowers without paying tribute to perhaps the most beautiful of them all, the red disa. This "Pride of Table Mountain" as it is called, the richest and rarest of the several species of disa found in the Cape Peninsula, has for many years excited botanists from all over the world. Originally found in the cool gorges of Table Mountain during the early eighteenth century, it reached Stockholm among seeds and pressed flowers sent by an employee of the Dutch East India Company to Petrus J. Bergius, a Swedish doctor and scientist, who named the fabulous scarlet orchid *Disa uniflora* in his published description of the flower in 1767.

However, Linnaeus the younger on good evidence changed

African wild flowers, drawing by Jan Juta: *left to right, Disa grandiflora, Protea cynaroides, Protea mellifera, Gladiolus spathaceus, Gladiolus debilis, Ixia duckittiae, Gerbera Jamesonii*

the name to *Disa grandiflora*, inasmuch as several examples were found with two or three flowers on each stem.

The flower is so dramatic, its color so vivid, the three-petaled form so perfect that it is no wonder that botanists have come from far and wide to see it in its native habitat. Before the bulbs were wantonly pulled up, and the flowers torn from their damp hideouts by both visitors and colored flower sellers alike, these exquisite orchids could be found in the stream-cooled gorges of the mountain in quantities.

Only once do I remember finding them, secret and resplendent, when my sister and I climbed the famous gorge in which they were known to flourish. The two scarlet velvet wings of the flower, flanking the striped pink center cup gives a unique splendor to this disa, which looks more like an exotic bird alighting on a stem than a shy orchid.

Even Charles Bunbury, the English botanist visiting Government House in Cape Town in 1838, was up early in the morning to join William Harvey, the colonial treasurer and an eager Irish botanist, in climbing the mountain in search of the renowned disa. It was Harvey, who had begun to compile his famous book, the *Flora Capensis*, who has left his name to posterity in the lovely harveyas found all over the Cape mountains, in pink and velvety white blooms.

Once while visiting friends in the Tulbagh valley I saw my first "chincherinchees," the lovely white ornithogalum or star-of-Bethlehem, as they are commonly called. I shall remember all my life the field of white, shivering flowers, heavy on the fleshy stalks blowing in the breeze. An orange variety, much less well known, grows in the same area, but lacks the pure white beauty of its cousin, which opens slowly in water and lasts for weeks when cut. The onomatopoeic name is surely African, though its origin is questioned and is supposed to resemble the sound of the fleshy stems rubbing together in the breeze, which sound Thunborg, the Swedish botanist, noticed more than 180 years ago. Today these invaluable flowers are exported in quantities to every flower market in the world, where they are in constant demand. But in their own unspoiled habitat their white purity is a memory to be treasured.

At some seasons, the flats would yield blazing mesembryanthemums, or from the lakes the scented blue water lilies. At others, from the mountains came the proteas, our national flower, of which there are over ninety species. Most people don't know that the silver tree (*Leucadendron*) is a protea, the tallest member of this huge family, with brightly shining, pointed leaves covered with a soft, hairy sheen that shines and sparkles in the sunlight. As children, we would carefully pick an inconspicuous branch when in flower, with its tight cone, delicately tinted and sweetly fragrant, nestling in a rosette of shimmering silver leaves. This we took home as the crowning glory of our bunch of wild flowers for Mama, most of which grew scattered under the silver trees, where they reigned supreme. Once upon a time, a small band of these lovely trees stood on the slopes of Wynberg Hill, supposedly their last stronghold, for they had been burned out of their other refuges. But now they are successfully grown from seed, not only privately in areas far removed from their natural habitat but in other countries as well, New Zealand and California, for example.

The brown-eyed colored ladies who sold the flowers had both ingratiating charm as well as a keen sense of bargaining.

"*Ach*, master," one would say, "come see what I have here, just what the master likes, these lovely crassula . . . *Ach!* Master, I had a long climb to get these, and they are so rare."

One was quite sure her wretched son or exhausted husband had had to clamber the slopes to find them for her.

"How much are they?"

"Well now, master, remember where they come from, how high it is to climb, yet I only ask you one and sixpence."

At the sound of the price, the rival next in line would pluck my sleeve.

"See, master, my beautiful watsonias," she would say, "all the way from the Muizenberg Mountains, a long way, master, and only one and threepence."

Thus it would go until one succumbed to all the blandishments and bought far more than one needed, but hardly anyone thought then of how the indigenous flora were being torn to pieces and plucked without a care for their rarity.

Both the Post Office and the flower sellers have been removed today to another area, and the preservation societies are fighting to keep the natural heritage of these unusual flowers from total extinction.

My curiosity only served to whet my appetite for what I believed lay ahead for me in Namaqualand, but nothing I had ever seen equaled what I saw there. By the time I went, I knew a little about the floral kingdom of my country but I think it was the scale of the landscape, the impact of the immense masses of color on my eyes and senses that I was not prepared for.

I had a friend, Hans, older than I was and allowed to drive his father's car. Together we planned that, when we both had a vacation and the flowers were in bloom, we would snatch the given opportunity to escape to Namaqualand. Hans studied maps for the most interesting routes and places to stay as near to the flowering areas as possible. A fortunate opportunity came through a friend of Papa's with substantial interests in a newly developed copper mine right in the midst of the flowering world in O'okiep, a small village of miners' cottages. His factor in charge of mining operations had the one really strongly built house in that huge desert area, and our friend offered to arrange for us to have a "shakedown" in his factor's house.

As our holidays grew closer, my excitement increased and the thought that we boys would be off on our own into an unknown paradise made me impatient and unmanageable. I counted the days and prayed for rain in the desert.

"I don't think you are old enough or responsible enough to go off like this," said Mama, and my spirits sank. "Remember what happened at Worcester?"

"I think he knows what we expect of him by now," replied Papa and my heart almost burst with gratitude for his understanding. He knew how much this chance meant for me, and, even if he too doubted, he supported the idea and calmed my mother's ever-watchful anxiety for her wayward son.

We took the easiest route up the west coast from Cape Town, past towns neither of us knew except by name. Very soon we began to see signs of the flowering season along the roadside.

The lovely arctotis, a native South African genus, was already in bloom, although I was yet to see the handsomest species in Namaqualand itself. It is a delicate daisylike flower with silvery foliage whose main stems lie prone, so that a single plant may festoon yards with its matlike growth. The flowers literally illuminate the landscape and come in browns, crimson, pink, and even a cream white. In Afrikaans they are called *gousblom*, *gous* for "golden" and *blom* for "flower." I think it must have traveled throughout the world, for I have met it in so many different lands, and it rivals in beauty its Namaqualand cousins, the gazania, venedium and ursinia, all golden-rayed to set the valleys aflame.

Here and there we saw outcroppings of some of the innumerable heaths for which the country is famous. I wish I knew more about them, for there are supposedly at least five hundred different species, with South Africa alone renowned for its waxen heaths, some of which Thunberg described in 1775.

The west coast route is not at all the area for the heaths, which long ago chose to establish themselves in the Ceres, Caledon, and Riversdale divisions. In the Caledon Wild Flower Garden, which is a most wonderful sight in the spring, many are easily being propagated as they also are in the National Botanical Gardens at Kirstenbosch. But in those early days there were only a few people, botanists or dedicated flower lovers like my father, who really cared about their extraordinary heritage at the Cape of Good Hope.

I stopped the car to pick one of the well-known varieties of heath that had strayed from its homeland right into our path, the lovely rosy pink and white fronds of the *Erica perspicua*, tall, elegant, graceful as a bird's feather. I know that there are over one hundred species of the *Erica* genus to be found in South Africa, but their story would fill several volumes.

It was sunset as we drove into Springbok, our goal on the map, and asked the way to the mine manager's house. The last rays of the sun were setting the whole landscape on fire.

"Oh, look," I said, breathless at the sight as we drove out of the village right into the setting sun. Gold, orange, red, and yellow swept across the valleys and up the hillsides to their rocky summits as far as one could see—nothing but this blazing color to the horizon in every side. We stopped the car and sat silent, overcome by such splendor.

"If it's flowers you are after, you've come to the right place," said our cordial host, "and at just the right moment," he added, as I silently thanked God for the rain.

"We heard you had had some rain," I said.

"Just enough to get the whole kingdom going," he went on. "I see you've brought your cameras."

"Oh, yes, we want to start out early tomorrow, if that is all right for you?" I asked.

"Coffee will be on the boil at the crack of dawn, and there's bread and butter."

I thanked him.

"We brought some stuff along with us," Hans said, "so we won't be back till sunset."

"Then you can tell us what you've found over dinner," said our hostess, a pale, blonde woman with gray eyes.

"But you've seen it all many times, I imagine."

"It's always exciting," she replied. "Something new turns up after the rains, and you never know."

"Have you been here long?" I asked.

"Seems long," she said wistfully. "Our eldest is getting on for five."

We crept out of the house to our car the next morning just as the first light began to fill the immense bowl of the pale gray sky. Taking the first sandy track from the house, we could see it winding faintly ahead of us through the acres of flowers.

We stopped before we had gone more than a mile.

"I must get out and look closer," I said excitedly to Hans. "Are there nothing but daisies?"

I was quite mistaken. There seemed to be layers of flowers, from small, bright things prone on the desert floor enmeshed with others, taller, though the arctotis dominated, tallest of all; the whole was woven of sunlight in yellows, orange, and gold into a solid carpet made of flowers, laid over the landscape for miles and miles around us.

"I never imagined it could be so vast."

"It looks endless," Hans agreed.

There were some open patches where lemon-yellow grielum occupied the earth; a five-petaled open flower, first cousin to the oxalis, an immense family, some low and single in pinks and lavenders, others taller, with three or four blooms on the stem and three leaflets, making it look like clover. They seemed to grow wherever there was space enough to clasp the sunlight.

I could name a dozen other flowers I found in among the arctotis but will only mention the many varieties of lobelia, tall, medium or shrublets, struggling on the earth's surface or erect, some pale or ultramarine blue; and the nemesia, now hybridized the world over but that there form sweeps of color, dark maroon or bicolored in gay yellow or pinks.

Suffice to say that, when we returned to the Cape after daily traveling through rolling desert country where the flowers grew right up the sides of the hillocks or *kopjes* to end almost in a straight line where the cupriferous rocks maintained their own domain, I took with me a bucket full of species I didn't know. These I spread out before the botanical authorities at Kirstenbosch, which Cecil Rhodes had bought in 1895, planting it with camphor and chestnut trees, and which has become the model for the other botanical centers throughout the peninsula. There I spent much time with pen and paper.

It was years before I saw the glory of Namaqualand again. Facilities in that area have changed. Roads are now well maintained, and the copper mines flourish for the benefit of the world. So do the extraordinary flowers of the district, which, as if by a miracle, leap up from the desert sands the moment one drop of rain touches them—that otherwise lie, dormant and unseen, waiting—asleep but alive—until God sends them the rain in another year or two.

8. Visitors

I wish I could remember all the interesting and unusual people who came to my father's house. They were so varied and as I have said, came from all over the world: diplomats, musicians, artists, and sportsmen, the famous and the unknown. All benefited by Mama's generous hospitality, all enjoyed our lovely garden, the good food, the happy atmosphere my family created. Some of the guests were merely a duty, though many developed into lifelong friends, like Philip Kerr, who was one of Lord Milner's * oncoming young men from England, and later, having inherited his title of Lord Lothian, was appointed British ambassador to Washington, D.C. I remember him playing tennis with my sisters and drinking whiskey and sodas with Papa

* Lord Alfred Milner, governor of the Cape Colony.

while discussing Rhodes's vision of South Africa. I was very young, but I never forgot him.

My sister and I were often critical of our parents' guests. Some we found ridiculous and made rude remarks about them, others so charming that we longed for their return. It naturally depended on how they treated us.

The most exciting guests from our point of view were those we only heard about from letters of introduction: the English, the distant relatives from Scotland, the Americans who, through Rhodes's friend, John Hays Hammond,* the mining engineer, found their way to our house. Mama would read aloud to us parts of some letter she had received introducing this or that individual to her hospitality. "Here's another one," she would say, "who sounds really interesting, a musician sent to us by Lady Davenport, who says he is charming and so talented. Perhaps we can get him here to play for us. Wouldn't that be exciting?" Her own enthusiasm was always conveyed to us, as listening to the descriptions we would guess what the newcomers would be like and make bets on their living up to our expectations.

My memories range over such a variety of people, many now long dead, but the pictures of some of them remain like sharply

---

* Mr. John Hays Hammond, the famous American mining engineer, came frequently to our house during Papa's early association with Cecil Rhodes. He had become associated with Barnato Brothers in 1893 and came out to South Africa as a consulting engineer for the Consolidated Goldfields Company of South Africa. As a boy I only met him some years later. He was a prominent leader in the Rand faction that led to the famous Jameson Raid, and in 1896 he was arrested, tried, and condemned to prison. His sentence was later commuted and he was released on payment of a fine of $125,000. He returned home to the United States, where he undertook a variety of important posts connected with mining properties both in the United States and Mexico. Years later after I had come to America I met his family. John, his eldest son, a brilliant inventor; Richard, a musician; and Natalie, their most gifted sister. John, Jr., had built himself a medieval castle on the coast of Gloucester Harbor, Massachusetts, where I visited frequently with my hostess, Miss Cecilia Beaux.

cut vignettes, vivid and alive because of their effect upon me, my thinking, and, in some cases, my whole life.

During the Boer War, it seemed that everyone connected with England or the British army came to our house. I still remember for one reason or another many of those who stayed at "Mon Desir."

No one who had ever seen Lord Kitchener could possibly forget his mustachios! Papa also had them, for they were then the fashion, and I can recall our butler, John, telling us in great excitement how the English "Lord" looked "just like your pa." It was the greatest compliment he could pay Papa.

The Balen-Powells lived in a charming old-fashioned house called "The Vineyard," not far from ours, and Miss Baden-Powell would bring her very aged mother to tea with Mama and tell us fascinating stories of her amazing brother. I remember seeing a letter she wrote to my mother on paper that had her famous brother's photograph printed on it, together with the words "The Hero of Mafeking" below the picture. Even then it struck me as very strange and ostentatious.

On what was called the "Camp Ground" at Rondebosch, another suburb of Cape Town, there was a hospital donated by the duke of Westminster, presided over by many titled ladies of the British aristocracy, most of whom had sons or husbands fighting in "the frightful war" against the Boers. Mama used to go over and help as an aide, and became friends with many of them, bringing them back to our house for possible consolation. I can still see Lady Edward Cecil, and lovely Lady Romilly, who used always to talk to us, for she had children of her own in England; she wore delicious scent that lingered in our drawing room for hours after tea with Mama.

Though I didn't see him, my sisters talked enthusiastically about Mr. Winston Churchill, who was taken by Papa to see our new Basuto pony lately imported from Basutoland for my eldest sister to ride. Mr. Churchill, with a sharp eye for a good horse, bought several of the same breed for his polo stable in

England on the strength of that introduction. No horses are swifter or more surefooted than the ponies bred by the Basutos for their high mountainous country.

Of all the many famous people that the Boer War brought into our circle, the one who had interested Mama the most was Winston Churchill's mother, Lady Randolph Churchill. That she was an American, though the widow of an Englishman of title and distinction, only added to the glamour that had always surrounded that extraordinary lady. Mama talked about her with enthusiasm.

"She was the most wonderful woman I had ever met, and the most beautiful," said Mama, her eyes bright with the excitement of remembrance.

In 1899, when the war was at its worst and the British forces were suffering severe reverses, Lady Randolph had conceived the exciting notion of gathering funds from the American women in Great Britain to equip and furnish, with staff and medical stores, a hospital ship called the *Maine* for the relief of the sick and wounded British soldiers in South Africa.

"Only someone with a genius for organization could possibly have done it," said Mama in admiration when telling me about the dark days of the war long after it was all over. She described how Lady Randolph had called together a committee of distinguished ladies, gathered funds, took her American staff to be presented to Queen Victoria, who was vitally interested in the whole idea, and had the personal honor of being invited to dine with the queen and stay at Windsor Castle.

It was on December 23, 1899, that the *Maine* moved out through the English fog on her mission of mercy. On the deck stood the woman responsible for the whole enterprise, her heart full of anxiety for her two sons, Jack and Winston, both already in the war against the Boers in South Africa. It was well known that America under President McKinley was strongly pro-Boer, but Lady Randolph, doubtless with her loyalties somewhat divided, had been determined to have both the Union Jack, as well as the Stars and Stripes, well supported by the Red Cross banner, flying at the mast of the ship she had been so instrumental in obtaining.

In Cape Town the whole staff of the *Maine* were invited to a reception given in their honor at the Mount Nelson Hotel which had always been and still is the best-known hotel in the city and the center of every sort of activity. Mama, representing her Cape of Good Hope Society, went to the party and joined in the welcome for this intrepid American adventure.

"They were such exciting days," she said. "Lord Roberts as commander in chief had inspected the ship, and Lady Randolph was delighted by his approval of everything." But Lady Randolph was most concerned about her sons, who had both joined the South African light horse regiment after Winston had escaped from his capture by the Boers while a war correspondent for the *Morning Post* in London. He was determined to get to the fighting front in any regiment that he could join.

Before the ship sailed from Cape Town to Durban, Mama had invited Lady Randolph and some of her ladies to tea at "Mon Desir." I unfortunately missed my chance of meeting the famous lady, but my mother remembered "that most beautiful woman" all her life. In July 1900 Lady Randolph married Lieutenant George Cornwallis West, who though much younger than she was, had wooed her ardently through many years.

I have said that my father was a keen cricketer who took an active part in anything to do with the game and, indeed, played with his cronies from "the bench" until his eyesight began to fail. It was natural that he hoped I, too, would enjoy the game and play it well but, though I was taught by the best available professional, and practiced hard at the nets, I never developed any real enthusiasm for it but much preferred tennis and football.

I remember a charming, gentle man who came for a weekend to our house, bringing me a cricket bat signed and dated. He was George Lohmann, the most famous all-around cricketer of his day. Tall, fair, and good-looking, he played for Surrey, coming to South Africa with the visiting English team, who were considered unbeatable and toured Australia with repeated success. How flattered I was by his present, and how my insides sank with a kind of shame in front of Papa, who wished so much that I would be worthy of the gift. Poor Lohmann came back to South Africa to die of tuberculosis, which even then had begun to destroy his lungs.

Later, he was followed by "Plum" Warner, who captained the MCC team, bringing his pretty wife to stay with us. Though he tried to teach me to bowl, I never became any good at it, despite my sisters' encouragement.

There were amusing incidents connected with some of the guests that still remain in my memory. There was one whose name was Archie. He had never been successful at anything, but came to ask Papa to find him a job. We children didn't think much of him . . . "He has such wet hands," said my sister with scorn. But because of some sentimental reason connected with his family, Papa was always being asked to help in some dire situation. The job was found, but Archie wrote asking for the loan of fifteen pounds sterling, as he had no teeth left and could not take the job without any! Generous as always, Papa sent him the money. I can remember so well my father's face as he read a letter from Archie telling us the horrible truth of how he had been sent from Cape Town to Port Elizabeth, a short but often very rough passage over stormy seas, and of how sick he had been, losing everything, so to speak, including the fifteen pounds' worth of new teeth, which went overboard together with everything else! Needless to say, we did not see Archie for some time, though we always laughed at any mention of his name.

Then there came another memorable visit from the famous Mrs. Cora Brown Potter, the great American actress. I still remember her arrival because I was waiting for her, hiding behind the hibiscus shrubs, anxiously looking forward to seeing this individual, about whom there had been so much discussion at the dinner table. Her success in the repertoire of plays then being performed in Cape Town had made her even more important in our eyes, but, above all, she was an American, coming from a land we knew little about but that was wrapped in a sort of exciting mystery, a land of fabulous wealth and wonderful creativity. We children always associated it either with Red Indians, whose legends we loved to read, or the dramatic history of the Revolutionary War, with the picture of George Washington crossing the Delaware before our eyes.

We had met very few Americans—the consul, and Mr. Hammond, the mining engineer among them—but nothing had prepared us for Mrs. Brown Potter, a wraith in black chiffon and an enormous hat, clutching in her arms her pet monkey, who was an unexpected guest. As she stepped out of Mama's carriage, which had been sent to meet her, and swept up the steps to our front door, where John the butler was bowing a welcome, a sudden wave of excitement flooded over me at the sight of this most exquisite creature. I saw for the first time the grace, the gestures, the affected assurance of a great actress whose slim, sinuous hands had woven enchantment around the world since first she had deserted society in America for the stage. For some reason I can't recall, Mrs. Potter was not performing that Saturday night, so my parents were giving a dinner in her honor. As usual, my sister and I were relegated to the morning room for our meal, but not before we had heard all about the arrangements for the welfare of Sacha, the monkey. It seemed that Sacha always slept in his mistress's bedroom in a satin-lined basket, but, if left alone, tied by an elegant leash, he contented himself with his many toys and "never got into any mischief." My father was not entirely happy about this unexpected visitor, for the monkey disturbed the dogs and frightened our very domestic cat almost to death, none of them having ever seen a monkey before.

But as we watched Mrs. Potter flow downstairs that evening,

swathed this time in lavender lace, her neck encased in pearls
—"She had a rich lover in Chicago," gossiped my sister—
leaving a trail of exquisite perfume hanging in the air of the
hall, she seemed so romantic, so different and beautiful, that we
hardly gave a thought to Sacha.

He evidently found himself in surroundings he didn't particularly like, so, seeing the bedroom door slightly ajar, he slipped
his bejeweled collar and decided to go for a little survey of our
house. Unfortunately he made for Mama's bedroom, where the
lights had been left on and the door open. Mr. Sacha scampered
in to find, to his delight, a dressing table full of all the things he
had been used to in his mistress's room yet somehow different,
with new smells, new shapes and textures to pick up and play
with. My sister and I had gone to bed, and the guests were con-
tinuing their gay conversation in the drawing room, when a
loud shriek woke us with a start. We rushed onto the landing in
our dressing gowns to find Mrs. Brown Potter calling desperately for Sacha.

"He is gone," she said dramatically. "O my Sacha, where are
you, my darling?" she called, as she raced in and out of every
room.

Quickly, I darted into Mama's bedroom at the end of the corridor to find the dressing table a shambles and Sacha sitting
among the ruins of scent bottles, jars, vases, and brushes, his
whole face white with Mama's favorite powder, his little fingers
all scarlet with creams and rouge. I ran to fetch Mrs. Potter,
who, caring nothing for the damage, snatched Sacha to her
bosom and covered his powdery face with kisses. It must have
been difficult for her to apologize enough to Mama for all the
breakage, although I know she offered to replace every broken
item. But the memory of Sacha's escapade has remained to this
day.

I never saw Mrs. Potter act, although Papa, who had met her
in London, where Henry Irving had befriended her, often spoke
of her talent, her beauty, and the quality she possessed to bring

to life Juliet, Ophelia, and the many other Shakespearean heroines she played.

Her first season in Cape Town, where her company was playing at the Exhibition Theatre supposedly for six months, was brought to a tragic end by a strange catastrophe. For suddenly, one Sunday evening, the theater burned to the ground with everything in it—scenery, manuscripts, costumes, music—everything except Mrs. Potter's magnificent wardrobe and personal possessions, which had been removed only the day before to her rented villa. This had been the result of an unexpected warning she had received from an unknown source.

Two days before the fire, as Mrs. Potter was leaving the stage door surrounded by many admirers, an unknown woman had given her a large bunch of flowers, to which was attached a note. Hastily, she had put the note into her handbag and not, until some hours later, even bothered to read it. The writer, after saying how much she admired the star, her lovely voice, and superb acting, warned her to move everything she possessed from the theater, as it was going to be burned. Hastily, Mrs. Potter instructed her secretary-companion to have all her clothes, papers, and possessions moved at once to her own house, in spite of the protests of her friends and her leading man, Kyrle Bellew, who teased her mercilessly for believing such nonsense. But the following evening the theater, which was an old-fashioned wooden building, together with some attached offices, was burned to the ground.

The tragedy upset the whole town. Everything the company possessed was destroyed, and, although only halfway through the season, they were obliged to return to England, suffering great financial loss. The management as well as the people of the town offered to help them in their predicament, but Mrs. Brown Potter and company sailed away brokenhearted. It was rumored that only the star herself had been somewhat compensated, by the generous gift, from Alfred Beit, the mining millionaire, of two superb diamonds the shape of dewdrops, which he told her were the tears of her captivated audiences, sad at her departure.

I was only reminded of the whole incident when, years later, I was taken by Papa to a performance by a well-known orchestra in the theater at Monte Carlo, and there in the audience he suddenly recognized Cora Brown Potter, very aged by that time but still lovely, with her profile so finely cut, her dark eyes burning, still alive with old remembrances; and her hands, once so poetic, now veiled in white lace mittens. Papa was amazed; pointing her out to me, he remarked, "Those hands in mittens, like Venus in white gloves."

He reminded me of the fire and together we laughed over the memory of Sacha in Mama's bedroom. I gazed at the ghost of lovely Mrs. Brown Potter, making friends with time but still somehow surrounded by a mystery that does not wither or grow old. They call it "charm," though no one can explain it. Sir James Barrie once defined it as "the bloom on a woman without which she is of little account." Cora Brown Potter obviously possessed it, and kept it until her dying day in 1936.

From the opposite end of the theatrical scale came another lady, of a very different type. Known as Mrs. Lester, she had come to South Africa years before with a music hall troupe, had married there, and ultimately remained to end her days in complete penury. How she ever entered Mama's circle we never knew, but then we seldom discovered how Mama met the various people she did or how they ever found her. So often she thought her ducks were swans; so often she was disappointed, but no one ever asked her aid without it being given generously and joyfully.

Regularly once a year, Mrs. Lester came to our house among artists of other categories to entertain a chosen group of friends. She evidently had acted in every sort of play, taking all types of parts, for her repertoire consisted of recitations with titles such as "Little Dorrit" (three voices), "The Cabin Boy" (five voices), "The Wreckers" (six voices, including the boatswain's mate).

Her normal voice was as deep and resonant as a man's, but with some gift of ventriloquism she could produce the gentlest, most feminine tones. As I remember her, she was old and ugly but possessed of a curious fascination—like a witch, we used to say—and there was no doubt that, once her audience had recovered from their surprise at her appearance, she held them interested, amused, and amazed by her versatility.

At the end of her performance, after an announcement about her career and worldwide experience, she would perform her "speciality number," which consisted of playing some very simple tunes on her teeth by hitting them rhythmically with her nails. We always wondered whether she had had each tooth made of a different content, because there was no doubt that, when tapped, each one made a slightly different sound—hardly a musical note, but a sort of click of a different tone. The effect was very like castanets, and she could play a clattering rhythm at extraordinary speed. The whole effect was so surprising, the sight of her hitting her teeth so fantastic, that her audience invariably clapped out of sheer astonishment or embarrassment. But Mrs. Lester never failed to win them in the end, despite her unattractive appearance. She would come off the stage, hot with pleasure and exhaustion, saying in a hoarse stage whisper to us children, "That's my ten-thousandth performance—good going, wouldn't you say?"

Another couple of great renown who stayed with us were Dame Clara Butt and her husband Kennerly Rumford. Madame Butt had been discovered by another Clara, named Novello Davies, the famous mother of a much more famous son, Ivor Novello Davies, internationally known as a writer, actor, and composer. Gifted with a phenomenal contralto voice of very limited range, Clara Butt had been trained by Madame Davies, whose individual method of voice production had created in her pupil a voice of extraordinary depth and beauty. For years, Clara Butt filled the Albert Hall in London to overflowing with audiences, drawn from every class, who came to listen en-

thralled, often weeping at Madame Butt's organlike tones boom-
ing out "Abide with Me" or the famous aria from Saint-Saëns'
opera *Samson and Delilah.*

She had never been able to sing in grand opera, being at least
six feet two inches tall, too tremendous not to dominate any
mere male tenor of the operatic stage, but her phenomenal success in oratorio and in concert followed her all over the world
on tours that even included South Africa, which in those days
was not considered very musical.

Kennerley Rumford, tall, handsome, and as black-haired as
his wife, was a charming man with a light voice, a singer of
popular ballads of the day. His duets with his wife invariably
brought down the house.

I can see them standing in our drawing room, imposing and
impressive, Madame Butt tremendous in a black velvet dress
edged with black ostrich feathers, worn as a compliment to the
then-successful trade in South African ostrich feathers flooding
the European market.

Mama gave a large reception in their honor, at which they
stood, backed by a huge arrangement of flowers, and shook
hands with every musical person of our acquaintance, many of
whom begged a signature on programs or albums alike. A
young friend of ours, a girl who aspired to becoming a professional musician, came running to me after having obtained the
diva's cherished signature. "Look," she said to me, "her name
has filled a whole page of my album!" Indeed, the signature was
as tremendous and dramatic as the lady herself.

One visitor to our house who made a deep impression upon
me and my thinking at that time was a Protestant priest, the
Reverend Douglas Ellison, who had come to South Africa to
lead the Railway Mission, as it was called. The purpose of this
mission, financed and administered by the Church Missions in
London, was to carry the Gospel and Christian teaching to the
many workers on the railway line between Cape Town and Johannesburg, a distance of 957 miles via Kimberley. This line, of

narrow gauge compared to today, traversed long stretches of the lonely karroo, where the houses of the railway workers built beside the line were the only habitations or sign of human life in hundreds of acres of wild desert. Next to these houses stood the water tanks and coal sheds where the engines, hauling their heavy load up the tortuous route over mountain passes and through valleys, could stop to refuel.

The workers were often English, or Dutch but English speaking, who lived in almost complete isolation except for their one link with life through the daily passing trains going either north or south. But their contacts were of very short duration —time only for a chat with the engine drivers, to collect newspapers or messages from friends—and were followed by lonely solitude as the train puffed slowly over the horizon, leaving them in the immense expanse of the African night.

Sometimes, if there was an emergency, a doctor would be dropped by one train to be picked up by the next, and they would have the chance of a visit, or best of all would come the missionary car with the *predikant*, or priest, who read prayers to them or gave them Holy Communion in his car. The men in charge at these stops could never leave their posts except when their turn came for a vacation, so the mission priest had various roles to fill. He was counselor and friend, legal adviser, doctor in an emergency, even registrar of births and deaths. But above all, as Douglas told us, "he was able to take to those people the everlasting mercy and hope through the redemption of Christ, with love and understanding that they lacked and so badly needed."

It was a mission that appealed to every one of us who knew the railway journey to the north, across the apparently endless wastes of the karroo, and had some idea of what the lives of the railway workers must be like. Everyone rallied with a will to help, led by Mama, who organized a large fete to raise badly needed funds for further expansion.

Douglas, as we grew to call him, came often to our house,

and I can still recall the impression he made on me. His gentle personality, coupled with his humor and enthusiasm, quickly endeared him to everyone who met him. Above all, I admired his complete dedication to his purpose, his utter self-denial. Here was someone like Hugo Naude, immersed in something much more important than himself, something in which he believed with all his heart and soul, a man to follow, I thought; if only I could have done so! As he described his life to us, I kept thinking how wonderful it must be to do so many things for other people that would give them joy, personal things as well as those for their hearts and spirits.

I lay awake long into the night thinking about the sort of life our friend led. Did God pick and choose the special men to do His work, or did one prepare oneself through long denial for such a calling? Douglas was so unlike our parish rector, who lacked the zeal, the enthusiasm, the vitality of our new friend; there was something so stimulating in the joy of the missionary priest who realized what he was taking to the people who needed him.

I asked Papa about missionaries, remembering the various religious groups I had heard about who had faced murder and annihilation by the Bantu in a black pagan world.

"Yes," said Papa, "they have a special calling, and are given extra courage, extra spiritual strength to face what they have to cope with, and, of course, their faith sustains them."

Only years later did I discover that, though he appreciated the Christian call for missions, he was apt to suspect the role of the missionary in the secular world from the unfortunate experiences he had had in dealing with them in his professional life.

Douglas invited us to visit his mission car, which was stationed at a siding in the railway junction called Salt River near Cape Town. I looked forward to this visit with intense excitement, for it was like being taken to someone's house, getting to know them so much better, and we wanted to see what he had described as his "home."

At one end of the car was an altar in the small sanctuary, with font and movable Communion rail complete. A crucifix and candlesticks added to the religious atmosphere. At the other end, beyond two or three rows of chairs, were two small cabins with toilet and basins, a tiny kitchenette plus office desk filling the remaining space.

"You see," he said, "I am completely at home here. I have everything so compact in here, even room for my books," he added, pointing under his bunk to stacks of reading matter.

"How long do you stay in one place?" Luia asked him.

"That all depends. Sometimes I have a baptism or a funeral service. I've even had a marriage in this car. The train drops me off at some convenient siding and I do my job from there. Sometimes they have to come and fetch me from miles away to hold a prayer meeting in one of the houses. We even buried one poor fellow out in the lonely karroo, because he wanted to lie near the fruit trees he had planted and watered every day. They literally struggle to live, those poor people. The train is their only lifeline."

Some of them, it seemed, tried to maintain contact with each other by keeping a donkey (feeding a horse under those conditions was too expensive), but there was only one dusty, sand road along the line from one point to another, no water, no shade, nothing but the limitless karroo. The workers could manage to keep chickens; some even had goats or sheep, for at least they had water from the tanks, filled by the windmills scattered around the rail stop.

"Why would anyone want to work under those conditions?" asked Luia.

"You may well ask," answered Douglas. "That is why most of them are 'down and outs,' wretched, uneducated, but desperately needing your help and mine."

I promised then to send him the contents of my money box!

Some years later, when Douglas somehow learned that I was going up to Oxford, which had been his alma mater before he joined the Church, he sent me a letter of good wishes and enclosed a poem, which I reprint here. After reading it I thought for a long time about its content, about the dedication it required to live the sort of life Douglas had chosen, totally immersed in the miserable lives of his flock, where his awful aloneness was only relieved by his burning faith.

Why had he sent me the poem? Was it advice, or warning? Was it because self-denial, the cornerstone of his faith had left him full of regrets, his heart full of longing at having missed a dream, lost a vision? Our friendship faded with the years, but I often wondered whether it was the faint example of Douglas that sent me onto my knees in the stony chapel of the Cowley Fathers at Oxford and led me ultimately to the high-perched monastery of Monte Cassino in Italy, where the ordered picture of the celibate priesthood almost clouded my vision of myself as an artist, free, full of the love of living, sinful and selfish.

I chose the latter path.

THE COST

If Love should count you worthy, and should deign
One day to seek your door and be your guest,
Pause . . . ere you draw the bolt and bid him rest
If in your old content you would remain;
For not alone he enters; in his train
Are angels of the mist, the lonely quest;
Dreams of the unfulfilled and unpossessed;
And sorrow and life's immemorial pain.
He wakes desires you never may forget,
He shows you stars you never saw before,
He makes you share with him for evermore
The burden of the world's divine regret.
How wise you were to open not . . . and yet
How poor if you should turn him from your door.

—S. R. LYSAGHT

Of the many young men who courted my sisters and were constant visitors at our house, I have a vivid memory of only two or three. Some were considered totally unsuitable by Papa because they could not support his daughters in their accustomed manner; others were rejected by Mama as having no "background" on a level with our own. But she quite naturally was also interested in their financial position, which was usually below par. There were charming, good-looking, penniless sons of the best families in England, either in the army stationed at the Cape or in the navy, but they could not be considered as suitable husbands.

One exception to these rejections was "Whisp" Leveson-Gower, the future Lord Granville and a relative of Mama's. He was a gay, gangling, laughing lieutenant on the flagship of His Majesty's Navy stationed at the local port of Simonstown. Whisp, encouraged by Mama, was a constant visitor. He rode to hounds, danced well, played a good game of tennis, but like most of the others was somewhat impecunious. He fell in love with my sister Réné, and though she was rather swept away by his big, generous enthusiasm, I feel sure she found it hard to take him seriously. He seemed immature even to me, as I helped him off with his riding boots, noted his frightfully untidy room, and summed him up as a not very dangerous contestant for my sister's hand.

Then there came into our circle a man of an entirely different type, with a very definite personality. Born of a Welsh family, short, intelligent, spoiled, the fair-haired boy of the great Baron Von Reuter, who predicted a brilliant future for his protégé, Sir Roderick Jones, who became a great friend of the family. He had position, money, brains, everything a mother could want for her daughter. But Mama forgot to question the daughter, whose heart had already secretly been given to another, and could not therefore consider this persistent suitor. It so happened she was in love with his best friend. Even when he discovered it, however, he continued to take my sister out riding, despite Mama's objections.

"I shall keep him as a friend," Réné announced with finality.

So Roderick continued to call. He did indeed remain a friend, even when my sister's romance ended in heartbreak, death, and tears. In time, Roderick was called to London, where later he married the brilliant writer Enid Bagnold.

Then one day, there arrived from England a man who made a marked impact on us all, Frank Broughton Webb, bringing letters of introduction from our English relatives. He was traveling through South Africa with a business friend but, having fallen in love with the Cape Peninsula, he decided to stay on, and settled down with a motorcar, a hunter on which to ride to hounds, and a native servant to look after him. He was six feet two in his socks, and moved with the grace of a leopard. In fact, we nicknamed him "the black panther" because of his ink-black hair and eyebrows, which arched over his light, animal eyes, and his long, swinging stride.

At once the household was in a flutter. Frank wasn't like anyone else. His shy charm fascinated all the ladies, particularly my second sister, who rode with him, danced, and played tennis while Mama watched, wondering. Only Papa seemed suspicious and criticized this captivating stranger, who he thought was "dissolute."

Papa's criticisms of people invariably made me fly to their defense regardless, so I championed Frank, who became my friend and confidant despite the difference in our ages. He taught me a great many things, particularly how to jump a horse by letting me mount his precious hunter, Topaz, for he was an expert steeplechaser, and had won many races both in England and locally since his arrival. He loved his horse with a passion and with an understanding I gradually grew to appreciate.

"Talk to him slowly, Johnny," Frank said, "and he will understand, and treat you as a friend," as, when out riding together, we would change horses so that I could take Topaz over the easy ditches and low fences. This reminded me of Kosi, who had taught me to ride with the same understanding for the need of intimacy between animal and man.

But Frank and Topaz were like twins. I could almost feel the shiver that rippled the golden coat of the horse as Frank mounted him, sometimes even whinnying his pleasure as he set out from the stables.

"Why did you call him Topaz?" I asked.

"He looks like one, don't you think, golden, amber, and so shining."

My friendship with Frank was exactly what I needed at that time. My sister Luia had left for school in England, so I, more alone without her companionship, felt in Frank the sort of adventurous spirit, the love of life, the inquiring mind I wanted to share.

Perhaps he was also lonely, despite his many interests. I found out later that his marriage had been a failure, and that he had divorced without having had a child, which he had longed for. He found himself comforted in our family life—in my sister a deep sympathy, in me a potential protégé whom he wanted to teach, encourage, and develop. One day he brought me a paint box.

"You have talent," he said. "You must use it, for one day you might be a great painter."

I asked Mama if I could accept such an expensive present.

"Frank is very fond of you," Mama said. "You would hurt him if you did not accept his gift."

I used the paint box for years after Frank had gone out of our lives.

Papa seemed more than ever involved in his work as judge president, with little time for me except to bring his judgment to bear on the unsatisfactory grades I continued to get in mathematics at school.

"You don't even seem able to add," he said in exasperation, "and as for your algebra, it's a disgrace."

I knew it, but hated to tell him how much I loathed working with those tiresome little symbols. So I failed to get the necessary marks, and was sent to a tutor to be taught mathematics.

Frank understood. He also hated maths and had never found work at school sympathetic.

His affair with my sister did not what Mama called "culminate," which meant an engagement ring, together with the necessary assurances.

"She's wonderful, much too good for me. She's such a fine person, Johnny, I could never keep up," he confided in me.

I longed for them to marry, for I felt that I would then keep Frank in my life forever. But fate planned it otherwise, and Topaz became the destructive agent.

It was the day of the big race at Kenilworth Race Course. Frank had entered Topaz in two races, the second the big steeplechase for a large stake. He was to ride Topaz, as always, for he would never allow a professional jockey to mount him. It was a Saturday, so I was allowed to go to the races with my sister and a party of friends. We went to see Frank in the ring before the first race. He was tense, white, but gay and careless of everything except his horse.

"He's in great form. Aren't you, Topaz?" he said, patting the golden neck. "We're going to win both races, aren't we?"

The horse turned his bright eyes to the man he loved.

"Of course you will," said my sister. "You always win."

I put out my hand. "Good luck," I said quietly.

Frank grinned at me and whispered, "Keep your fingers crossed over those jumps, Johnny," he said.

We went back to our seats in the stands. We had watched Frank ride many times to win flat races, and I had even won some money from the bookies that Frank had bet on himself in my name, but steeplechasing was a different matter and my sister and I sat tense as the first race was called.

Frank galloped in ahead of the whole field, with the golden tail of his beloved Topaz flying straight behind him. The crowd cheered, and we took it as a personal compliment.

"I knew he would win," said sister Helen.

But I was cold with excitement, and time seemed to stop for the following races until the steeplechase was announced. Then my heart pounded with such agitation that my hands turned clammy, and deep down in my bowels fear began to creep over me. As the horses rode past the grandstand, I noticed that Frank's number was seven, which I knew was not a number he liked. Topaz was prancing, beautiful, powerful, impatient to be off.

I prayed silently to myself, "Lord, please let him win and keep him safe." I did not dare look at my sister, but I knew she was saying the same prayer.

They were off, and she quickly focused her glasses on the horses.

"He is moving up," she said excitedly. "He is third in line now, and passing, passing quickly. He is neck to neck in the lead with number four."

I remembered that four had been the favorite. I held my hands clenched in my coat pockets, my mind racing with the horse and the man, tearing around the course and over the jumps to lead the field by several lengths. At the last jump he stumbled and crashed. I had no glasses, but the sudden intake of breath by the excited crowd and the agonized cry that my sister uttered warned me of disaster.

"He has fallen," she gasped.

My heart stopped. "Oh, God, not killed," I said to myself, "not dead, please Lord."

The race ended as we rushed down, fighting through the clamoring mob in time to see Frank carried on a stretcher into the jockeys' quarters. My sister grabbed my hand as we pushed our way through. At the gate we were stopped.

"Mr. Webb—is he all right?" she faltered. "We are relatives," she lied, "we must go to him."

They let us past, but the doctor came to the door, shutting it silently. He was a man we had known for a long time.

"Why, Miss Juta," he said, surprised at seeing us. "He is

going to be all right. He has concussion, though nothing broken, as far as I can detect now."

"Can't we see him?" she asked.

"Better not," he said. "Perhaps later on. I shall move him to the hospital at once," he told us consolingly.

As we left the jockeys' quarters, I suddenly realized that in all our anxiety about Frank I had never given a thought to Topaz.

"What happened to Topaz?" I asked my sister as we went back to find our party.

"I don't know how badly he was hurt," she said.

I turned and rushed back to where we had been below the grandstand and bumped into a jockey still in his varicolored silks.

"Do you know what happened to the horse that fell in the steeplechase?" I asked him hurriedly.

"He broke his neck," he said, and went on.

The words sank right through me. Broke his neck, he had said. "Oh Topaz, Topaz," I said to myself, "what has happened to you? You can't leave Frank, you can't go."

I stopped in the corridor, hardly able to breathe as I realized what such news would mean to Frank. He might not even want to live once he knew he had killed his horse. I could not believe it and walked on, not even caring in which direction I was going.

Frank recovered physically after a long stretch in hospital, but spiritually he was wounded for the rest of his short life. I went alone to see him in the hospital, as Mama did not think it suitable for sister Helen to visit him until he was convalescent. He looked white and drawn, somehow much older, I felt, but I was nervous, afraid of any mention of Topaz.

"Hello, Johnny," he said, quite cheerfully. "Good of you to come. When I'm allowed out, I'm going away. The doctors think a change would put me right. I thought I'd try the Transvaal."

"Can't you go to the seaside?" I asked, not caring to let him know I didn't want him to go so far away. "And what about your house, and, and—" I stopped suddenly, realizing.

"Oh, I know about him," Frank said. "I don't expect to ever race again. Nothing could be the same without him."

That was all that was said. As soon as he was allowed, he left for the north and went to Johannesburg; we never saw him again.

My sister got a letter written the night before his departure. In it he told her he would come back when he was better and looked forward to seeing us again. I don't know what she felt, for she never talked of him.

In Nyasaland he caught typhoid fever and, strangely enough, was nursed in the local hospital by a great friend of my sister's. She later told us much about his last struggle to live and how often he talked of us.

The tragedy of Topaz, followed so soon by Frank's death, left an indelible mark on me. As he had said, for a long time afterwards nothing was the same as it had been.

By a strange twist of fate, there came to stay in our house an American lady who, for years afterwards, was remembered by us with mixed feelings—Miss Elsa Maxwell. She has written her own reminiscences of the first extraordinary years of her varied career, so my memories only record a personal experience.

Coming to South Africa as the accompanist to a female singer, Dorothy Toye, who was touring the music halls billed as "The Double Voiced Phenomenon," Miss Maxwell quickly realized that her remarkable talents were being wasted, and soon found ways and means of changing her career.

In Johannesburg, while performing at the local theater, she met Sir Lionel Phillips, a charming, gifted, rather lonely man, who had made millions in both gold and diamonds but who thought of himself as a man with a frustrated talent, one who should have become a great musician, an organist in fact. As he was a small man, this choice of instruments was interesting.

Lady Phillips, a gifted, intelligent woman, was a most charming hostess. But it so happened that, when Miss Maxwell came to Johannesburg, Lady Phillips was about to set out on a trip abroad, leaving Sir Lionel with fewer social obligations than when his wife was at home.

My sister, Réné, who was a friend of the Phillips's daughter, Edie, went to stay with them in Johannesburg, where she caught scarlet fever and was confined to one wing of their house for several long weeks of quarantine. Before her illness, she had met Elsa, who during her convalescence was attentive and kind, so it was natural that she should write to my parents introducing Elsa, who was coming to Cape Town on what was supposedly a business trip. For by this time she had retired from her music hall commitments and undertaken the editorship of a "magazine" she had persuaded Sir Lionel Phillips to finance. The magazine was called *The State* and ran quite successfully for a few months.

Mama, having heard how kind Elsa had been to her convalescing daughter, asked her to stay with us for a few days. I remember so well the effect she made on us when we first met her. My other sisters were abroad at the time, so I was alone at home with my parents when Elsa arrived in a taxi all the way from Cape Town, a forty-five minute drive in those days. She looked like a "cottage loaf," we all agreed afterwards, short, fat, in an ill-fitting coat and skirt, wearing a most unbecoming beret with a jaunty feather in it. But she had charm; Mama and I were soon captivated by her enthusiasm, her humor, and her delightful manners.

Not so Papa, who from the first retreated from Elsa's very personal approach. But later, even after the debacle of her magazine and her rather hurried departure from South Africa, he had to admit her talents, as well as her extraordinary musical ability.

For she was a sensitive musician who could interpret almost any composer with feeling and understanding. She herself had composed a number of songs, for which she had also written the words. So she frequently went to the piano, sometimes to play her own interpretations of Wagner's music from the *Ring*, or sing some of her own songs in a half-speaking, husky voice. I would sit there, fascinated by this odd, persuasive personality, who seemed to have come from another world of great names, people of renown, a variety of international acquantances, though they were then nothing to what she later accumulated.

I think Papa became suspicious of her easy flow of conversation, which so subtly became infinitely flattering to herself and her abilities. She in turn became wary of his gimletlike eye, and must have realized that, unlike Sir Lionel, she had no easy prey to deal with.

Mama entertained for her with enthusiasm, inviting the socially prominent, the musical, the intelligent world to meet the now-considered unusually talented Miss Maxwell. The impact of her personality upon our friends we only gradually began to realize; but she played charmingly for them, flattered and cajoled them all, talking endlessly about the United States and her success, though she never said a word about her family or her past except as a musician.

Time went by, and Elsa seemed to have settled into our house for a much longer visit than had been expected. Though asked to stay for a weekend by this or that friend we had introduced to her, she always returned with wonderful stories of future contributors to the magazine or articles she now intended to write on some lately discovered subject.

She used to write late into the night a voluminous correspondence of apparently great urgency. Her room, which was across the passage from mine, was constantly littered with papers, cuttings, manuscripts, none of which the maids were allowed to touch. Through the fanlight over her door, I often saw smoke blowing out into the passage, and, though I knew she smoked packets of cigarettes, much to Mama's disgust, I never knew the real cause of all the smoke until one night, when she came to my door and called me to see if I was awake.

"Come in, Johnny, and listen to this," she said. So slipping on my dressing gown and slippers, I went into her room to find her dressed in scarlet silk pajamas, with an enormous cigar in one hand and clutching a batch of papers in the other.

"I've just finished a poem," she said, "and I want you to be the first to hear it. Sit down and I'll read it to you," thus flattering even me.

Words came so easily to Elsa, and the rhythmic verses carried me away by their cadence. I sat entranced, dreaming of love, of passion I knew little about then, of the pain of unrequited longing, which it seemed the poem was all about.

"It's marvelous," I said.

"It's so real, so full of me," she continued, "but I could only write it because of this one I just got today. Just listen to this and see if you don't think this is wonderful, the sort of thing practically no one ever has said to them . . . Just listen!"

She started to read ecstatically from the pages of blue paper she was clutching, which I could see were covered with a bold, scrawled handwriting. This poem in turn seemed equally passionate, and, as she read on, I kept wondering who it could be from, what sort of person had written these lines of love and longing to this strange woman, who seemed totally without physical allure, and whose voice grew huskier and huskier as she puffed volumes of smoke from her cigar.

"There," she finished, exhausted, "isn't that marvelous? Imagine having those things said to one!"

"They must love you very much," I said, for want of something to say.

"Oh, they do, Johnny," she answered, "much more than I deserve. And now, you must be off to bed—and by the way," she added, "let this be our secret, shall we? I mean, don't tell anyone what I have read you. I just thought I *had* to share something so lovely, that's why I called you in, but your mother might not like my keeping you up so late."

"Oh, that's all right," I said, feeling rather boastful. "Thank you for reading to me; I'll never forget the poems." And after all these years I never have forgotten them.

After that first visit, I was often invited into Elsa's room. She used to talk to me about her ideas for the magazine as though she were threshing out her thoughts to herself, about her plans for the future, the friends she loved and wanted to see again, never hesitating to mention them by name. Above all, she seemed interested in my own longings to be an artist. I felt I had become her confidant, and was rather proud as well as flattered by her apparent interest in my own budding talents.

The climax came one night while we were sitting in her room, Elsa smoking her usual cigar, filling the place with smoke. Someone knocked loudly on the door. It was Mama.

"I smelled smoke," she said rapidly, "and came to see if everything was all right. . . . It's time for you to be in bed," she said sharply to me. Elsa, sensing her disapproval, tried to excuse my presence, explaining that she had only asked me to come in to discuss a new idea she had for the magazine. Nothing was said about our previous visits.

I was never invited to her room again. Mama said she thought it was a mistake for me to visit a lady's room in my dressing gown even though I was invited, hinting that I was too old to behave so casually, and that such things were not done by gentlemen. Little did I know, yet naturally obeyed.

Only the return of my sister, recovered at long last, prompted Elsa, somewhat abruptly, to leave our house. Mama thought it very strange that, after so long, she would not even stay to greet Réné on her return but left for Johannesburg, much to Papa's relief.

I did not see Elsa again in South Africa, for she left to go to England, and only years later did we meet again, when I found her at the top of the social tree among the smart, rich set of

Americans in Paris, where I was studying painting. She was always gracious and hospitable, but now busy with schemes of far-reaching importance. I always felt my presence, whether in Paris, London, or New York, reminded her of a past she much preferred to forget. She may even have remembered the many things she had told me in bursts of confidence about herself and other people during our midnight talks at the Cape.

Her influence was widespread; many people never forgot her. I am among those who have remembered much that she said to this very day. Indeed, I never met anyone like her in all my travels, no one with such a sense of humor, who nevertheless counted on the sound of a distinguished title or an equally distinguished bank account to stimulate her. Society, as it is called, she assailed until she was accepted as a star performer might be. I think deep down she despised them because at heart she was an artist.

Her return to the United States, famous and sought after at last, under the painstaking guidance of her champion, Elsie de Wolfe, who as Lady Mendl for years had avoided her, was Elsa's ultimate triumph.

I have always wondered what Papa would have said had he heard of her worldly success.

We had regular visits from an Afrikaner friend of Mama's, a woman of character, intelligence, and a peculiar charm. She was born of a distinguished Dutch family but had married an English South African, much against her family's wishes. He had the much criticized concern for the dark indigenous people that the Dutch Afrikaners considered a kind of weakness in the British. When he died, he left his wife with an inherited sense of "mission." This she assumed with all the ardor of a convert, for, though her family was strictly Dutch Reformed, she had been so persuaded by her husband that she defied convention and worked in one Anglican mission station after another, adopting the Anglican Church along the way.

BACKGROUND IN SUNSHINE

We loved Mrs. van X., her childlike enthusiasms, her laughter, and her tremendous love of life, which endeared her to us children, with whom she always took the trouble to spend much of her time. Even Papa, who had christened her Salvation Nell, critical of her insistent "do-goodness," grew to appreciate her mind and her humor. For she would laugh loudly, unabashed, at things about life she found so funny.

She talked rather broken English, having been brought up in Afrikaans, and what with a good deal of dental trouble and trying to cope with the two languages, her conversation was at times confusing. Occasionally, her words "shlipped," and she would excuse her dilemma by saying, "*Ach, wat,* Jesus won't mind if I have no teet." Almost everything she said began with either "*ach, ja*" or "*ach, wat,*" or more insistently "*ach, nie,*" all Afrikaans ejaculations.

Having assumed the role of a missionary, Mrs. van X. always wore either black or dark blue dresses, her hair parted in the center, and very flat black leather shoes.

"*Ach,* Helen," she would say to Mama, "I can't think how you have time to keep so fashionable! But you mustn't forget," she would add, "Jesus doesn't care about our appearance—it is the spirit that He wants."

My sister and I found her constant reference to our Lord almost embarrassing, but Mrs. van X. included Him in everything, and we began to accept this idea, which was exactly what she wanted us to do.

She was careful to avoid any mention of politics when staying in our house, and Mama had told us that she was in a delicate position, belonging as she did to a family divided in itself. Her own relatives were resentfully anti-British, as so many were, but her husband's family, his brother and sisters, were strongly in favor of England's policies.

As children invariably do, we knew how many of our friends belonged to completely divided families, where even parents and children violently disagreed, to the sorrow of all concerned. But Mrs. van X. steered her boat through these dangerous waters with Jesus at the helm; she diverted every argument, with a dexterity we all marveled at, into some safe channel with one saying or another direct from the Gospels.

Occasionally when she was alone with us children, she would talk of the missions to the Bantu or the colored people.

"*Ach, wat,*" she would say, "you young people must never forget that these darkies are like our children, they are our responsibility. Why do you think God sent us into this heathen land except to teach about Jesus, and bring these people into His fold?"

"Didn't God accept them even if they hadn't heard about Christ?" asked Luia. "After all," she went on, "they are human beings made in His likeness."

"Of course, God accepted them as His children," Mrs. van X. replied, "but they were still in darkness until the white man came to teach them the Truth and the Way."

"But only people like you seem to want to teach them," I said wondering.

"That is just why we need more people who will understand and care for them," she said. "That is what I want you children to remember."

She threw up her hands and went on. "It can't go on like this, these dark people must evolve and grow to take their place in this great land. Terrible things may happen when they do, because remember—we white people are very few by comparison, and, unless we are careful, they will resent us more and more as they develop."

She spoke like a prophet with a prophetic vision into the future of "*ons land,*" this plain, outspoken Afrikaner woman with her glowing eyes and her spirit radiating the force of her faith.

Luia and I would have long discussions after Mrs. van X. talked to us, for she always stimulated our thinking even if we thought that she exaggerated on her own subject.

"Do you really believe everyone has to be a Christian?" I asked Luia after one of her talks.

"That is what the Bible says," she answered.

"But what about all the millions of Moslems and Hindus and all those Chinese with their own religions?" I asked.

"They have to be taught about Christ eventually, that is what we were told to do."

We didn't discuss the point of view of our guest with our parents. We knew Papa would not agree with her, thinking she was jumping ahead too quickly, thereby making the dark people discontented with their lot, when, according to him, they were not by any means ready to assume a more important place in the structure of the colony.

"*Ach*, dat is just it, we don't give them a chance," we could hear Mrs. van X. saying.

As for Mama, she took her cue from my father, and, though she was happy to play the Lady Bountiful asking Peter, the gardener, about his wife's miscarriage or sending her some jellies when she was recovering from one of her countless childbirths, she never allowed herself to become involved, as Mrs. van X. wanted her to do.

It should be remembered that I am writing of a time when the color line was closely held to, when the white man assumed, not only authority as his right, but a natural superiority over the indigenous peoples. They were all around us, as I have said, but their place and position was clearly established. The relatives of our colored butler, maids, and cook all visited our house, but they stayed in their appointed place, eating in the kitchen and never coming beyond that boundary. We white people as the ruling race were expected to be tolerant, kind, and an example, which many were certainly not, but not to do as Mrs. van X. would have had us do, claim those of the dark races as "our brothers and sisters in Christ" and draw no line between us all as children of God. Mama found this difficult to accept, always conscious as she was of Papa's position.

Unfortunately, Luia was away staying with school friends when came the memorable day that Mrs. van X. put us to the test. I was obliged to face the issue alone.

Visitors

"I am delighted to come to tea in your lovely garden and visit you," wrote Mrs. van X. to Mama, "and, knowing your generous hospitality, I am bringing two friends, one of whom I think you know, the Reverend Pieter Smidt, a most splendid man and a remarkable leader. You will like him more as you get to know him better." Nothing prepared Mama for the other visitor.

When they arrived, ushered into the drawing room where I was with Mama, awaiting them, it can be imagined with what surprise Mama greeted the unknown guest, a very dark but handsome Negress, joyously introduced by Mrs. van X. as "my great friend, Mrs. Umzumvubu, whom I want you to know."

Whatever discomfort or embarrassment Mama may have felt, be it said to her great credit that she shook hands cordially with the unexpected guest, who spoke perfect English and was most polite, without showing any sign of surprise, though I am sure it was the first time a dark person had ever come socially into our living room and been treated on an absolutely equal footing. I did not dare glance at John, nervously passing cups of tea, though he had never seen such a confrontation in all his life. The Reverend Smidt, a *waare Afrikaner*, humorous and kindly, took a chair next to Mama and proceeded to flatter her with oblique references to Papa. I found myself passing cucumber sandwiches to Mrs. Umzumvubu, John having fled from the scene, obviously unable to cope with the situation. I was charmed by the black lady with her melodious voice, her bright flashing eyes, and exquisite white teeth.

After tea, we went into the garden, where Mrs. van X. maneuvered herself with her friend to Mama's side. I was left to bring up the rear with the Reverend Smidt. He was cordial, kindly, and not condescending to the youth I was. He asked me about my school, my interests, sports, and whether I had plans for my future. Without any calculation, I told him I wanted to be an artist. This brought forth an enthusiasm I little expected from a Dutch Reformed minister.

"That is splendid," he said. "We need more artists, creative minds of all sorts to come out of this country. We have it all latent in us, in the Dutch and the Huguenot background. It is all there, and only needs encouragement. . . . You know," he added, "art is very close to religion—they are both an aspect of God."

He sounded more like my friend Douglas Ellison, who though a priest by profession was by nature an artist, combining the two into one great paean of praise. To find this encouragement from a member of a church I had always thought of as cold, filled with Calvinistic, Lutheran ideas, stripped of all the emotional appeal that art gives, was wonderful to me, who always expected the criticism I generally got when I talked to our friends of becoming a professional artist.

That evening I know that Mama reported the whole experience to Papa over his glass of sherry before dinner. I found them sitting alone on the *stoep*, and immediately sensed the strait of a "situation."

Later Mama told me that my father was very cross with Mrs. van X. for having put her in such an awkward position without any warning.

"He doesn't think it is time yet to treat either the coloreds or the Bantu as our equals," she said. "but I think our guest was a charming person, so alive, so genuine. I really enjoyed meeting her."

My heart went out to Mama for her generosity of spirit, her natural graciousness.

"I admire Mrs. van X. very much for all she is doing, as you know, but I don't think I will join her group . . . just yet," she added as an afterthought.

We did not see the lady for quite some time after the incident. But her talks to us had disturbed my thoughts about human relations and what they meant in the huge boiling pot of nationalities that we were living in. We had been taught, more by example than instruction, how we were expected to deal with the nonwhites, what we could expect from them, and how we were to behave toward them.

But I was already revolutionary, had always been to some extent, and my conscience had been stirred by Mrs. van X.'s ardent exposition of what she called the "responsibilities" we had assumed. I wondered whether the white man had always exploited the indigenous people he had conquered in all the many parts of the world he had explored, once he had "christianized" them and the Church had established herself. The missionaries had been the conscience of the dominant powers; they had taught, helped, guided the supposedly converted native peoples, but we, the white conquerers, were really responsible. Had we been cruel, harsh, and intolerant of everything we didn't understand, that we thought of as "barbaric," without giving a thought to the "rights" of the people we found with their own degree of civilization, low though we thought it was?

I longed to be able to talk to someone other than my father about the ideas surging through my young brain. Mrs. van X. had opened a door that we, as children, never knew existed. Suddenly I had been made conscious of the world of people around me, black, brown, yellow, and white.

We had never questioned the situation but had taken it all —the position, the relationships—for granted. We moved among the people of color, but we never, never mingled. The dark people and their children were never in our "circle"; they were always there, but always outside, where we had been taught they belonged. We never imagined that in later years we would have questioned how these different races, with their barriers of culture and education, were going to live together in one country, or that we might have to face the future possibility of black "domination" in a country that could by then have become "mixed" in color.

I remember the gossip at school when it was reported that the grocer's white assistant was courting, and in fact sleeping with, a darkly colored girl; the expressions of disgust, of offended prerogative, at the outrage considered by just a group of boys to have been committed by one of our own race against his "people" is difficult now to believe. Racial domination by the white

271

world was taken for granted, and it was never thought that any people, let alone any nonwhite, would ever threaten that dominion. But there were those who thought differently.

Mrs. van X. said we had no right to the exclusivity we assumed as ours except by fortunate advantage. Given a chance, the dark people might have the advantage, and then where would we be, the few, the cultivated, educated white people, swamped in a morass of black natives striving for a place in the sun?

I knew no one to whom I could talk about this problem, which somehow seemed to have been given me to think about, except my tutor, a Scotch South African who was coaching me for my examinations into Oxford. I called and asked if I might see him, for he lived only a few blocks from our house, and I hurried there on my bicycle.

"Hello," he said, greeting me at the door. "Is anything the matter?"

"I'm sorry to disturb you, sir, "I said. "I know it's Saturday, but I do need to talk to you. Nothing is really the matter, except that I must ask you some questions."

"Fire away," he said. "What sort of questions—nothing personal, I hope?"

"Oh, no, it's about this country, and—and the future," I answered.

I told him everything Mrs. van X. had said to us; about Papa's reactions, about our multiracial staff at home, and how I now felt I had to make up my mind about what I believed, and if necessary how I should act were the pattern of living to alter.

"Don't worry, Jan," he said consolingly. "You are much too young—and I didn't say stupid—to come to any conclusion about a matter I believe is going to cause endless difficulties, even civil war, before it is resolved sometime in the future."

"Then you do think that tremendous changes are bound to come about?" I asked.

"Certainly I do, but I know you can't solve the problems, or yet decide how you will feel and act under different circumstances."

"Mrs. van X. says we ought to prepare for these changes by treating the Bantu and the colored people quite differently."

"Oh, perhaps, but not yet."

"Do you believe that Christianity, I mean God, has something to do with all of this?"

"But of course," he said, "God has to do with everything. He may ordain an entirely other pattern for our life here on earth."

"D'you think we ought to pray for guidance, as Mrs. Van X. says we should?"

"I do, but you ought to get educated first," he ended snappily.

I left him, still not really sure about what I should believe or do. Only his attitude that time might heal rather than create wounds gave me some consolation.

The next day was Sunday, Whitsunday, the birthday of the Church, we had always been taught, the day on which we commemorate the mysterious coming of the Holy Spirit. I used to feel a little uncomfortable about the Spirit; this breath of Christ, this "mighty rushing wind," this eternal force sent by God to go on and on throughout the world made me wonder; and why did Christ give it to the world in an "upper room" and not in the temple, or at least among all the people?

We all went as usual to Church, I to sing in the choir, my mind full of strange misgivings. The world of black, brown, yellow, and white people whirled through my brain. Then came the sermon hymn:

> *God of justice save the people from the clash of race and creed,*
> *From the strife of class and faction make our nation free indeed,*
> *. . . Till it finds its full fruition in the Brotherhood of Man.*

There it was, everything Mrs. van X. had said; there it was in the Epistle to the Corinthians; and there was I, full of pride and prejudice, class conscious, intolerant, doing nothing to build a bridge for the Brotherhood of Man, not even sure that I should. . . .

Bending below the choir stalls, I had to stuff my handkerchief into my mouth to stifle my sobbing. But on that Whitsunday I grew much older.

9. Tot Siens—Au Revoir

THE last year that I lived in my home was perhaps the most eventful of my young life. I was alone with my parents, as all my sisters were scattered abroad, two of them married in England and my sister Luia still studying for the opera in Paris. I was happy to be free of their influences and on my own to do the things I enjoyed, and see the people I liked without their watchful eyes upon me.

I had not done well in my examinations, much to Papa's disappointment, and I was being tutored before going on to some university or other. For, though the question of my future was often discussed, particularly my desire to study abroad to become a painter, Papa remained adamant on the question of my education in the usual sense of the word. It seemed useless to argue with him that I should be educated in the profession that

I persisted in wanting to adopt for my future, for he always said that art could come later, after I had been properly educated along the usual lines. At the back of his mind, I think he always hoped I could be persuaded that to become a barrister following the family tradition would mean security and give me a stable position in society, rather than risk all the uncertainty of an artist's life.

I knew that his views were sensible and wise, only my spirit rebelled against the imagined monotony of practicing the law and longed for what I thought would be the freedom of the creative life. Sooner or later I knew we would have to come to some decision, and I dreaded the day when my future would have to be decided upon.

Several things occurred to bring about the decision. One was my desire to go away from South Africa to a university in another country if it was ultimately decided that I should study law. Another was the fact that two of my friends were leaving the Cape to go to universities, one in Holland and the other in England.

Papa jumped at this inducement, suggesting the university of either Leyden or London, where he himself had passed his examinations so successfully. I could foresee the inevitable—a compromise was my only hope. I spent anxious hours working out what I should say when I made the proposition to my father that I study to become a lawyer, provided that, once I was fully fledged, he would give me three years of art training in any school of my choice. He agreed, and I chose to go to Oxford rather than London, for I had read quite a good deal about Oxford, where one of my brothers-in-law had distinguished himself both as a cricketer and on the river, and I had become interested in the history of the university. Thus I was entered for Christ Church College, with the entrance examination looming ahead of me in the autumn of the year.

"You'll have to take some extra coaching and really work hard for your entrance exam or you'll never pass," said Papa,

Jan Juta at work on one of two mural paintings (36' by 15') commissioned for the Council Chamber, City Hall, Pretoria, South Africa, 1938

casting a shadow onto my hopes. For once it had been settled that I should study law, I set aside my dream of painting in Paris for the time being, determined to make the most of this chance of studying in so great an institution as Oxford University. Particularly, I relished the thought of Christ Church, whose corridors, I felt convinced, must still be haunted by Cardinal Wolsey in his rustling robes.

Almost as though I had some premonition of future events, I relished every moment I now had at home. I rode a great deal, went to parties with my friends, played tennis regularly, reveling in the sunshine of that last summer at the Cape before facing the climate of England, which I already feared, knowing it from many visits to Britain with my parents.

Several girls with whom I danced, played, and dated from time to time attracted me, but I was rather cavalier about them, feeling nothing very serious about any girl—until I met Deirdre.

That was a name that had always charmed me, a name I had read in books of Irish verse and legend—and that curiously conjured up an image of the sort of beauty one could dream about, but somehow never expected to meet.

I remember when I met her, and saw her loveliness face to face for the first time, my breath seemed to stop as though something had caught my throat. It was at a dance given by friends with whom she was staying on a visit from her home in the Transvaal. As I came into the ballroom and joined a group of friends, I saw her suddenly, standing apart, talking to our hostess, Mrs. F. She was tall and dark, her head set high on a lovely neck and shoulders, wearing pinky-beige lace.

Every nerve in my body seemed conscious of her presence in the room; then, with my blood pulsing in my head, I went forward quickly to greet my hostess and manage an introduction to this stranger I already felt I knew, though I had only just seen her. I can still see it all so clearly, as she turned to greet me and I looked into her eyes, which were unlike any I had ever seen, like blue-gray water shining limpid through a mist of black lashes. From that first look, I was lost in a turmoil of emotion.

As I think back to that meeting, through all the events and crises of a long life, past the ecstasy and tears that marked the procession of the years, I know nothing I ever felt afterwards resembled that first extraordinary flooding of emotion, my first feeling of love. Everything, my ideals, my longing, my loneliness, my need—all came together at once, focused on this lovely human being I did not even know but who somehow both spiritually and physically seemed to be my dreams incarnate.

"Shall we dance?" I asked her, as the orchestra started to play.

Putting my arm around her, holding her as closely as I dared allow myself to, we glided away into a rhythmic world I felt was hardly real, so perfect to me seemed our unity of movement. What we talked about at that first meeting seems unimportant now. I was only interested in finding out how long she was staying, how available she might be, and whether or not she was as interested in seeing me again as I was to be with her.

Everything that has ever happened to a young man involved in his first love affair happened to me. I was irritable, moody, starry-eyed, utterly lost to reality. I know I was difficult at home, and Mama, sensing the truth, I am sure, turned on me one day.

"I don't know what's the matter with you," she said. "You seem so unreasonable—besides, you never remember anything I ask you."

With my heart bursting, I longed to tell her, but couldn't find the right moment or the mood.

I borrowed our car, having just obtained my license to drive, and asked Deirdre to come out driving with me. I took her to my favorite places, the high road over the Constantia neck, from where the sweep of Houts Bay could be seen lying sapphire and emerald below; up through the avenues of pines and oaks to Kirstenbosch, the botanical gardens, the scene of happy picnics and my mountain climbs; then, for a change, across the flats to the long, lonely beaches beyond Muizenberg, where the waters of False Bay sweep the soft sands in lines of curling breakers. We sat almost silent on the dunes, in such apparent harmony that I began to think she cared for me, though I was still far too afraid to ask her. I only talked of things that interested me in the desperate hope I would discover the sort of congeniality I longed for.

I found she was older than I was and, being a girl, far more evolved within herself than I. But she loved the things I thought important; she read verse, enjoyed books, rode to hounds, danced like thistledown on the ballroom floor, laughed when I laughed, above all seemed interested in the arts and in my wanting to paint. Every day with her enriched my own spirit; every experience shared had an added poignancy; every sunset watched together had a greater brilliance, a new intensity.

Mama was becoming more and more concerned about my obvious infatuation, for, although I didn't want to talk about Deirdre at home, I knew my mother sensed what was happening to me. Papa merely watched and was silent, though I don't doubt he discussed the matter with Mama when I was well out of the way. I couldn't talk about this girl because I didn't want her thought of as just another acquaintance, just someone else I enjoyed taking out to dance. But I knew perfectly well that the moment was daily getting nearer when I would have to introduce her to my parents, and I steeled myself to have to hear her discussed, possibly criticized, by Mama, who could tease me so easily, often hurting me by her sharp perception and quick wit. She usually took a dislike to the girls I grew interested in and invariably managed to make me feel I had not chosen very well, for one reason or another. Fundamentally she was proud of me, and was determined that I only attach myself to someone she thought worthy of me.

Papa, who was so much wiser, never concerned himself with my friends unless for his own good reasons he disapproved of them. Then he was sharply outspoken.

But this was different, this was unlike anything that had ever happened to me, so naturally I wanted Mama's support, her encouragement, her approval of Deirdre. I wanted to tell her I was so in love with this girl that nothing else seemed to matter. I couldn't stand the idea of ever hearing her criticized, or of having any little imperfection pointed out. If there was any, I knew my mother's sharp eyes would discover it, but I didn't want to hear about it.

I tried to think of the best way to bring about their meeting through some other means than my direct intervention, and decided to go to our mutual friend with whom Deirdre was staying and beg her help as an ally in my cause. She was younger than Mama, but they "visited" on occasion and met at other women's tea parties. It took a certain courage even to go and talk to her, but I was so afraid that time would run out. I knew that Deirdre was only visiting her friend for a few weeks, so I felt I had to clinch matters and not lose my opportunity.

Mrs. C. was very understanding. She herself loved and admired Deirdre, and I think she sensed my sincerity, perhaps even discerned how deeply involved I was. Besides, she knew Mama and could appreciate the necessity of having her on my side, if I was to pursue the affair and be allowed to follow my impulse never to let Deirdre escape me and return as planned to the Transvaal. How wise she thought it was from Deirdre's viewpoint I never knew, but at least she agreed to ask Mama with a few other friends, to tea, when she would introduce Deirdre as her house guest.

I was so nervous about this meeting that I felt I must warn Deirdre of how important I thought it was that she should like Mama, and for my mother to appreciate her. I think it was at that conversation that Deirdre fully realized how much she meant to me, though I had not yet had the courage to put my feelings for her into words—only casual mention of my appreciation, my admiration for her looks, my need to see her as often as possible—though she must have sensed my joy in her companionship.

"You say such strange things to me," she said one afternoon. "Things no one has ever said, at least not the way you say them."

"What sort of things?" I asked, wondering in sudden fear how many others had wooed her, how many boys she could choose from, and whether there was anyone she particularly favored. I was too afraid to ask outright.

"Oh, about my looks," she said casually, "the way I dance, and my hands—you are always admiring my hands."

"It's because I think they are so beautiful," I said. "You don't mind my telling you, do you?"

"Of course not, you silly boy. Naturally, I love to be admired, every girl loves that."

"But I really mean what I say to you," I ventured. "It's not just flattery."

"I hope you do mean all you say. I don't like flattery or pretension," she said, with a sort of finality in her voice.

On the day of the tea party, which I knew Mama had accepted, I was up and out of doors even earlier than usual. Around and around in my mind circulated only one thought: Mama and Deirdre, their reaction to each other and the effect of their meeting upon my ideas. "I must think," I kept saying to myself, while my dog and I wandered through the garden as the sun set the mountain alight with the first rays. "What am I to do, what shall I do?" I asked myself over and over again, longing for someone to either guide or admonish me, comfort or advise me, I, who didn't know my own mind.

The obvious person ought to have been my father, but, as I have said, I was afraid of Papa. Though I knew he loved me, I had never been on a level of intimacy with him that made me feel free to discuss anything to do with my inner emotional life.

Apart from rather cold advice as to my behavior, always reminding me of what was expected of me, my background, and the code of ethics that governed gentlemen of our social level, he never ventured to seek any intimacy with me. I can only recall one unexpected step in this direction when, in the midst of some discussion, he suddenly said, "Remember I was also a young man once."

Perhaps I should have grasped this offered hand there and then; perhaps our relationship would have changed from being one of respect, admiration, and fear to one of human understanding wherein we could have talked as man to man—or at least as friend to friend. But I was so surprised that I missed the moment, and thereby probably lost the wisest, most loving friend a boy could ever have. I know now how shy my father was, how defensive—for reasons I have never fathomed. How, in spite of his innate loving kindness, he found it so difficult to bridge a gap between personalities on any but a purely objective basis. He seldom talked about people, rarely criticized openly, controlled his judgment unless roused to anger by evil, injustice, or inhumanity between people. But I also realized that I really did not *want* him to know me. I was not then prepared to be "known" by anyone—except that this unexpected love had suddenly reversed my desire for remoteness.

I now wanted to give all of myself, and be known in all the ugliness, the beauty, the evil, and the good that made up my nature. But this was not for anyone except the person I loved— least of all for Papa. Had I gone to him for advice, he would have counseled me, possibly consoled my anxiety; he would have perhaps become my ally when Mama began her subtle campaign to separate me from Deirdre. But I didn't seek his advice. Rather, I worried about how best to win over Mama to accepting my choice as something serious, something of a permanent nature, unlike any experience I had ever had.

Going to the stables to saddle my horse, I had the sudden

thought that a gallop over my favorite hillside would somehow clarify my mind, perhaps even solve the problem.

I was not even educated. I had no profession, my future was not assured or secure, as far as I knew. How could I dare to speak of the future or my longings or my dreams to anyone, even if I loved them and yearned for them to share my life? I had never thought seriously at all about marriage, feeling it was something to be dealt with in the future, when the time came. I had never calculated on love, and didn't realize what it meant —in fact, despite all I had read and heard about it, I had never imagined that one could be caught by a current of such power that one would be swept away, out of contact with the security of the mainland of sense and reality, so far out into wild, turbulent waters of passion and desire that one seemed beyond control, helpless, ecstatic, floundering for an anchor.

I wanted this girl more than I had ever before wanted anything; I wanted to give her all of myself, all I had to offer, but I knew how little that entailed. What had I but dreams of a future? I couldn't ask someone like Deirdre to wait until I found my feet, until I could support her as I knew a husband was expected to support a wife. Besides, I wanted to paint, to live a creative life, and all the risks that entailed had been underlined.

Without thinking, I had cantered up over the hillsides to the heights on the slopes below Table Mountain. Daisy knew her way without my even guiding her; instinctively, she sensed I would go to my favorite hideaway, where we would stand as usual, I sometimes dismounting and tethering her to a mimosa tree while I climbed the big Hen and Chickens rocks to look over the flats, still floating in blue shadow.

"What shall I do?" I kept repeating in my anxiety, knowing in the back of my troubled mind that there was only one possible, honorable answer. I should confess my love, but should go away and leave her, not daring even to suggest that, if she loved me, we would somehow be together again in life. I had no right to propose this. But sitting there on that day, looking over the valley where the vineyards lay folding over the hills in neat array, where the blue waters of the bay curved into the misty horizon, I was suddenly overcome by the thought that soon I should be leaving all of it, all those things of my childhood that I loved: the countryside, my home, my horse, and now the person I loved as well. All of it was to be left behind when I started off on the first lap of my future course. Perhaps I would never come back, but if I did nothing would ever be the same again because I would be different. Would the valleys be the same, the woods I had wandered, the hidden pathways of the heart? Would I find Deirdre the same bright flame to set my whole spirit alight with the consuming longing I now felt? As my heart welled up into my throat with the emotion of the thought, I knew it could be so.

I rode home in a calmer state of mind. Chastened by my introspection, I had decided that I had to tell Deirdre how I felt, even at the risk of hearing that she didn't feel the same way about me.

Depending on how Mama felt about her after their meeting, I might have to look for an ally. No friend of my own age would be any help; besides, the only person who could influence Mama at all was my father. "At least," I argued to myself, "there is nothing to be ashamed of, nothing he could blame me for, and perhaps out of his natural sympathy he would support me, understanding my confused emotions."

It is strange how one can remember incidents out of the past with a clarity and precision that astonishes one. Moments of pain and pleasure that somehow retain their brilliance, their color, their very scent through the years.

I can recall every word of the conversation about Deirdre that I was waiting impatiently to have with Mama. Though I had come home calmer, more prepared, I was too nervous to appear quite natural, I am sure; Mama would be the first to notice any slightest change in me. She had a psychic sense where I was concerned, and often forestalled my remarks, showing how well she knew what I was thinking. Later that evening I joined her in the drawing room as casually as I could. At once she broached the subject, which made my insides tremble with excitement as she spoke.

"I met a very charming girl this afternoon at Mary C.'s tea. She said she knew you. I don't remember your telling me about her—what's her name?"

"Deirdre Martin," I said. "She comes from the Transvaal."

"Oh, yes, Mary said she knew her parents in Johannesburg. I thought she was awfully pretty."

"I think so, too," I said bravely.

"Why didn't you tell me you had been seeing her? She seems to think she knows you quite well."

"I met her at that dance at the Felthams'," I said, as casually as I could. "She dances beautifully."

"I thought you might like to ask her here with some of your friends one day, but it seems she is going away quite soon."

I felt almost choked with apprehension. Had plans changed? Was Deirdre going sooner than I knew? When could I see her to find out, when could I be with her to tell her all I had been preparing to say?

All these questions crowded into my mind at once. I got up, wondering how I could maneuver to get to the telephone, speak to Deirdre, and ask her to see me without Mama overhearing me.

I reached Deirdre by telephone.

"How was the tea party?" I asked at once.

"Oh, very nice. I think your mother is perfectly beautiful, but she terrified me," Deirdre said.

"You will have to know her better. She isn't really like that. She liked you and thought you so pretty. But I want to see you," I insisted. "Could we drive tomorrow afternoon? I have something important to tell you." I hoped that would encourage her inquisitiveness.

"I don't feel awfully well," she said.

"Have you caught cold?" I asked quickly.

"I don't think so. I'll be all right. Yes, let's go to our favorite view. What time, about three-thirty? The light is so lovely then."

That was the sort of response I loved, her pleasure in the things that mattered to me: the light, the landscape, our mutual appreciation, the joy of sharing experience. "I love you so," I murmured under my breath, "your spirit, your looks, the cadence of your voice."

"Splendid," I said. "I'll be there—and Deirdre," I added, "take care of yourself, get better."

"I will," she said, "good-bye."

How I hated those words. All my life I had resented this necessity of parting, of leaving, of having to go away from what gave one joy, or satisfaction: the garden, my trees, my dog, the places and the people I loved—always this having to go away, even from the glory of the sunset, always having to say goodbye to something precious. Would life never allow one to stay?

Late into that night I lay thinking about what I should say the next afternoon; how best to express all I wanted Deirdre to know; how she could be convinced that my feelings for her had altered my very thinking, my whole outlook on my future, which until then I had envisaged as alone. Perhaps a poem, with all the imagery of poetry, which we both loved, would better convey my feelings than my hesitant words.

For hours I was changing and perfecting the words and rhythm.

In the back of my mind, I knew my outlook was unrealistic, but swept by an emotion that consumed me, all practical issues were put aside. But I had not correctly estimated Deirdre's reaction to my proposal. I drove up to fetch her at exactly the hour agreed on, my heart beating so hard by then it was almost impossible to hide my feelings. No doubt my words came tumbling out in confusion, for Deirdre kept saying, "Oh my dear, my dear," as my thoughts of our future, our ultimate togetherness, my passion, and my longing for her happiness all flooded over her. I held her hand, kissing it from time to time.

"I love you so," I said.

"I understand, and it's all wonderful, but there is your future to decide, which may influence our plans if we are to have any. You are still very young, you know," she said, rather wistfully I thought.

"But I can't lose you," I said. "I can't let you go now, unless you tell me you will wait a while for me. It won't be terribly long, really it won't," I insisted.

"You don't know how you will feel in a year's time, especially at Oxford, nor do I have any idea how I shall feel about you."

"But you do love me now?" I asked her. "Enough to say you will wait and see?"

"That wouldn't be fair," she said. "I am fond of you, Jan, you aren't like anyone I've ever met—but I can't promise you anything, not now, anyway."

At that moment my heart began to crack.

That evening before dinner, while Papa was having his glass of sherry in his library, I went down the long, dark corridor leading to his room, a passage we had always held almost sacrosanct, one we had always rather feared as well as respected. On that evening, sustained by a sort of courage born of bravado, I walked quite boldly down it and knocked on his door.

"Well, come along in," Papa said, surprised to see me, I felt sure.

Only anxiety sent words to my mind as I mumbled, "I want to talk to you a moment. I'm very troubled."

The tone of my voice must have conveyed my state of mind, for he said, "What is it, my boy?" He drew up a chair beside his writing desk.

"It's a girl," I said, "but don't worry—there's nothing wrong," I added quickly, lest he misunderstand the reason for my anxiety.

"Sit down and tell me," he said. And at that moment he touched my heart as never before by his gentle voice, obvious concern, and his smile.

"I know this is a bad time," I said. "I realize all the uncertainty of my future, but I've fallen in love. I am not certain what I ought to say or do, so I've come to you."

"Perhaps I can at least advise you," he answered. "I know what it's like." And he smiled at me.

"I've told her how I feel," I went on.

"Does she feel the same way about you?" he asked.

"I don't think so, though she might grow to in time, but what worries me is, have I the right to ask her to wait for me—it all seems so long, so far away, with Oxford and my exams?"

"Do your mother and I know her or her family?" Papa asked.

"Mama met her just the other day—she's staying with the C.'s—that's where I met her. She's wonderful, Dad, she really is."

"I'm sure she is, if you love her," he said, flattering me.

Something in his phrase caught at my heart; I felt lifted into an arena of approval.

"What shall I do, Dad?" I asked despondently.

"It strikes me," said Papa, weighing his words, "that perhaps your having to go away is a most fortunate thing. It may sound harsh to you, my son, but it will give you both time to think from a distance."

"But she will forget me," I interrupted. "There are bound to be lots of others, and if I'm not there—"

I must have sounded hopeless, for he said, "You know, being 'in love' as we say, is not always the best basis for any sort of future happiness with someone you love."

"One wouldn't marry somebody one was not in love with," I objected.

"You might be surprised," Papa answered. "The thrill changes, often dies, but in its place can grow something much more lasting, more worthwhile, where admiration, sympathy, and understanding all take the place of that first thrill."

"You still haven't told me whether you think I can ask her to wait for me."

"I don't think it fair for either of you to be bound by promises. They can cause such heartbreak. Besides, if you fall out of love, promises are no use anyway."

"I know I'll lose her if I leave her," I said, feeling as though it had already happened.

"Don't worry," Papa said. "If you each find you really need the other, you will get together. Fate is a curious thing."

"I'll never love anyone as much as I do Deirdre. I didn't know it could be like this," I said.

"Good luck to you," Papa said. "I only hope you find the sort of happiness I found."

I left him, wondering what sort of happiness he had found, suddenly realizing I was analyzing my parents' marriage, trying to view them both in true perspective, my enormously gifted European father and my beautiful, spoiled, talented mother. Had they each found what the other needed? How could anyone ever know? We seemed such a happy family, how could one see behind the facade, so well presented to the world they lived in? I thought of Deirdre, pale, gray-eyed, sure of herself, a goddess, brought by me into an alien world, the unconventional untidy world of the arts where I knew I belonged. Could she face that, with or without money?

As a result of all my anxiety over my love affair, I became aware for the first time of the two very different people within my personality; the dark side of my nature, full of calculation, selfishness, and ambition kept intruding into the secret discussions I had with myself over my future. I realized the battle going on within me over what I wanted to have and wanted to give.

Suddenly, without warning of any change, I was unable to talk to Deirdre when I called her as usual on the telephone, being told she was ill, in bed, and unable to speak to me.

At once I called her hostess to inquire further, only to be told the same thing.

"She has a bad cold on her chest," said Mrs. C., "but I'll give her your messages."

I have often wondered in the days that followed whether she ever did, and whether Deirdre ever again heard from me. I thought, chafing under the separation, if I could only be with Deirdre, I would make her well at once. Here was the person I loved, ill, and I should be allowed to tend her, comfort her, heal her; my vanity knew no boundaries. I was not allowed to see her, and my anxiety increased when I was told she had been moved to our local hospital.

I asked Mama to call Mrs. C. to find out what the matter was, and whether she could do anything for Deirdre.

"You seem very concerned," Mama said to me.

"I am afraid she is dangerously ill," I answered anxiously.

"Oh, she'll be all right," Mama said, comforting me. "She has Dr. Liss to look after her. I expect she will be out in a week."

My mind was flooded by appalling anxieties—suppose she was not well in a week, suppose she never came home, suppose I lost her before I had ever gained her!

Within a few days, she died of double pneumonia, with some complication of pleurisy. I heard it directly from the nurse in charge at the hospital where I had gone to inquire. There was no warning, nothing to spare me the shock—nothing.

"I'm sorry to have to tell you," the nurse began, and my heart stopped beating as the whole devastating fact dawned on me.

"It isn't possible," I cried out to the nurse. "They cured me of pneumonia, she can't have died!"

"There were various complications," the nurse continued. "I'm very sorry indeed. She was so young and lovely."

At those words I left abruptly, ran to the car and tore up the mountain road to our favorite lookout, my tears burning my throat, my mind unwilling to accept this fate.

"Oh, my darling, my darling," I kept repeating. "You can't have left me, not now, not yet."

It had all happened so quickly: her coming into my life; the emotion she kindled in me, which swept me away beyond the boundaries of reason—the first fine, careless rapture I had ever known, clasping a star that, as I was about to grasp it, fell, and with its falling broke my heart.

Now suddenly I remembered some lines by Bobbie Burns that Mama used to say to me. She loved Burns, who no doubt appealed to her Scotchness. "After all," she would say, "no other poet I've ever heard of bothered to write a poem to a mouse, and with such charm," she added characteristically.

But the lines she used to say to me when I was depressed or disappointed rushed now into my head:

> But pleasures are like poppies spread;
> You seize the flower, the bloom is shed;
> Or like the snowfall on the river,
> A moment white, then melts forever.

What a fearful disillusion lay in those words; was this what all this loving was about, "white as the snowfall on the river" and then gone? I clenched my nails into the palms of my hand to stop the lump rising in my throat.

Everything seemed suddenly to have changed; what was the point of Oxford and England, all our thinking and planning? I was back where I had started, only I was not the same person. It was as though a light, a lovely, penetrating light, that had shone through the maze of my uncertainty had now been put out. I didn't see the path any more, and cried out in a pain I had never felt before. I was sure that there would always be moments when her face would come before me, her pale eyes and the exact tone of her voice would suffocate my senses; times when I would see her again as on the last time we were together, so vivid, so gentle, with the light emanating from her into my gloom. I didn't know how I could go home and calmly face my parents, or stop the pounding of my heart, where memories so ached and ached that everyday things became unreal and out of focus. Now it meant leaving my home, all my youthful, sheltered life, everything I most loved, with my heart shattered by the loss of this one person, the only girl I then believed I would ever want to have share my life.

I had to go home and I knew what to expect, though Papa with only a look yet hardly a word quietly said he wanted to see me in his library.

Mama, I felt sure, was almost glad that the problem of Deirdre had been solved without her having to assume any part in the finale. She was sorry, sympathetic, trying to be kind, but without any realization of the state of my mind and heart. On the other hand, Papa knew how I felt, for I had confided in him.

"I'm deeply sorry you have had to suffer this," he said as we sat later in the quiet of the library, "but you've got to take it like a man and control your grief. There is only one thing in your favor—you are still very young and your greatest friend is time."

"Nothing will ever be the same," I said.

"Of course not, but that is growth; through this you will learn, and nothing teaches one so thoroughly as suffering. From now on, you'll be grown up and I'm proud of you."

There was so much he left unsaid, so much he never told me or advised me about as I wish he had, but at that moment we were closer than we had ever been. He took me in his arms, where I sobbed uncontrolled, until he said:

"Now, that's enough—chin up, and show what you are made of. *Florens in arduis* you know," he ended, quoting our family motto with a smile.

Deirdre's mother had come from Johannesburg when she heard of her daughter's illness. She was staying with Mrs. C., I was told, and was with her child until the moment she died. I did not meet her until years later when I returned to South Africa. Then we only casually mentioned the tragedy of Deirdre's death. I don't think she had ever heard of me in connection with her daughter, though she wrote a little note to Mama thanking her for the hospitality and kindness we had shown her daughter. But at that time I was enclosed in my own grief, numb to everything, unable to concentrate on any of my lessons, and hardly caring what the future was going to be. They had taken my girl away in her coffin, back to her home, where there was a memorial service at her burial.

I had no part in the drama, for nobody really knew what had happened between two young people. Nor could they have understood how, by its intensity, it had changed the life of one of the protagonists. Only Deirdre and I knew, though even she had found it difficult to believe: for even in those days young love was relegated to the realm of romance and hardly considered serious. But the scars from that first wound still mark my heart.

The date of my departure grew closer and closer. I was to sail on the Union Castle mail steamer, together with my friend Geoffrey, who was to enter the University of London. With a sort of sentimental premonition, I clung to every moment that drew me nearer to my departure. I was determined to go to each of my favorite haunts once more before I left: the woods, the lily ponds, the flats where Daisy and I had cantered into countless sunsets, the old Dutch house, "Stellenberg," whose every curve of architecture was engraved on my mind.

I can remember so clearly the last morning I stood in the dawning light in front of our house, my father's house. It had seen every phase of my young life: in it I had watched sorrow and joy; within the shuttered rooms I had cried tears of pain and heartbreak; along the corridors I had run laughing in carefree happiness. Through the wide open doors had flowed a whole world, colorful, exciting, unusual, a world of people of interest who had influenced my outlook on life. Would I ever see it again? Would I encounter it again in the memories of the many friends who had visited, enjoyed, but never forgotten the atmosphere of my home? Though I didn't imagine it then, I was to meet it over and over again in my life in different parts of the world, in France, Italy, Holland, and England, where I was to contact memories in every stratum of society. It had been a center of comfort and refuge to so many.

And now I was to leave, with all the plans for my future overturned by Deirdre's death, and a certain premonition I would never live in our house again. Always, I had envisaged myself as inheriting by rights what had been my father's estate. But on that morning I felt quite sure that that was the end of my sojourn in my father's house.

My last ride on my beautiful black horse took me up the mountainside to the lookout from the Big Rock. I had to keep one final tryst with Deirdre at the place I shall always associate with her.

I stood on the rock, my heart flooded with memories as I looked out across the flats to the Hottentots' Holland mountains, which guard the north. The mysterious north of Cecil Rhodes, where he had finally gone to rest among the turbulent Matopos Hills; the north that had also claimed Frank, and now Deirdre, together with many others who had marked my life so vividly. Over those mountains lay the whole gigantic continent, swarming with dark vitality: the immense plains where the animals still reign as kings of their own domain, the forests, and the thousands of singing hills, all the Africa I had known and loved.

Would I ever make a rendezvous with it again?

GLOSSARY

BIBLIOGRAPHY

Glossary of Words in Afrikaans

Afrikaans—the language of Dutch South Africans
Assegai—a native spear
Bantu—the generic term for the immense family of negroid African peoples
Biltong—strips of venison or other meat, salted and dried in the sun
Boers—Dutch South African farmers
Bokmakierie—the Bush Shrike, with black and yellow feathers
Baas—master
Boerboom—schotia, with panicles of crimson flowers
Brandewijn—brandy
Donga—gully or dried water course
Doek—head kerchief
Kopje—rocky hillock, or literally "little head"
Konfijt—preserves or jam
Kraal—a group of native huts, the village of a Chief, an enclosure for cattle
Kappie—cotton bonnet worn by the Dutch
kloof—a natural cutting through rocky mountains
Kist—chest or trunk
Kaffir—the name given the African natives by the early Arab traders, literally "unbelievers"
karroo—open desert
Knobkerrie—a short stick with knobbed head, used as a weapon
Rondawel—a round hut of "adobe" and thatch built by the natives

GLOSSARY OF WORDS IN AFRIKAANS

Stoep—a raised paved verandah

Scheeps–jongen—able seamen . . . the crew

Trek—to move, travel, go . . . as a noun e.g., The Great Trek, being
the migration of the Boers 1836–1848

Tolk—an interpreter

Uitspan—a place to rest, and unharness the oxen

Uitlanders—literally foreigners from another country

Voortrekker—pioneer

Vlei—a small lake or pond

Water-uintjie—a water weed with scented white flowers

Wildebeest—the brindled gnu

Bibliography

BARNARD, LADY ANNE. *South Africa a Century Ago (1797–1801).* Oxford: Basil Blackwell, 1925.

BENT, JAMES THEODORE. *Ruined Cities of Mashonaland.* London: Longmans & Co., 1892.

BRUWER, A.J. *Zimbabwe, Rhodesia's Ancient Greatness.* Johannesburg: Hugh Keastland, 1965.

BULLOCK, CHARLES. *The Mashona and the Matabele.* Cape Town: Juta & Co., 1950.

EVANS, J. DAVIES. *Malta.* London: Thames & Hudson, 1959.

FOUCHÉ, LEO, ed. *Mapungubwe.* Cambridge, England: The University Press, 1937.

HALL, RICHARD NICKLIN and NEAL, W. G. *The Ancient Ruins of Rhodesia.* London: Methuen & Co., 1904.

HARDEN, DONALD. *The Phoenicians.* London: Thames & Hudson, 1962.

JOHNSTON, SIR HARRY HAMILTON. *The Opening Up of Africa.* New York: H. Holt & Co., 1911 and London: Williams & Norgate, 1912.

JUTA, RÉNÉ. *The Cape Peninsula.* London: A. & C. Black, 1910 and Cape Town: Juta & Co., 1910 and John Lane, 1927.

JUTA, RÉNÉ and JUTA, JAN. *Cannes and the Hills.* Boston: Small, Maynard & Co., 1928.

JUTA, RÉNÉ and JUTA, JAN. *Concerning Corsica.* London: John Lane, 1926.

KRIGE, E. JENSEN, and KRIGE, J. D. *The Realm of the Rain Queen.* Oxford: Institute of African Languages and Cultures, 1939.

BIBLIOGRAPHY

LEIPOLDT, CHRISTIAN LOUIS. *Jan Van Riebeeck: A Biographical Study*. London: Longmans, Green & Co., 1936.

MACIVER, RANDALL. *Mediaeval Rhodesia*. London: Macmillan & Co., 1906.

MARAIS, EUGENE N. *The Soul of the White Ant*. London: Methuen, 1937.

MARAIS, EUGENE N. *My Friends the Baboons*. London: Methuen & Co., 1939.

MARAIS, EUGENE N. *Burgers van die Berge*. Pretoria, S.A.: J. L. van Schaik, Ltd.

RAWLINSON, GEORGE. *Phoenicia*. London: Ernest Benn, Ltd., 1885.

—, *The Story of Phoenicia*. New York: G. P. Putnam's Sons, 1889. 1890, 1891, 1893.

SELOUS, FREDERICK C. *A Hunter's Wanderings in Africa*. London: Macmillan & Co., 1911, London: R. Bentley & Sons, 1890.

SUTHERLAND, CAROL V. H. *Gold*. London: Thames & Hudson, 1959.